Teacher's Guide

LEVEL F

Comprehension PLUS

Dr. Diane Lapp
Dr. James Flood

Modern Curriculum Press

Program Reviewers

Carmen Arzt
Reading Recovery/Resource Teacher
LaPuente, California

Meg Ballantyne
Literacy (Reading) Specialist
Commerce City, Colorado

Sharon Bonner
Literacy Resource Teacher
Glen Ridge, New Jersey

Alison Heath
Classroom Teacher
Houston, Texas

Carrie Jefferson
Teacher on Special Assignment
Antioch, California

Bonnie Nadick
Reading Specialist
Chicago, Illinois

Sr. Mary Jean Raymond
Teacher/Educational Consultant
Cleveland, Ohio

Bess Ann Sommers
Language Arts Consultant
Canton, Ohio

Fran Threewit
Reading Specialist
Kenwood, California

Celebrity Authors

Joyce Annette Barnes, "Kids in Space," Lesson 21
Ann Hodgman, "Carrot Cupcakes," Lesson 4
Norma Johnston, "The Labors of Stacy," Lesson 26
Betsy Sterman, "Redcoats and Homespun," Lesson 3
Lou Ann Walker, "Was There Really a King Arthur?," Lesson 1

Program Development

Executive Editors: Leslie Feierstone-Barna, Magali Iglesias
Supervising Editor: Cindy Kane
Teacher's Guide Editor: Mary Bulkot
Design Development: MKR Design, New York, NY
Illustrations: T51: Dan Larson/Mapping Specialists, Ltd.

ISBN: 0-7652-2191-8
Printed in the United States of America

14 15 16 17 18 V0YM 17 16 15 14 13

Modern
Curriculum
Press

Pearson Learning Group

1-800-321-3106
www.pearsonlearning.com

Contents

Overview of Comprehension Plus T4
Using the Comprehension Plus Teacher's Guide T5
Using the Comprehension Plus Student Edition T6
Scope and Sequence of Skills T8
Skill Index Chart T9
Using the Comprehension Plus Tests T10
Tests Answer Key T12
Class Record-Keeping Chart T14
Progress Record Chart T16
Tests 1–6 . . . . .T18

Teacher's Guide Lessons

1 Main Idea and Supporting Details T53
2 Drawing Conclusions T54
3 Identifying Sequence: Order of Events . . .T56
4 Identifying Sequence: Steps in a Process . .T57
5 Predicting Outcomes T59
6 Recognizing Cause and Effect T60
7 Using Context Clues T62
8 Comparing and Contrasting T63
9 Summarizing .T65
10 Paraphrasing .T66
11 Recognizing Author's Purpose T68
12 Statements of Fact and Opinion T69
13 Making Judgments T71
14 Point of View .T72
15 Identifying Text Structure T74
16 Understanding Author's Viewpoint T75
17 Making Generalizations T77

18 Outlining T78
19 Persuasive Devices and Propaganda T80
20 Literary Elements: Character T81
21 Literary Elements: Plot T83
22 Literary Elements: Setting T84
23 Literary Elements: Theme T86
24 Synonyms T87
25 Antonyms T89
26 Using Figurative Language T90
27 Analogies T92
28 Connotation and Denotation T93
29 Using a Map T95
30 Understanding Charts and Tables T96
31 Using Graphs .T98
32 Using a Dictionary T99
33 Using an Encyclopedia T101
34 Using a Library Card Catalog/the Internet . .T102

Graphic Organizers Blackline Masters

Story Sequence Chart T104
Summarizing Chart T105
Prediction Chart T106
Main Idea and Details Chart T107

Cause and Effect Chart T108
Fact and Opinion Chart T109
Story Elements .T110
Venn Diagram for Comparing and Contrasting . .T111

Annotated Student Edition 113

Overview of COMPREHENSION PLUS

Comprehension Plus is a six-level comprehension program that provides explicit instruction and practice in major comprehension skills and strategies students need to derive meaning from written text. The Student's Editions and Teacher's Guides for grades 1–6 (Levels A–F) are designed to help students master the most frequently tested comprehension skills. *Comprehension Plus* provides another plus by giving students opportunities for application of comprehension skills in related study skill areas. For example, after students have developed skill in recognizing main idea and supporting details, they are given the opportunity to apply this skill to related study skills such as outlining, summarizing, paraphrasing, and using an encyclopedia.

Thorough Instruction

The basic lesson plan in *Comprehension Plus* provides another big plus. It is based on a simple, fundamental premise: Students can be taught the strategies that will help them comprehend written text. Recent studies have shown that in order to improve in a specific comprehension skill, students must be aware that the skill exists. They must also understand the dynamics involved in applying the skill in a meaningful context. Instruction directed to the students and accompanied by meaningful practice improves proficiency in comprehension.

The biggest plus in *Comprehension Plus* is that students are given much more than practice. They are given direct instruction in the strategy behind each comprehension skill as well as practice activities that allow them to apply the skill in a meaningful context.

Comprehensive Scope and Sequence

The focus skills that comprise the scope and sequence of *Comprehension Plus* are widely accepted as the most important comprehension skills students need to understand a variety of written texts. Students learn the skills that are tested on the following major standardized tests:

• Stanford Achievement Test (SAT-9)
• California Achievement Test (CAT-5)
• TerraNova
• California Test of Basic Skills (CTBS-5)
• Iowa Test of Basic Skills (ITBS-M)
• Metropolitan Achievement Test (MAT-7)
• National Assessment of Educational Progress

The Skills Index on page T9 of every Teacher's Guide provides a complete listing of every focus skill and maintenance skill and lists the lesson in which the skill can be found.

Range of Text Difficulty

All reading passages included in *Comprehension Plus* have been evaluated using either the Spache or Dale-Chall formula for determining text difficulty. The following chart provides the range for each level of the program.

Comprehension Plus Level	Grade Level	Range of Text Difficulty Formula	Range of Scores
A	1	Spache	1.0 – 1.6
B	2	Spache	1.8 – 2.6
C	3	Spache	2.8 – 3.6
D	4	Spache	3.8 – 4.6
E	5	Dale-Chall	4.8 – 5.6
F	6	Dale-Chall	5.8 – 6.6

Using the COMPREHENSION PLUS Teacher's Guide

The Teacher's Guide has everything you need to help students learn and practice the comprehension strategies, study skills, and word study skills they need to succeed. Carefully sequenced instruction, application of focus skills, maintenance skills, and assessment tests help students master the key comprehension skills and strategies necessary for them to understand written text.

Focus Skill
• The focus skill and instructional objective are clearly presented at the beginning of each lesson.

Teaching Tips
• Provide valuable information about the purpose for teaching each skill.
• Help you pinpoint students' understanding of each focus skill.

Reviewed and Maintained Skills
• Two or three comprehension skills, one phonics skill, and one writing skill are maintained within each lesson.

On Your Own Practice
Easy-to-use teaching tips help you assign and assess five practice opportunities:
• **Introducing Vocabulary** Aids students' understanding of the passage by preteaching the key words.
• **Reading the Passage** Prereading discussions help students get ready to read the passage and learn the focus skill.
• **Checking Comprehension** Expands on the answers to the two comprehension questions in the Student Edition to help you determine if students understood the passage.
• **Practicing Comprehension Skills** Provides tips to help students apply the focus skill.
• **Practicing Vocabulary** Reviews key words in each passage and identifies the words that focus on the featured word study or phonics skill.

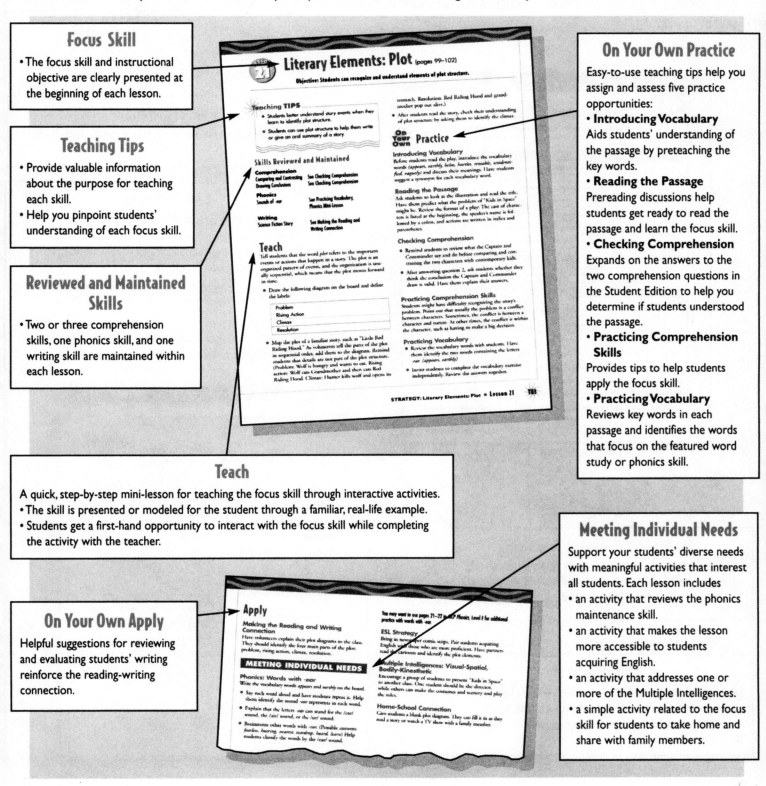

Teach
A quick, step-by-step mini-lesson for teaching the focus skill through interactive activities.
• The skill is presented or modeled for the student through a familiar, real-life example.
• Students get a first-hand opportunity to interact with the focus skill while completing the activity with the teacher.

On Your Own Apply
Helpful suggestions for reviewing and evaluating students' writing reinforce the reading-writing connection.

Meeting Individual Needs
Support your students' diverse needs with meaningful activities that interest all students. Each lesson includes
• an activity that reviews the phonics maintenance skill.
• an activity that makes the lesson more accessible to students acquiring English.
• an activity that addresses one or more of the Multiple Intelligences.
• a simple activity related to the focus skill for students to take home and share with family members.

Using the COMPREHENSION PLUS Student Edition

Student-friendly and designed to create meaningful reading experiences, each lesson in the Student Editions is designed to help students master a skill in context.

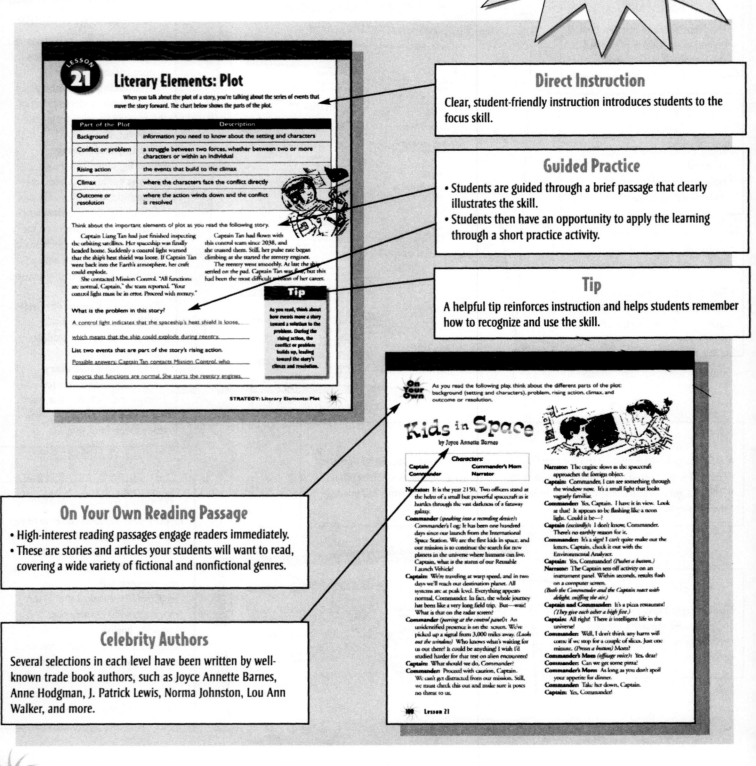

Direct Instruction

Clear, student-friendly instruction introduces students to the focus skill.

Guided Practice

- Students are guided through a brief passage that clearly illustrates the skill.
- Students then have an opportunity to apply the learning through a short practice activity.

Tip

A helpful tip reinforces instruction and helps students remember how to recognize and use the skill.

On Your Own Reading Passage

- High-interest reading passages engage readers immediately.
- These are stories and articles your students will want to read, covering a wide variety of fictional and nonfictional genres.

Celebrity Authors

Several selections in each level have been written by well-known trade book authors, such as Joyce Annette Barnes, Anne Hodgman, J. Patrick Lewis, Norma Johnston, Lou Ann Walker, and more.

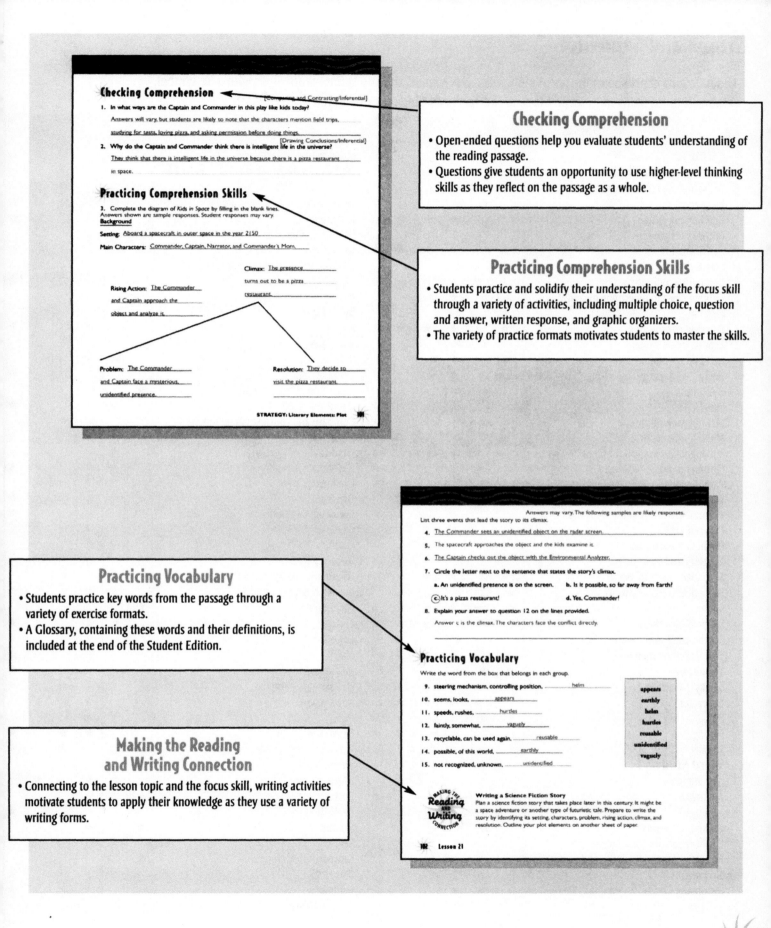

Checking Comprehension
[Comparing and Contrasting/Inferential]

1. In what ways are the Captain and Commander in this play like kids today?

   Answers will vary, but students are likely to note that the characters mention field trips,

   studying for tests, loving pizza, and asking permission before doing things.
   [Drawing Conclusions/Inferential]

2. Why do the Captain and Commander think there is intelligent life in the universe?

   They think that there is intelligent life in the universe because there is a pizza restaurant

   in space.

Practicing Comprehension Skills

3. Complete the diagram of *Kids in Space* by filling in the blank lines.
   Answers shown are sample responses. Student responses may vary.
   Background

   Setting: Aboard a spacecraft in outer space in the year 2150

   Main Characters: Commander, Captain, Narrator, and Commander's Mom.

   Climax: The presence turns out to be a pizza restaurant.

   Rising Action: The Commander and Captain approach the object and analyze it.

   Problem: The Commander and Captain face a mysterious, unidentified presence.

   Resolution: They decide to visit the pizza restaurant.

   STRATEGY: Literary Elements: Plot 101

Checking Comprehension
- Open-ended questions help you evaluate students' understanding of the reading passage.
- Questions give students an opportunity to use higher-level thinking skills as they reflect on the passage as a whole.

Practicing Comprehension Skills
- Students practice and solidify their understanding of the focus skill through a variety of activities, including multiple choice, question and answer, written response, and graphic organizers.
- The variety of practice formats motivates students to master the skills.

Answers may vary. The following samples are likely responses.

List three events that lead the story to its climax.

4. The Commander sees an unidentified object on the radar screen.

5. The spacecraft approaches the object and the kids examine it.

6. The Captain checks out the object with the Environmental Analyzer.

7. Circle the letter next to the sentence that states the story's climax.

   a. An unidentified presence is on the screen.   b. Is it possible, so far away from Earth?

   c. It's a pizza restaurant!   d. Yes, Commander!

8. Explain your answer to question 12 on the lines provided.

   Answer c is the climax. The characters face the conflict directly.

Practicing Vocabulary

Write the word from the box that belongs in each group.

9. steering mechanism, controlling position, helm

10. seems, looks, appears

11. speeds, rushes, hurtles

12. faintly, somewhat, vaguely

13. recyclable, can be used again, reusable

14. possible, of this world, earthly

15. not recognized, unknown, unidentified

appears
earthly
helm
hurtles
reusable
unidentified
vaguely

MAKING THE Reading AND Writing CONNECTION

Writing a Science Fiction Story
Plan a science fiction story that takes place later in this century. It might be a space adventure or another type of futuristic tale. Prepare to write the story by identifying its setting, characters, problem, rising action, climax, and resolution. Outline your plot elements on another sheet of paper.

102   Lesson 21

Practicing Vocabulary
- Students practice key words from the passage through a variety of exercise formats.
- A Glossary, containing these words and their definitions, is included at the end of the Student Edition.

Making the Reading and Writing Connection
- Connecting to the lesson topic and the focus skill, writing activities motivate students to apply their knowledge as they use a variety of writing forms.

Scope and Sequence

The following chart shows the Focus Skills with a ☆ symbol and the Maintenance Skills with a ★ symbol. A more detailed Skills Index is provided in the Teacher's Guide for each level.

LEVEL	A	B	C	D	E	F
COMPREHENSION						
Strategies and Skills						
Activating prior knowledge			★			
Analyzing		★	★			
Author's purpose	☆	☆	☆★	☆★	☆★	☆★
Author's viewpoint			☆	☆	☆	☆
Cause and effect	☆★	☆★	☆★	☆★	☆★	☆★
Classifying	☆★	☆★	★			
Comparing and contrasting	☆★	☆★	☆★	☆★	☆★	☆★
Context clues to determine meaning	☆	☆	☆★	☆	☆	☆
Details	☆★		★			
Drawing conclusions	☆★	☆★	☆★	☆★	☆★	☆★
Expressing opinions		★	★			
Fact and opinion		☆	☆★	☆	☆	☆
Fantasy and realism	☆	☆	☆			
Hypothesizing		★	★			
Main idea	☆★	☆★	☆★	☆★	☆★	☆★
Making generalizations		★	☆	☆★	☆	☆★
Making inferences			★			★
Making judgments about ideas and text		☆★	☆★	☆★	☆★	☆★
Outlining and Notetaking					☆	☆★
Paraphrasing		☆	☆	☆	☆	☆
Personal opinions			★			
Persuasive devices and propaganda					☆	☆
Point of view		☆	☆	☆	☆	☆
Predicting outcomes	☆★	☆★	☆★	☆★	☆★	☆
Problem and solution			★			
Sequence: order of events	☆★	☆	☆★	☆★	☆	☆
Sequence: steps in a process	★	☆	☆	☆	☆	☆
Summarizing	☆	☆★	☆★	☆★	☆★	☆★
Supporting details		☆★	☆	☆★	☆★	☆★
Synthesizing information			★			
Text structure: method		☆	☆	☆	☆	
Visualizing	★	★	★			★
Story Structure						
Character	☆	☆★	☆★	☆★	☆★	☆
Plot	☆★	☆	☆★	☆	☆★	☆★
Setting	☆	☆	☆	☆	☆★	☆★
Theme		☆	☆	☆	☆★	☆
Word Study						
Alphabetizing	☆	☆				
Analogies						☆★
Antonyms		☆	☆	☆	☆	☆
Compound words		☆	★			
Connotation and denotation				☆	☆	☆
Figurative language: simile and metaphor			☆	☆		
Homonyms		☆			☆	
Synonyms		☆	☆	☆	☆	☆
Suffixes			★			

LEVEL	A	B	C	D	E	F
Using figurative language					☆	☆
RESEARCH AND STUDY SKILLS						
Charts and tables		☆	☆	☆	☆	☆
Dictionary		☆	☆★	☆	☆	☆
Encyclopedia			☆	☆	☆	☆
Following directions	☆★					
Graphs	☆	☆	☆	☆	☆	☆
Library card catalog/the Internet					☆	☆
Maps		☆	☆	☆	☆	☆
Picture maps and clues	☆★					
WRITING						
Article			★			★
Bar graph	★					
Book report		★	★			
Campaign speech						★
Cause and effect sentences	★					
Character sketch	★	★	★			★
Compare and contrast paragraph			★	★		
Description		★	★			★
Description of a setting		★	★			
Descriptive paragraph			★		★	★
Dictionary page					★	
Directions			★		★	★
Eyewitness account						★
Fantasy		★	★	★	★	
Graph			★			
How-to paragraph				★	★	
Informative paragraph		★	★	★		
Journal entry		★	★	★		★
Label Book	★					
Letter		★	★		★	★
Log entry			★			
Myth					★	★
Movie review						★
Narrative paragraph			★	★	★	★
News report			★		★	
Note		★	★			
Paragraph			★	★		★
Persuasive paragraph				★		★
Picture map	★					
Poem		★	★		★	
Poster			★			
Realistic story						★
Riddles	★		★			
Sentences	★	★				
Sentences that compare	★					
Story		★	★			★
Summary			★	★		★
Tongue twister		★				

Skills Index

The following chart shows the lessons where the Focus Skills and the Maintenance Skills are presented in the Student's Edition and Teacher's Guide of Level F.

The first column lists the skills. The second column lists in boldface type the lesson numbers where the Focus Skills are presented. The third column lists the lesson numbers where the Maintenance Skills are presented.

Each Focus Skill is presented in the Strategy section of the lesson in the Student's Edition. The "On Your Own" section, which begins with a reading selection, provides further opportunities to apply the Focus Skill to a new context. The Maintenance Skills included in each lesson are those skills that were presented as Focus Skills in earlier lessons in Level F, as well as Levels A, B, C, D, and E.

Strategies and Skills	Focus Skills	Maintenance Skills
Comprehension		
Author's purpose	11	5, 13
Author's viewpoint	16	
Cause and effect	6	1,8,10,12,13,18,22,25,26,28,31
Character		14, 15, 23
Classifying		8, 16
Comparing and contrasting	8	2, 3, 6, 7, 9, 21, 26, 31, 32, 33
Context clues	7	
Drawing conclusions	2	1, 3, 4, 5, 8, 9, 10, 15, 16, 17, 20, 21, 22, 23, 24, 25, 27, 29, 33
Fact and opinion	12	
Main idea and details	1	2, 6, 13, 14, 16, 18, 19, 32
Making generalizations	17	11
Making inferences		27
Making judgments	13	1, 4, 11, 12, 17, 19, 24, 29, 30, 33
Making predictions		7, 20, 34
Notetaking		9
Outlining	18	9
Paraphrasing	10	
Persuasive devices and propaganda	19	
Point of view	14	
Predicting outcomes	5	
Sequence: order of events	3	
Sequence: steps in a process	4	
Summarizing	9	34
Text structure	15	
Visualizing		22, 24
Story Structure		
Character	20	14, 15, 23
Plot	21	30
Setting	22	28
Theme	23	
Word Study		
Analogies	27	25
Antonyms	25	
Connotation and denotation	28	
Synonyms	24	
Using figurative language	26	
Research and Study Skills		
Library card catalog/the Internet	34	
Understanding charts and tables	30	
Using a dictionary	32	
Using an encyclopedia	33	
Using graphs	31	
Using a map	29	

Using the Comprehension Plus Tests

Assessment Tests are provided in the Teacher's Guide for each level of the program. There are six tests in Level A, five tests in Levels B–D, and six tests in Levels E and F. Each test is designed to measure students' proficiency on four to six skills taught at each level. The tests may be used as pretests or posttests depending on the students' needs and the teacher's instructional style. If students answer two out of the three tested items correctly, they are considered to have mastered that skill.

In addition to the tests, *Comprehension Plus* provides the following management tools:
• Class Record-Keeping Chart (pages T14–T15)
• Progress Record Chart (pages T16–T17)

There are a total of six tests offered for this level of *Comprehension Plus*. You may want to use them to evaluate how well students have mastered the 34 focus skills taught in the lessons. As the following chart summarizes, each test includes three passages. Students will answer six comprehension questions for each passage. Each set of six questions will test students' understanding of two focus skills.

To administer the test:

• Make as many copies of a test as you need.

• Have students write their names on each page.

• Explain that students will read three test passages and answer six questions for each passage.

• After students read the first passage, you may want to review their answers to the first test item to make certain they understand what is expected of them.

• Use the Answer Key on pages T12–T13 to score each test.

• You may want to record the test results on the Class Record-Keeping Chart on pages T14–T15.

Test	Passage Number	Lessons	Skills
1	1	1 & 2	• Main idea and details • Drawing conclusions
	2	3 & 6	• Order of events • Cause and effect
	3	4 & 5	• Steps in a process • Predicting outcomes

Using the Comprehension Plus Tests, *continued*

Test	Passage Number	Lessons	Skills
2	1	7 & 8	• Context clues • Comparing and contrasting
	2	9 & 11	• Summarizing • Author's purpose
	3	10 & 12	• Paraphrasing • Fact and opinion
3	1	13 & 14	• Making judgments • Point of view
	2	15 & 16	• Text structure • Author's viewpoint
	3	17 & 18	• Making generalizations • Outlining
4	1	20 & 24	• Character • Synonyms
	2	21 & 22	• Plot • Setting
	3	23 & 26	• Theme • Using figurative language
5	1	19 & 25	• Persuasive devices and propaganda • Antonyms
	2	27 & 28	• Analogies • Connotation and denotation
	3	33 & 31	• Using an encyclopedia • Using graphs
6	1	32 & 30	• Using a dictionary • Understanding charts and tables
	2	29 & 34	• Using a map • Using a library card catalog/ the Internet

Answer Key

Test 1 (Passages 1, 2, and 3 numbered sequentially)

1. **Liza wants a picture of Tori Vale for the school paper.** Main idea
2. **Liza asks Mick to take a picture.** Main idea
3. **The high jump is set up across the field.** Main idea
4. **He knows Mr. Carter has a camera.** Drawing conclusions
5. **track meet** Drawing conclusions
6. **She is writing a story for the school paper.** Drawing conclusions
7. **fastened his shoulder straps** Sequence: order of events
8. **They went up the ramp.** Sequence: order of events
9. **streaked across the sky** Sequence: order of events
10. **She is late to pick him up for an important game.** Cause and effect
11. **they can't travel halfway across the galaxy in time** Cause and effect
12. **the game won't start until he gets there** Cause and effect
13. **Get permission to go on private property.** Sequence: steps in a process
14. **pass out gloves and garbage bags** Sequence: steps in a process
15. **visit every few weeks** Sequence: steps in a process
16. **They might be injured or cause an environmental hazard.** Predicting outcomes
17. **Everyone can enjoy the pleasant habitat.** Predicting outcomes
18. **The animals and plants that inhabit the stream will die.** Predicting outcomes

Test 2 (Passages 1, 2, and 3 numbered sequentially)

1. **sudden idea** Context clues
2. **expect** Context clues
3. **pot** Context clues
4. **They both take catnaps.** Comparing and contrasting
5. **He works around the clock.** Comparing and contrasting
6. **the sun** Comparing and contrasting
7. **Sally Ride applied to NASA in 1977 and was one of 35 people accepted into the space program that year.** Summarizing
8. **Sally was the first American woman in space.** Summarizing
9. **Sally grew up in Southern California.** Summarizing
10. **to inform** Author's purpose
11. **The author gives information about Sally Ride's life and accomplishments.** Author's purpose
12. **a biography of a famous scientist** Author's purpose
13. **It was a chilly winter evening, and the people of Nome, Alaska, weren't very hopeful.** Paraphrasing
14. **The drivers and their dogs endangered themselves to help people they didn't even know.** Paraphrasing
15. **A yearly event, the Iditarod, honors their courageous accomplishment.** Paraphrasing
16. **Nome is a lonely little town.** Fact and opinion
17. **Seppala traveled 260 miles.** Fact and opinion
18. **The serum left Anchorage on a train.** Fact and opinion

Test 3 (Passages 1, 2, and 3 numbered sequentially)

1. **She loves the game.** Making judgments
2. **She is not a very good sport.** Making judgments
3. **They played fair and had fun.** Making judgments
4. **a young girl** Point of view
5. **I, me, my** Point of view
6. **The events would be told in the third person, using words such as *she* and *they*.** Point of view
7. **compare and contrast** Text structure
8. **on the other hand, but, however** Text structure
9. **It would have included specific events in the sequence in which they happened.** Text structure
10. **I am just like a cork bobbing in the deep blue ocean.** Author's viewpoint
11. **They make her feel curious and hopeful.** Author's viewpoint
12. **excited** Author's viewpoint
13. **Peasants usually paid rent in return for work, food, and protection.** Generalizations
14. **He always used his woods for hunting.** Generalizations
15. **Most peasants had more opportunities when towns began to grow.** Generalizations
16. **How an Estate Was Set Up** Outlining
17. **Working on an Estate** Outlining
18. **Opportunities for Work in Towns** Outlining

Test 4 (Passages 1, 2, and 3 numbered sequentially)

1. **helpful, friendly, caring** Character
2. **She helps a stranger.** Character
3. **They are more concerned about themselves.** Character
4. **useful** Synonyms
5. **reward** Synonyms
6. **desperately** Synonyms
7. **Matthew must secretly get information for the Sons of Liberty.** Plot

Answer Key, *continued*

8. **climax** Plot
9. **Matthew turns over information that leads to the Boston Tea Party.** Plot
10. **a street of shops in Boston** Setting
11. **"Thanks to Matthew, December 16, 1773 will go down in history."** Setting
12. **colonists** Setting
13. **There are rewards greater than money.** Theme
14. **Yori feels great when he makes a sick child happy.** Theme
15. **A student volunteer enjoys spending Saturday afternoons reading to blind people.** Theme
16. **simile that means Yori's unhappiness spread to those around him.** Using figurative language
17. **metaphor comparing the girl to a toy.** Using figurative language
18. **He was ready to give up any dreams of becoming a musician.** Using figurative language

Test 5 (Passages 1, 2, and 3 numbered sequentially)

1. **amazing, paradise, cozy** Persuasive devices and propaganda
2. **If you choose to join these many adventurers, the Florida Everglades promises a vacation to remember.** Persuasive devices and propaganda
3. **sweeping generalization** Persuasive devices and propaganda
4. **wet** Antonyms
5. **descend** Antonyms
6. **expert** Antonyms
7. **Muggsy** Analogies
8. **team** Analogies
9. **part-to-whole** Analogies

10. **pint-sized** Connotation and denotation
11. **great** Connotation and denotation
12. **adored** Connotation and denotation
13. **Carson's Life, Writings and Warnings** Using an encyclopedia
14. **Writings and Warnings** Using an encyclopedia
15. **Environmental Protection Agency** Using an encyclopedia
16. **They went steadily down.** Using graphs
17. **The pesticide levels found in Americans has been falling since the EPA was set up in 1970.** Using graphs
18. **About half of those surveyed were very concerned about pesticide residues in foods.** Using graphs

Test 6 (Passages 1 and 2 numbered sequentially)

1. *rapid* and *rash* Using a dictionary
2. **a different word history** Using a dictionary
3. **entry number 1, definition number 1** Using a dictionary
4. **identify characteristics of four rare dog breeds** Understanding charts and tables
5. **hairlessness** Understanding charts and tables
6. **Xoloitzcuintli** Understanding charts and tables
7. **Ashland** Using a map
8. **northeast** Using a map
9. **mile 21** Using a map
10. **Boston Marathon, History** Using a library card catalog/Internet
11. **subject** Using a library card catalog/Internet
12. **call number that helps locate the book** Using a library card catalog/Internet

Comprehension Plus • Level F **T13**

Class Record-Keeping Chart

The following chart can be used to record the number of items each student has answered correctly for each skill tested. Students need to answer correctly two out of the three tested items per skill to be considered to have mastered that skill. Write in each cell the number of items answered correctly by the student. Add the total of correct answers in the bottom cells.

Test	Items	Strategies and Skills										
1	1–3	Main idea and details										
	4–6	Drawing conclusions										
	7–9	Sequence: order of events										
	10–12	Cause and effect										
	13–15	Sequence: steps in a process										
	16–18	Predicting outcomes										
2	1–3	Context clues										
	4–6	Comparing and contrasting										
	7–9	Summarizing										
	10–12	Author's purpose										
	13–15	Paraphrasing										
	16–18	Fact and opinion										
3	1–3	Making judgments										
	4–6	Point of view										
	7–9	Text structure										
	10–12	Author's viewpoint										
	13–15	Making generalizations										
	16–18	Outlining										
4	1–3	Character										
	4–6	Synonyms										
	7–9	Plot										
	10–12	Setting										
	13–15	Theme										
	16–18	Using figurative language										

Name

Total Correct

Class Record-Keeping Chart, *continued*

Test	Items	Strategies and Skills											
5	1–3	Persuasive devices and propaganda											
	4–6	Antonyms											
	7–9	Analogies											
	10–12	Connotation and denotation											
	13–15	Using an encyclopedia											
	16–18	Using graphs											
6	1–3	Using a dictionary											
	4–6	Understanding charts and tables											
	7–9	Using a map											
	10–12	Using a library card catalog/the Internet											

Name

Total Correct

Progress Record Chart

Name_____

The following chart can be used to record students' progress upon completion of the Comprehension/Study Skills, the Vocabulary Skill, and the Writing Skill activities for each lesson. The symbol ✔, +, or – can be used or any numerical system devised by the teacher to indicate students' work as satisfactory (✔), very good (+), or needs improvement (–). Page references for each Strategy and Skill are provided for convenient reference.

Lesson	Focus Skill	Comprehension Study Skills		Vocabulary Skills		Writing Skills	
		PAGE	✔, +, –	PAGE	✔, +, –	PAGE	✔, +, –
1	Main idea and supporting details	5–6, 8–9		10		10	
2	Drawing conclusions	11, 13		14		14	
3	Sequence: order of events	15–16, 18–19		20		20	
4	Sequence: steps in a process	21, 23		24		24	
5	Predicting outcomes	25, 27		28		28	
6	Recognizing cause and effect	29, 31		32		32	
7	Using context clues	33, 35		36		36	
8	Comparing and contrasting	37, 39		40		40	
9	Summarizing	41–42, 44–45		46		46	
10	Paraphrasing	47, 49		50		50	
11	Recognizing author's purpose	51–52, 54–55		56		56	
12	Statements of fact and opinion	57, 59		60		60	
13	Making judgments	61, 63		64		64	
14	Point of view	65–66, 68–69		70		70	
15	Identifying text structure	71–72, 74–75		76		76	
16	Understanding author's viewpoint	77, 79		80		80	
17	Making generalizations	81, 83		84		84	
18	Outlining	85, 87		88		88	
19	Persuasive devices and propaganda	89–90, 92–93		94		94	
20	Literary elements: character	95, 97		98		98	
21	Literary elements: plot	99, 101		102		102	
22	Literary elements: setting	103, 105		106		106	
23	Literary elements: theme	107, 109		110		110	
24	Synonyms	111, 113		114		114	
25	Antonyms	115, 117		118		118	
26	Using figurative language	119, 121		122		122	
27	Analogies	123, 125		126		126	
28	Connotation and denotation	127, 129		130		130	
29	Using a map	131, 133		134		134	
30	Understanding charts and tables	135, 137		138		138	

Progress Record Chart, *continued*

Name_____

The following chart can be used to record students' progress upon completion of the Comprehension/Study Skills, the Vocabulary Skill, and the Writing Skill activities for each lesson. The symbol ✔, +, or – can be used or any numerical system devised by the teacher to indicate students' work as satisfactory (✔), very good (+), or needs improvement (–). Page references for each Strategy and Skill are provided for convenient reference.

Lesson	Focus Skill	Comprehension Study Skills		Vocabulary Skills		Writing Skills	
		PAGE	✔, +, –	PAGE	✔, +, –	PAGE	✔, +, –
31	Using graphs	139, 141		142		142	
32	Using a dictionary	143, 145		146		146	
33	Using an encyclopedia	147, 149		150		150	
34	Using a library card catalog/the Internet	152–153, 155		156		156	

Read the story below. Then answer the questions on the next page.

Get the Picture

Mick had just finished the long jump. He was changing his shoes and was putting on his warm-up jacket when Liza came running up from out of nowhere. As usual, Liza was in a big hurry.

"Liza is just who we need on this team," Mick thought. "She could be a first-class sprinter if she were not so busy working on the school paper."

Meanwhile, Liza was clutching her pen and notebook and huffing and puffing to catch her breath.

"Hey, Mick," she said, gasping. "Have you got your camera? Tori Vale is having a totally awesome day, and we really need a photo of her final jump. It looks like she might break the record. I want to get this story."

Mick looked at the high jump set up across the field. He could see the officials adjusting the bar.

"How awesome?" he asked.

"She just cleared 5'3" without even trying," said Liza, "and that was her first jump."

"Wow," said Mick. He didn't have his camera equipment with him, but he knew someone who never went anywhere without his gear. "OK. You get back over there. I'll meet you in a minute."

"Don't let me down, Mick. This is big," said Liza.

"I won't. See if you can catch a quick interview with Tori before the jump, and try to stall the guy with the clipboard.

Get a quote from him, too."

"Got it," said Liza. She headed back through the crowd.

Mick turned and scanned the stands. He was looking for Mr. Carter's green cap. When he spotted it, he ran across the track and up into the bleachers.

"Mr. Carter," yelled Mick, leaping up the steps two at a time. "Can I use your camera, please? Tori Vale is about to jump. I've got to get the picture."

Mr. Carter didn't hesitate. He handed his camera over to Mick.

"You'd better get moving," he said. "She's up for her second jump just as soon as Liza runs out of questions and gets out of the way."

Mick put the strap over his head. He grinned. "Thanks, sir," he said. Then he hurried back down to the track.

Mick ran back across the field and caught up with Liza, scribbling away in her notebook. Tori was getting ready to jump.

"Perfect timing," said Mick. "Did you get something juicy for the caption?"

"Of course," said Liza. "Tori always has something brilliant to say. Now hurry up and get set. You don't have a moment to spare. Is the camera loaded with film? Are you focused?"

"You just take notes and leave the camera business to me," said Mick, adjusting the lens. "I've got it under control. The only one around here who needs to be focused is Tori."

Fill in the circle next to the words that answer the question or complete the sentence.

1. Which of the following statements best states the main idea of this story?

    ◯ Liza wants a picture of Tori Vale for the school paper.

    ◯ Liza asks Mick to take her picture.

    ◯ Mick asks Mr. Carter if he can borrow his camera.

    ◯ Mick prepares to take a picture of Liza.

2. Which of the following statements supports the main idea of this story?

    ◯ Mick puts on his warm-up jacket.   ◯ Mr. Carter has a green cap.

    ◯ Liza asks Mick to take a picture.   ◯ Mick knows Mr. Carter.

3. Which of the following statements does NOT support the main idea of this story?

    ◯ Mick borrows a camera from Mr. Carter.

    ◯ Mick grabs the camera and hurries back across the field.

    ◯ Mick adjusts the lens and prepares for the shot.

    ◯ The high jump is set up across the field.

4. Why does Mick scan the stands looking for Mr. Carter's green cap?

    ◯ He knows Mr. Carter has a camera.   ◯ He thinks Mr. Carter knows Tori.

    ◯ He knows Mr. Carter loves sports.   ◯ He needs Mr. Carter's cap.

5. Mick and Liza are at a _____.

    ◯ horse show   ◯ track meet

    ◯ car race   ◯ softball game

6. What is Liza doing?

    ◯ She is working for the coach.   ◯ She is writing a story for the school paper.

    ◯ She is trying to make the team.   ◯ She is trying to break the high jump record.

Comprehension Plus ● **Level F** **T19**

Read the story below. Then answer the questions on the next page.

Running Late

Dan was putting his two-way timer back into his jacket pocket for the tenth time just as his mom drove up on her scooter. She pulled up beside him and gave the horn a little blast.

"Well, if it isn't Dan the Man, champion goalie of the Super Novas!" said Mom. "Fancy meeting you here. How about a lift to a certain playoff game?"

Dan was in no mood to be cheerful.

"Where in the galaxy have you been?" he yelled. "I've been waiting for you for ages. I thought you told me you'd be here by 1315 and not a minute later! That's what you said! 'You be waiting for me, Dan. I will be there at 1315 and not a minute later.' How come you're late?"

"My apologies," said Mom in a voice that was perfectly calm and serene. "I had to make a brief, unscheduled stop to pick something up at Pod 3, and it took me a little longer than I thought it would, that's all."

"Now we won't make it on time," Dan said dejectedly. "There is no possible way in the whole wide universe." Dan shook his head.

"Oh, sure there is," said Mom. "Don't worry, honey. We'll take the ferry. You just hop in and hold on tight. I'm in total control of the situation, and I won't let you down."

Dan jumped into the scooter, buckled his helmet, and fastened the shoulder straps while Mom set the coordinates. They whizzed into the commuter lane of the orbiter tube, zipped around the edge of the space station, and arrived at the terminal just in time to zoom up the ramp and onto the ship. Once they were safely on board, the doors closed behind them with a hiss, and soon they were streaking across the red sky.

Dan looked at his timer again. "Look at the time! It is well after 1400, and we have to travel halfway across the galaxy. We'll never make it, Mom, not in a million light-years."

"Just relax, Dan, no one will care," said Mom, flipping through a magazine.

"I will," said Dan. "I will care a whole lot! Maybe you think this is just another dumb game, Mom, but I don't. This game is important to me."

"Well, of course it's important, Dan, and I know how much you care about it, too. I didn't mean that," said Mom. She put her arm around Dan's shoulder and gave him a hug. Then she started laughing as she reached down into her tote bag and pulled out a soccer ball. "This is the game ball, Dan. Coach Brill asked me to pick it up on my way over. They can't start without it, so I doubt they will start without you."

Fill in the circle next to the words that answer the question or complete the sentence.

7. What did Dan do after he buckled his helmet?

○ looked at his timer   ○ jumped in the scooter

○ fastened his shoulder straps   ○ waited for his mom

8. Where did Dan and Mom go after they zoomed around the space station?

○ They went to Pod 3.   ○ They went to Coach Brill's house.

○ They went into the orbiter tube. ○ They went up the ramp.

9. The doors closed, and then the ship _____.

○ whizzed into the commuter lane   ○ streaked across the sky

○ zipped around the space station   ○ stopped at Pod 3

10. Why is Dan annoyed with his mom in the beginning of the story?

○ She apologizes for going to Pod 3.

○ She never lets him drive.

○ She laughs and holds up a soccer ball.

○ She is late to pick him up for an important game.

11. Dan thinks he will be late for the game because _____.

○ they can't travel halfway across the galaxy in time

○ Mom is setting the coordinates

○ he buckled his helmet and fastened his shoulder straps

○ he forgot about his game

12. Since Dan's mom has the game ball, _____.

○ his mom stopped to pick it up   ○ the game won't start until he gets there

○ Mom will watch the entire game   ○ he jumped into the scooter quickly

Read the story below. Then answer the questions on the next page.

Stream Clean-Up

A community stream clean-up is a good project for a scout troop or science class. If you have a stream in your area, chances are it could use some help. The following tips can help get you started.

A few weeks before clean-up day, get permission to tromp around on private property. See where you want your team of volunteers to work and what sections of the stream need the most help. Give nearby homeowners plenty of advance notice about your project. Some of them might even be willing to help you out if you explain what you are doing.

On clean-up day, begin by setting up a place where trash can be sorted. You will need to be able to sort litter that can be recycled and litter that can be reused and litter that will need to be hauled away. Then assign volunteers to different sites along the stream. Each volunteer should have a buddy, and you should try to spread people out to cover the largest area possible. Finally, pass out gloves and garbage bags and tell everyone to get busy.

Have volunteers begin by picking up litter, such as cans, bottles, and paper. They can then sort what they find for recycling. Other garbage, including items such as tires and furniture, can be set aside for proper disposal. Volunteers should refrain from picking up anything that they are unable to lift or identify. Tell the health department, hazardous materials team, or environmental quality office if anything looks dangerous or suspicious. If you are in an industrial area, you have to be especially careful not to try to move any large cans or barrels that you find. You might not be able to tell what is in these containers and, if they are disturbed, they could leak unknown waste into the stream.

Pay attention to what you are taking out of a flowing stream, and don't remove everything. Shady pools form around logs and rocks. A dumped tree stump may be the perfect perch for a river otter. The bedsprings may provide a hiding place for some unseen creatures. It might be more destructive to disturb the stream bottom than it would be to leave old junk in place. Find out how deep the "garbage" you want to remove is buried. If it is more than 50 percent buried, consider it part of the stream habitat.

Once you have cleaned up the stream, continue to watch it. Make a schedule so that you can monitor the stream on a regular basis. A quick litter pick-up every few weeks will help you stay ahead of pollution, and it will give you a chance to explore and appreciate a lively habitat.

Fill in the circle next to the words that answer the question or complete the sentence.

13. What should you do before clean-up day?

    ○ Call the health department.   ○ See how deep garbage is buried.

    ○ Look for river otters.   ○ Get permission to go on private property.

14. After you assign each volunteer a clean-up site, _____.

    ○ call the hazardous materials team   ○ get permission to go on private property

    ○ set up a place for recycling   ○ pass out gloves and garbage bags

15. After you have cleaned up the stream, _____.

    ○ visit every few weeks   ○ call the environmental quality office

    ○ take away things you can't lift   ○ get permission to go on private property

16. Predict what might happen if people try to remove litter they can't identify.

    ○ They might have to recycle it.   ○ They might continue to watch the stream.

    ○ They might find a shady pool around a log or rock.   ○ They might be injured or cause an environmental hazard.

17. Predict how a stream clean-up might help a community.

    ○ The scouts can earn a badge.   ○ Everyone can enjoy the pleasant habitat.

    ○ The clean-up will provide money for the volunteers.   ○ People won't have to pick up their own trash.

18. Predict what might happen if a stream is never cleaned.

    ○ The stream will become a fast-flowing river.   ○ The stream will become inhabited by wild animals.

    ○ Community members will use the stream for fishing.   ○ The animals and plants that inhabit the stream will die.

Read the story below. Then answer the questions on the next page.

Martin's Duties

My name is Martin. I am employed in Mr. Edison's laboratory. Mr. Edison is a world-famous inventor, and he has lots of people working with him. Everyone who works here is busy developing different ideas day in and day out. My primary responsibility is to run errands, like going to the library and post office, and picking up packages at the train station. When I am around the laboratory, I have to anticipate Mr. Edison's next whim and be ready with whatever he needs before he even knows he needs it. I try to think of the details because Mr. Edison has a lot of things on his mind. He likes to invent something small every ten days and something significant every 6 months. I am one of the people who is dedicated to helping him stay on schedule. When you look at it that way, you might say that Mr. Edison couldn't do anything without me!

For now, I also am in charge of keeping the lamps lit, but this job won't last much longer. Mr. Edison has been working on an electric light bulb, and every day he gets closer to finding the key ingredient for his invention. He is experimenting with different materials to find a filament that will burn at a high temperature for a long time. I don't really understand all of the details, but I know that the filament is what heats up and glows to light up the glass bulb. I have seen some of the things that Mr. Edison has tried, and I'm sure that light bulbs will be amazing when he finds the perfect solution. Some of the filaments he has used make a terrific flash and then instantly fizzle. But some of the filaments burn so brightly and so long, it's as if the sun is shining in the middle of the night. It seems impossible to believe unless you have witnessed it yourself, but you'll just have to take my word for it.

Other folks who work in the laboratory with me and Mr. Edison arrive early and stay late, but most of them return home to their families in the evening. Mr. Edison works around the clock because he doesn't need much sleep. Whenever he wakes up, he always wants a cup of tea. My catnaps have to be just a tiny bit shorter than Mr. Edison's so that I can put the kettle on.

"Tea, my boy!" he'll say. "I feel an idea brewing."

I like working for Mr. Edison because he is a great man. When he is curled up on one of the workbenches or lab tables or desks, he is dreaming about ways to change the world, and when he wakes up, anything is possible.

Fill in the circle next to the word or words that answer the question or complete the sentence.

1. The word *whim* means ___.

  ○ need   ○ sudden idea

  ○ achievement   ○ interruption

2. The word *anticipate* means ____.

  ○ expect   ○ delay

  ○ investigate   ○ rethink

3. Another word for *kettle* is _____.

  ○ bottle   ○ mug

  ○ teacup   ○ pot

4. How are Mr. Edison and Martin alike?

  ○ They both take catnaps.   ○ They both run errands.

  ○ They both invent things.   ○ They both drink tea.

5. How is Mr. Edison different from other folks who work in the laboratory?

  ○ He keeps the lamps lit.   ○ He likes to drink tea.

  ○ He works around the clock.   ○ He arrives early.

6. What are some of Mr. Edison's filaments compared to in this story?

  ○ the night   ○ the sun

  ○ brightly   ○ the key ingredient

Read the story below. Then answer the questions on the next page.

Sally's Goals

When Sally Ride was a little girl growing up in a Southern California suburb, she did not dream of becoming an astronaut. She did not foresee that she would be the first American woman in space. However, she did hope to achieve something important. From a very early age, she was the sort of person who set high standards for herself. She also showed a willingness to work hard and make sacrifices in order to meet her goals. In a word, Sally Ride was unstoppable from the start.

Sally Ride was born on May 26, 1951. As a youngster, she proved to be a very talented and dedicated athlete. Tennis was her favorite sport, and she was so skilled that she reached the top 20 of the junior national level. For a while she thought of making tennis a career, and she left college to see if she had enough ability to make the women's tennis circuit. She soon realized that she could not control exactly where the ball landed and how it bounced. Without that level of control, she would never be the kind of tennis player she needed to be. She gave up tennis in favor of returning to school and studying physics. Before she was finished with her college years at Stanford University, she had earned four undergraduate and graduate degrees.

In 1977, Sally was looking for work in astrophysics when she happened to read an article in the Stanford *Daily* about a call for NASA astronauts. Prior to this time, NASA had trained pilots to be astronauts into space. These were the men with the "right stuff." But NASA now needed scientists to serve as mission specialists. These people had to be exceptional in their fields of study as well as able to meet the tough mental and physical qualifications—the right stuff—required of astronauts. More than 8,000 candidates applied for the program, and of that group 1,000 applicants were women. From this pool of talented, eager young people, only 35 were chosen for the training course. Sally Ride was one of the six women accepted into the space program that year.

When Dr. Sally Ride became the first American woman in space in 1983, she served as a mission specialist aboard a six-day mission on the space shuttle *Challenger*. She had the following words to say about her historic flight: "I'm sure it was the most fun I'll ever have in my life."

When she was a little girl, Sally Ride did not dream of becoming an astronaut, but she surely aimed for the stars when she set her life goals. Amazingly, she actually did reach the stars, but for her, nothing less would do.

Fill in the circle next to the words that answer the question.

7. Which statement best summarizes the third paragraph of this article?

○ Sally Ride was talented and eager when she was chosen for the space program in 1977.

○ Sally Ride applied to NASA in 1977 and was one of 35 people accepted into the space program that year.

○ Sally Ride was looking for work in astrophysics when she applied to NASA in 1977.

○ Sally Ride was chosen to be one of 35 people accepted into the space program.

8. Which statement should be included in a summary of the entire article?

○ Sally was on a shuttle for six days.   ○ Sally read the Stanford *Daily.*

○ Sally liked tennis.   ○ Sally was the first American woman in space.

9. Which statement should NOT be included in a summary of this article?

○ Sally grew up in Southern California.   ○ In 1977 Sally applied to be an astronaut.

○ Sally was one of six women accepted   ○ In 1983 Sally became the first
   into the space program that year.   American woman in space.

10. What do you think the author's primary purpose was for writing this article?

○ to entertain   ○ to inform   ○ to persuade   ○ to express

11. How were you able to identify this purpose?

○ The author gives information about   ○ The author tells funny stories about the
   Sally Ride's life and accomplishments.   life of Sally Ride.

○ The author wants to describe NASA.   ○ The author talks about astronauts.

12. Think about the way you read this passage. Which of the following selections would you be likely to read in a similar way?

○ a riddle book about the planets   ○ a poem about the beauty of the full moon

○ a biography of a famous scientist   ○ a science-fiction adventure story

Read the story below. Then answer the questions on the next page.

The First Iditarod

It was a cold winter night in Nome, Alaska. Hopes were dim. The year was 1925. A diphtheria epidemic was sweeping through the lonely little town. Children's lives were at stake. If the people did not get help in time, many would die. The children needed a serum. This special medicine was their only chance for survival. Nothing else could stop the disease. It would quickly spread from home to home. Two children had already died. More were suffering.

Doctors in Nome put out the call across the state. At last, they located a supply of serum in Anchorage. But Anchorage was 1,000 miles away, and there was no plane. The plane that usually made the run had been put in storage for the winter. Pilots offered to get the plane ready. They could try to make the dangerous trip, but they might not succeed. The governor quickly responded to the emergency. He ordered sled dog teams to be organized to deliver the serum. Mushers from all over agreed to help. The race for survival was on.

The box of serum was wrapped in a quilt and bound up in canvas. It left Anchorage on a train and went as far as Nenana. There, it was turned over to the first team of dogs and their driver. Across the icy wilderness, the precious cargo passed from team to team.

The 20 teams were made up of Eskimo, Russian, Norwegian, Irish, and North American Indian mushers. Each team had to fight danger and hardship. They traveled from 25 to 75 miles before handing the crate of serum off to the next musher and team. Eventually, the serum would be delivered to a sled dog team from Nome. That team was led by Togo and driven by Leonhard Seppala.

Seppala and his team traveled from Nome to the drop point. When they got there, they had planned to rest. But the team with the serum was waiting. So Seppala took the serum and quickly turned around. He headed his team into the icy wind. The dogs retraced their steps over the snow. At last, after an exhausting 260 miles, Seppala turned the serum over to the team making the final leg of the trip.

Gunnar Kaasen had 13 dogs. His lead dog was named Balto. Balto and the team ran the last 53 miles in less than 8 hours. They reached Nome on February 2. Only five days had gone by since the first musher started the trip. The teams had gone 674 miles in all. Balto was hailed as a hero. However, all of the mushers and dogs risked their lives to save the lives of strangers. Each year, the Iditarod is held to commemorate their brave deed.

Fill in the circle next to the words that answer the question.

13. Which of the following statements best paraphrases the first sentence in this article?

   ○ The winter is very harsh in Nome.   ○ It was cold and depressing in Nome.

   ○ On a cold winter night in Nome, Alaska, hopes were down.

   ○ It was a chilly winter evening, and the people of Nome, Alaska, weren't very hopeful.

14. Which of the following best paraphrases the second to last sentence from the article?

   ○ Therefore, all of the mushers and dogs risked their lives to save strangers' lives.

   ○ The drivers and their dogs endangered themselves to help people they didn't even know.

   ○ All of the mushers and dogs risked their lives. They wanted to save the lives of strangers.

   ○ All of the dogs were willing to risk their lives to save the lives of the people.

15. What is the best paraphrase for the last sentence in the article?

   ○ The annual Iditarod commemorates their honorable deed.   ○ A race is held to honor the men and dogs who participated in this activity.

   ○ A yearly event, the Iditarod, honors their courageous accomplishment.   ○ There is a race, the annual Iditarod, to commemorate this deed.

16. Which of the following is a statement of opinion?

   ○ Nome is 1,000 miles from Anchorage.   ○ The sled dog teams delivered the serum.

   ○ Nome is a lonely little town.   ○ There was a diphtheria epidemic in Nome.

17. Which of the following is a statement of fact?

   ○ The wind felt icy.   ○ Balto was a hero.

   ○ Seppala traveled 260 miles.   ○ The teams had to fight danger.

18. Which of the following is a statement of fact?

   ○ Everyone in Nome had lost hope.   ○ Balto was the strongest lead dog of all.

   ○ The serum left Anchorage on a train.   ○ Seppala and Togo had never been so tired.

Read the story below. Then answer the questions on the next page.

A Letter from Jenny

June 30

Dear Grandmother and Grandfather,

Thank you so much for your nice card. I always appreciate your support, and this time, your good wishes and your special gift really came in handy. As you know, I played softball all during spring quarter, and we just wrapped up a two-week all-star tournament. I have a lot to tell you about how it all went. We did not finish in first place, but we were victorious! It was quite an experience.

My team had a fantastic regular season, with 14 wins, 1 tie, and 4 losses. Everyone on the team could have tried out for the all-star team, but not everyone was in town. Two of our best players went on vacation as soon as school was out, and our best hitter fractured her wrist roller blading. The players who tried out were really good, though, and with such stiff competition, I felt lucky to have landed a spot on the team. Once the team roster was posted, we had to start practicing two and three hours a day. We only had two short weeks before the first game. There was plenty to learn, but Daddy played catch with me, and we visited the batting cages regularly. By the time opening day arrived, I was amazing. Of course, the lucky bat you gave me was an enormous asset!

Our first opponents, the Tricksters, were unbelievably talented. It was kind of frustrating for us to have such a difficult start, but after about four innings, their pitcher began to make some mistakes. We were able to catch up in the bottom of the fifth inning and ended up winning by a single run. What a squeaker! When the final out was made, we threw our hats in the air and cheered wildly. I think we were all relieved to see that game come to an end.

We triumphed in our next two games and then came up against a top-rated team that hadn't ever been beaten. When we tied things up in the top of the sixth inning, they were quite irritated. Their shortstop was crying, their second baseman was screaming, and their coach was turning purple. I was pitching, and we were truly remarkable, but they still wound up beating us by two.

We finished out our league tournament in third place out of 11 teams and were selected as recipients of the Sportsmanship Award. We each got a medal and a really awesome jacket. It was a terrific experience for everyone on the team. I can't wait to make the all-star squad again next year! I hope you'll be able to come watch some of my games.

Love,
Jenny

Fill in the circle next to the words that answer the question.

1. How does Jenny feel about softball?

○ She loves the game. ○ She only likes to play if she is winning.

○ She only cares about the awards. ○ She wouldn't mind quitting.

2. What judgment can you make about the shortstop in the fourth paragraph?

○ She is not a very good sport. ○ She doesn't take the game seriously.

○ She works hard to stay ahead. ○ She enjoys playing softball.

3. What does the Sportsmanship Award tell you about Jenny's team?

○ They were not gracious losers. ○ They played fair and had fun.

○ They would not congratulate the winning teams. ○ They did not make an effort to be friendly.

4. Who is writing the letter?

○ a grandfather ○ a grandmother

○ a young girl ○ a dad

5. What words tell you the letter is in first person?

○ *I, me, my* ○ *they, their*

○ *the girls* ○ *their pitcher*

6. How would this letter be different if Jenny's dad were writing the grandparents to tell them about Jenny's softball team?

○ The events would be told in the third person, using words such as *she* and *they*.

○ He would not include information about the Sportsmanship Award.

○ The events would be described in rich detail, and descriptive words would be used.

○ The events would be told in the first person, using words such as *I* and *me*.

Read the story below. Then answer the questions on the next page.

The Santa Fe Trail Journal

Well, we are nearly eight days out of Council Grove, and I feel so abandoned, lost, and lonely. I am just like a cork bobbing in the deep blue ocean. We are a million miles from nowhere, as far as I can determine, though Daddy assures me that we are making progress all the time. He says we will take the Long Route along the Arkansas River because that is the way that has water, which we need for our dusty old animals. He doesn't favor the Desert Route, even if it is days and days shorter, because it is too dry. We can't take any chances with the livestock.

Mama usually has an opinion about everything but, on this subject, she has few words to contribute. She says that if we go the Desert Route, we will encounter rough landscape. On the other hand, if we go the Long Route, we are likely to run across plenty of rough folks. Between the two choices, it doesn't make a shred of difference to her. She just wants to get going and get it over with. Uncle Dean was here during the war, so he's familiar with this country. He tends to agree with Daddy that the Long Route will be the best way even if it will take us an extra couple of weeks, but he says that the Cimarron Desert is a sight to behold when it blooms. He tells me that we can take the Long Route this time, but I should plan to travel the Desert Route someday. I hate to say it, but I'm not going to make this journey again anytime soon, and that is final.

Still, I am curious. I think about a dry, flat landscape and cannot picture so much as a petal surviving those conditions. If I were planted knee-deep in sand, would I grow? Would I bloom like the bright desert flowers that Uncle Dean tells me about? I hope I would, but I fear I wouldn't.

However, my Uncle Dean surely can paint a fabulous picture. He has told me about the pine woods and red rock canyons and snow-capped peaks that we will see when we eventually reach our new home. They sound so odd compared to the flat fields and pastures of Iowa, rolling out green without even so much as a bump to stop the breeze.

Daddy and Mama tell me not to let Uncle Dean fill my head with a lot of ridiculous ideas, but as I walk these dusty miles, I try to imagine everything Uncle Dean has described. I can't wait to get there and see it all for myself.

Fill in the circle next to the word or words that answer the question or complete the sentence.

7. What is the text structure of this journal entry?

○ problem and solution   ○ compare and contrast

○ cause and effect   ○ main idea and details

8. What clue words helped you identify the text structure the author used?

○ *on the other hand, but, however*   ○ *first, second, finally*

○ *because, since*   ○ *for example, the following*

9. How would this journal entry look different if the author had used chronological order to structure the text?

○ It would have described more problems the family had encountered.

○ It would have included more of the author's opinions.

○ It would have included specific events in the sequence in which they happened.

○ It would have stated a clear main idea and supported it in a variety of ways.

10. Which sentence helps you understand how the author feels at the beginning of the passage?

○ Well, we are nearly eight days out of Council Grove.

○ He says we will take the Long Route along the Arkansas River.

○ We can't take any chances with the livestock.

○ I am just like a cork bobbing in the deep blue ocean.

11. How do Uncle Dean's stories make the author feel?

○ They make her feel silly and playful.   ○ They make her feel curious and hopeful.

○ They make her feel bored and lonely.   ○ They make her feel unhappy and afraid.

12. Thinking about her new home makes the author feel _____.

○ lonely   ○ angry   ○ excited   ○ hopeless

Read the story below. Then answer the questions on the next page.

From Estate to Town

During the Middle Ages, the rural countryside of Great Britain was divided into a patchwork of individual estates. Each estate was owned by a wealthy landlord. The landlord and his family members lived in a large manor house on the property. The surrounding land was divided up according to its use. There were woodland areas. These small forests belonged solely to the landlord. He used this part of the estate for hunting. Meadows and fields were shared with the peasants who lived and worked on the property.

The peasants lived in small cottages or huts on the lord's property. The peasants paid rent, fees, and taxes to the landlord. They also had to follow his rules. In return, the landlord gave them work and protected them. The peasants were given a section of land where they could raise their own animals and have a kitchen garden. In addition, they had a share in the crops that they raised for the estate. Everything that the estate needed for day-to-day living had to be produced on the property. It took many workers doing a variety of jobs to keep the estate going. Of course there were workers needed to care for the animals. There might be cows, sheep, pigs, and chickens. Field hands planted, tended, and harvested the crops. There was often a flour mill on the property, as well as a blacksmith shop, stables, and a dairy.

Little by little, towns began to spring up across the countryside. Indeed, many of the early towns grew out of the large estates owned by the most successful landlords. Having a group of workers who shared estate lands began to decline. The development of these small towns gave peasants more opportunities for work. They could hire out for work beyond the boundaries and limits of a landlord's estate. Towns also passed laws that governed all of the people. The peasants did not have to follow one person's rules. This change took the ruling power away from the individual landlords. The landlords began to use estate lands to supply goods to towns.

Landlords stopped raising crops to take care of their own needs. They began to trade with merchants in the town centers. Some landlords saw this as a way to increase their income. They could simply hire the peasants to work the land and sell their crops at market, rather than giving them a share in the property and keeping the crops for their own use. In time, many peasants chose to leave the estates where they had lived. They struck out on their own as independent citizens.

Fill in the circle next to the words that answer the question.

13. Which statement is a generalization about the lives of peasants?

   ○ Peasants had to follow the landlord's rules.

   ○ Peasants usually paid rent in return for work, food, and protection.

   ○ Peasants grew their own food.   ○ Some peasants raised animals.

14. Which statement generalizes one role of the landlord?

   ○ He rented his property to peasants in return for work.

   ○ He charged the peasants taxes and fees.

   ○ He lived in the manor house on the property.

   ○ He always used his woods for hunting.

15. Which statement generalizes what changed estate life for peasants?

   ○ Estates began to supply goods to the towns.

   ○ Most peasants had more opportunities when towns began to grow.

   ○ Landlords hired peasants to work.   ○ Peasants followed town rules.

16. If you were outlining this passage, what would be the main topic of paragraph 1?

   ○ Hiring Peasants to Work   ○ The Relationship of Lords and Peasants

   ○ Living in a Manor House   ○ How an Estate Was Set Up

17. What would the main topic of paragraph 2 be?

   ○ Sharing Crops on the Estate   ○ Paying Rent to the Landlord

   ○ Working on an Estate   ○ The Life of Peasants and Lords

18. Which statement is a subtopic for From Estate to Town?

   ○ Opportunities for Work in Towns   ○ The Rights of Citizens

   ○ Protecting Private Property   ○ Supplying Goods to the Towns

Read the story below. Then answer the questions on the next page.

The Constructive Camper

For the last four summers, I've boarded the bus for Camp Thistledown with all the neighborhood kids. This year I turned twelve, which is a little old for a Thistledowner, so I decided to spend a summer in the city.

"Daphne, you should do something *constructive*," my parents said to me, fearing that their daughter wouldn't do anything useful for three solid months. *Constructive,* by the way, is their favorite word!

With their prodding, I signed up for a museum day camp. It's a cool program. Each week a counselor ushers campers to different museums. I get to visit different parts of the city as we travel by subway and bus. Last week we toured the Museum of Natural History. My parents consider museum visits a constructive pastime, but I would say the most constructive part of this day was my subway ride to the day's destination, the Museum of Modern Art.

"I hate modern art!" groaned my fellow camper Nina as we sped beneath the streets. "It's just big blobs of paint!"

"Have you been to the modern art museum?" asked Greta, our counselor.

Nina shook her head. "I won't like it," she scowled.

I gazed around the subway car. Personally, I was excited, and I didn't want grouchy Nina to dampen my spirits. That's when I noticed a passenger of about 70. The woman was frantically patting her pockets and the seat beside her. Clearly, she had lost something. Soon, she was peering under the seat. "No!" she gasped.

"Ma'am, are you okay?" I asked. "Can we help you?"

"It's my locket!" she explained. "It was a gift from my sister. I'm on my way to put it in my safe-deposit box, and I've been afraid to put it down. Oh, I dozed off and dropped it!"

I looked at my fellow campers.

"Don't look at me, Daphne," Nina whispered, "because I'll get motion sickness if I crawl around the floor. She'll find her trinket eventually."

Another camper, Nathan, was watching. "Heck, I'll help," he told me. "Maybe she'll offer a reward!" Nathan began searching the floor.

The woman was crying now, and I moved to sit beside her. When something jabbed me, I stood up. I saw a glint between the seat cushions, crammed my fingers in the space, and pulled out a silver locket.

"Dear girl, let me compensate you!" the woman exclaimed. She took out a twenty-dollar bill!

Strange as it may sound, I didn't want the reward. "No, thanks," I said. "I'm glad I could help!"

I moved back to my fellow campers.

"I should have found that locket!" Nathan said. "You're nuts!"

I might be nuts, but I'd say that today being nuts was very constructive.

Fill in the circle next to the word or words that answer each question.

1. Which list of words best describes the narrator, Daphne?

   ○ *quiet, shy, lonely*   ○ *energetic, athletic, intelligent*

   ○ *helpful, friendly, caring*   ○ *selfish, bored, greedy*

2. Which of Daphne's actions reveal the most about her character?

   ○ She visits museums.   ○ She rides the subway.

   ○ She helps a stranger.   ○ She stops going to Camp Thistledown.

3. How are the campers Nina and Nathan different from Daphne?

   ○ They are more concerned about themselves.

   ○ They are more generous and anxious to help others.

   ○ They are older and wiser than Daphne.

   ○ They have never been to summer camp before.

4. What synonym for *constructive* does the author of "The Constructive Camper" use in the story?

   ○ grouchy   ○ useful

   ○ valuable   ○ modern

5. The woman on the subway wanted to *compensate* Daphne. Which word is a synonym for *compensate?*

   ○ reward   ○ understand

   ○ meet   ○ befriend

6. The following words are all synonyms of *frantically.* Which synonym best matches the meaning of *frantically* as used to describe the actions of woman on the subway?

   ○ recklessly   ○ desperately

   ○ carelessly   ○ rashly

Read the story below. Then answer the questions on the next page.

The Printer's Apprentice

As Matthew Payne swept the doorstep, he heard bits of a conversation going on inside the print shop. The printer, Thomas Bishop, was talking with two men. Matthew recognized one as Samuel Adams. Adams led a group called the Sons of Liberty. Its members were against the high taxes that Britain demanded from the colonists. The younger visitor was about five years older than 12-year-old Matthew.

As a printer's apprentice, Matthew knew his place. He should stay out of private meetings. However, words such as *liberty* and *justice* kept him interested. They were important words that made the hairs prickle on Matthew's neck. When the printer called him inside, the boy responded quickly.

"Matthew, Mr. Bishop says you're a smart boy," Adams said. "He and I and Jonathan here want to end King George's tea tax! Others are ready to join us. The next tea shipment to arrive in Boston Harbor will never leave the dock! There are plans in the works, but we need help."

"What can I do?" Matthew asked eagerly.

Jonathan Downs spoke. "We must know exactly when that next shipment arrives. The merchants won't tell us. They make their living selling tea." He went to the door and pointed across the lane. Wagons loaded with crates stood outside a shop. One merchant, Mr. Grimes, shouted to boys unloading the cargo. "You can blend in with those boys, and can get the information we need."

Matthew's neck prickled again as he nodded.

Each day the merchant Grimes gathered boys from the streets and put them to work. Matthew easily joined the crew, and he waited quietly for a chance to gather information. Unfortunately, Grimes was never far from his leather-bound record book.

Just before closing, an elegant woman stopped at the shop. When she waved a gloved hand to Grimes, he flushed. He moved from his desk and joined her for a stroll.

Matthew darted inside the shop. He leafed through the ledger, scanning entries marked "December." His index finger traced columns of print.

"Tea . . . ." Matthew murmured. When would the cargo arrive? "That's it!" he exclaimed. Then he covered his mouth and peered around. The shop was empty. He closed the book and hurried outside.

That night, four Sons of Liberty were devising plans. There was Thomas Bishop, Samuel Adams, and young Jonathan Downs. And there was Matthew Payne.

"You've done it!" Jonathan praised Matthew.

"We have the date!" Mr. Adams said. "Thanks to Matthew, December 16, 1773, will go down in history. We'll give King George a tea party he won't forget!"

Name _____ **TEST 4,** *continued*

Fill in the circle next to the word or words that answer each question.

7. Which statement best describes the conflict in "The Printer's Apprentice"?

   ○ The colonists want to gain freedom from Britain.

   ○ Matthew must secretly get information for the Sons of Liberty.

   ○ Samuel Adams must convince Matthew to help the patriots' cause.

   ○ Matthew is unhappy working as a printer's apprentice.

8. At one point in the story, Matthew sneaks a peek in the merchant's record book. Which term describes this high point in the plot?

   ○ background   ○ conflict   ○ climax   ○ falling action

9. What is the story's outcome, or resolution?

   ○ The American colonists go to war with England.

   ○ Matthew leaves the print shop and goes to work for Mr. Grimes.

   ○ Samuel Adams organizes a men's group called the Sons of Liberty.

   ○ Matthew turns over information that leads to the Boston Tea Party.

10. Which phrase best describes *where* the main story events take place?

   ○ a street of shops in Boston   ○ a tea ship in Boston Harbor

   ○ a British seaport   ○ an unnamed American town

11. Which sentence from the story clearly states the time period when the story takes place?

   ○ Unfortunately, Grimes was never far from his leather-bound record book.

   ○ "Thanks to Matthew, December 16, 1773, will go down in history."

   ○ "We have the date!" Mr. Adams said.   ○ He closed the book and hurried outside.

12. Which of the following things mentioned in the story gives a *clue* to the time period?

   ○ colonists   ○ ships   ○ shops   ○ record book

Read the story below. Then answer the questions on the next page.

Making the Big Time

Yori frowned at his calendar and then picked up his guitar. His band had been together for five months. Everyone said they were fantastic, but they still hadn't gotten a paying job. Yori began to strum. Playing chords helped him think.

The trio had become acquainted in band class, and organizing a group had been Yori's idea. Yori played guitar and acted as leader, Latisha was on drums, and James was on the saxophone. The three sixth-graders got together just for fun. In fact, they named their trio Playday. But when fans praised their talent, they decided to turn fun into profit.

To make themselves known, Playday volunteered to entertain at birthday parties. They played for free at school assemblies. Oh, Yori loved the applause! He felt like a superstar!

"We have to practice every spare minute," Yori had explained to James and Latisha. At each meeting, they discussed young musicians who'd made it big.

"The Jackson Five were kids," Latisha said. "Michael shot to fame like a rocket!" she exclaimed.

"We can do it!" Yori encouraged the group. "People will say they knew us when."

But now, after months of keeping spirits high, Yori was tired. Playday hadn't had one paying job! What good was talent if it didn't make you a dime?

Yori's bad mood was like a bad rash. Soon Latisha and James caught the low spirits.

Playday decided to break up after one final volunteer job. Yori looked at the calendar square for the next day, April 25. His mother, a nurse at Children's Hospital, had asked Playday to perform for the patients.

"Once again, we'll play for free," Yori groaned.

The next day dawned drizzly and dank. "My music career is like a spring day!" Yori thought. "It's supposed to be bright but just doesn't come through!"

The trio set up in the hospital lobby, and the nurses brought in the audience. As Playday began its first number, Yori could feel their lack of spirit.

Then Yori spotted one patient sitting limply in her wheelchair. Her expression was vacant, but when music filled the room, this rag doll came to life. She sat up straight, and the light that sparked in her eyes kindled something in Yori. He felt the thrill he'd been missing. As Yori's playing caught fire, James and Latisha gained energy. Soon Playday was rocking as never before.

After the performance, the trio visited with patients. Yori spoke to the girl who'd inspired him to play so well.

"Wouldn't it feel great to be rich and famous?" she asked, eyes still bright. "Will you be a rock star?"

"Probably not," Yori answered. "But I'll never give up my music. It felt like the big time playing for you!"

Fill in the circle next to the words that answer each question or complete the sentence.

13. Which sentence expresses the main theme, or big idea, of "Making the Big Time"?

   ○ Music can brighten any day.   ○ There are rewards greater than money.

   ○ Money is the root of all evil.   ○ Hard work will surely bring success.

14. Which detail from the story supports the main theme of the story?

   ○ People tell the trio that they are   ○ Yori feels great when he makes a
     very talented.   sick child happy.

   ○ Playday can't get a paying job.   ○ Yori, James, and Latisha form a rock group.

15. The theme of this story might apply to which of the following situations?

   ○ A student volunteer enjoys spending Saturday afternoons reading to blind people.

   ○ An athlete finally makes it to a high-paying career in professional ball.

   ○ An ambitious sixth-grader gets a summer job mowing lawns.

   ○ A music store asks a group of sixth graders to vote on their favorite top ten hits.

16. The phrase "Yori's bad mood was like a bad rash" is a _____.

   ○ simile that means Yori's unhappiness   ○ metaphor that means Yori's mood
     spread to those around him   was improving as the day went on

   ○ simile that means Yori was sick   ○ metaphor that means Yori was mad

17. The phrase "but when music filled the room, this rag doll came to life" is a _____.

   ○ simile comparing the girl to music   ○ simile meaning that the music was loud

   ○ metaphor comparing the girl to a toy   ○ metaphor meaning the little girl sang

18. Which of these phrases is NOT an example of figurative language but literal language?

   ○ "My music career is like a spring   ○ He was ready to give up any dreams
     day!" Yori thought.   of becoming a musician.

   ○ Yori's playing caught fire . . .   ○ "Michael shot to fame like a rocket!"

Read the article below. Then answer the questions on the next page.

Your Everglades Adventure

Each year thousands of tourists drive southwest out of Miami through Florida farmlands. An hour's drive takes them into the beautiful swamplands of Everglades National Park. If you ever choose to join these adventurers, the Florida Everglades promises a vacation to remember.

The Everglades is like no other place on Earth. Actually, this amazing wilderness is a shallow, slow-flowing river. The area's 2,750 square miles will give you a chance to view some rare and endangered animals. Where else can you see crocodiles and alligators, giant turtles, and Florida panthers? In winter, the park is a bird lover's paradise. It attracts migrating birds from all over the country. The farther south you travel, the deeper into the wilds you go. You might be lucky and spot a rare green sea turtle or an American crocodile.

Travel south far enough, and you'll reach Flamingo. This is the southernmost place in the continental United States. Flamingo was once a quiet fishing village in the wilderness. Now the town offers many services for visiting tourists. You might stay the night at Flamingo Lodge and Marina. Its comfortable quarters include cozy cottages and lodge rooms. For extra fun, houseboats are available. You can cruise the waterways in style.

Enjoy the sights from your houseboat's rooftop sundeck.

A favorite way to explore the Everglades is by canoe. Rent one in Flamingo. Then spend the day gliding peacefully through marshes, creeks, ponds, and bays filled with tropical life. Expert guides offer camping, hiking, and canoeing tours. Experienced travel agents recommend Flamingo as the place to begin your Everglades experience. There you will find everything you could possibly want. You can rent canoes, kayaks, motorboats, fishing equipment, and bicycles. Be sure not to forget the binoculars! You won't want to miss seeing a colorful, exotic bird spread its glorious wings as it rises over the water.

The best time to visit the Florida Everglades is during the dry season from December through May. The temperature is cooler, and a lower water level draws more wildlife. Wet season runs from June to November. Then visitors will find much hotter weather, fewer migratory birds, and a lot more mosquitoes! Keep in mind that many services, such as houseboat rentals, are not available during the summer months.

Why not leave the busy city life behind for a while? Exchange it for the peace of Earth's most amazing wilderness area. There is only one Everglades. See it for yourself!

Fill in the circle next to the word or words that answer each question.

1. Which of the following are examples of "loaded words" intended to persuade the reader to visit the Everglades?

　○ *amazing, paradise, cozy*　　　　　○ *Everglades, Florida, tourist*

　○ *southwest, binoculars, river*　　　○ *canoe, wet, hike*

2. Which sentence uses the persuasive device called "bandwagon"?

　○ Travel south far enough, and you'll reach Flamingo.

　○ If you choose to join these many adventurers, the Florida Everglades promises a vacation to remember.

　○ The best time to visit the Florida Everglades is during the dry season from December through May.

　○ Actually, this amazing wilderness is a shallow, slow-flowing river.

3. The author states that in Flamingo "you will find everything you could possibly want." This is an example of which persuasive device?

　○ testimonial　　　　　　　　　○ bandwagon

　○ loaded words　　　　　　　　○ sweeping generalization

Fill in the circle next to the antonym for the underlined word.

4. The <u>dry</u> season is in the winter, and the _____ season is in the summer.

　○ busy　　　○ favorite　　　○ wet　　　○ hot

5. The tourists watched a bird <u>rise</u> over the water and then _____ to shore.

　○ decide　　　○ descend　　　○ fly　　　○ nest

6. The <u>inexperienced</u> visitors hired an _____ guide to show them around the marshes, creeks, and ponds.

　○ unusual　　　○ odd　　　○ expert　　　○ energetic

Read the article below. Then answer the questions on the next page.

Muggsy

What are the chances of a 5-foot-3-inch player becoming an NBA star? They're similar to the chances of snow in July or an elephant stampede in Central Park. But Tyrone "Muggsy" Bogues beat the odds. Since 1987, he has played basketball in a league of giants.

When the Washington Bullets drafted Muggsy Bogues, people were astounded. Muggsy himself was not surprised. He'd planned to make it as a basketball player since he was a kid. Muggsy remembers classmates choosing him last for playground teams. They called him "the cute little one" or "shorty." Being small was just another hurdle for Muggsy, who lived in a rough Baltimore neighborhood. He held his head high.

Muggsy may not have been able to dunk a basketball, but at Baltimore's Dunbar High, he was nicknamed "The Human Assist." Teammates racked up points, but it was Muggsy who passed them the ball. What Bogues lacked in height, he made up for in speed, ball handling, and confidence.

Bogues won the Most Valuable Player award at North Carolina's Wake Forest University. When he graduated, the team retired his number. No Wake Forest basketball player would wear number 14 again. It was a great tribute to Muggsy's spirit and ability.

Bogues set his sights on the pros. His dream came true when he was the twelfth man chosen in the NBA draft. Why were the Washington Bullets anxious to draft a 5-foot-3-inch player? For one thing, Bogues was good—no, he was great! Also, fans adored him! The Bullets knew people would flock to see the smallest player in NBA history.

Imagine the fairy tale character Jack climbing the beanstalk to a land of giants. The picture would be much like Bogues stepping onto an NBA court. When Muggsy first joined the league, sportswriters poked fun, calling him "pint-sized." No one joked for long. As Muggsy's career took him from the Bullets to the Charlotte Hornets, to Golden State, and on to Toronto, writers praised him. They wrote reports like the following:

The overtime clock was running down as the New York Knicks led the Charlotte Hornets by four. The Knicks' six-foot-seven, two hundred pound Anthony Mason had the ball, and Mason was headed for a slam-dunk!

Streaking down the court came lightning-fast Muggsy Bogues! Bogues caught Mason and knocked the ball away. The amazing move saved the Hornets and sent them to a 110-106 victory.

Sportswriters no longer emphasized such words as *short* and *small*. They replaced them with terms such as *amazing*. According to Charlotte teammate Larry Johnson, Muggsy sparked the Hornets' energy in the same way that a spark plug sparks engine fuel.

So, what were the chances of a "shorty" making it in the NBA? Muggsy Bogues ignored the odds and became an NBA legend.

Complete each analogy by filling in the circle next to the correct answer.

7. land of giants : Jack :: NBA court : [_____]

○ Muggsy   ○ Hornets

○ Larry Johnson   ○ sportswriters

8. spark plug : engine :: Muggsy Bogues : [_____]

○ fans   ○ team

○ basketball   ○ free throw

Fill in the circle next to the correct answer.

9. The "spark plug" analogy above shows which kind of relationship?

○ opposites   ○ cause and effect

○ part-to-whole   ○ categories

10. Which word or words has the most negative connotation?

○ short   ○ small

○ pint-sized   ○ slight

11. Which word has the most positive connotation?

○ good   ○ okay

○ great   ○ adequate

12. Which word suggests the strongest feeling?

○ liked   ○ loved

○ adored   ○ appreciated

Read the following encyclopedia entry and the graphs that follow it. Use information from the entry and graphs to answer questions on the next page.

CARSON, RACHEL (1907–1964) was an American scientist who studied the effects of chemicals on oceans, lands, and wildlife. Carson was an author who wrote about respecting and protecting the environment.

Carson's Life

Rachel Louise Carson grew up on a Pennsylvania farm where she learned to love the outdoors, nature, and writing. She published her first story when she was 10 years old. At Pennsylvania College for Women and Johns Hopkins University, Carson studied marine biology. She combined her interest in science and nature with her love of writing by composing her own books. For most of her adult life, Carson worked for the United States Fish and Wildlife Service. When Rachel Carson died in 1964, she left the public with a new awareness of the effects that human actions had on nature.

Writings and Warnings

Rachel Carson spent most summers at an ocean research center in Woods Hole, Massachusetts.

There she studied tide pools and ocean currents. Her books about the wonders of the sea include *Under the Sea Wind* (1941), *The Sea Around Us* (1951), and *The Edge of the Sea* (1955). Carson remains most well-known for *Silent Spring* (1962), a book that warns about dangerous pesticides. Carson cautions that certain chemical poisons can kill more than insects. They destroy many birds and fish. She also suggests that these pesticides not only poison the food supply of animals but also pollute the human food supply. In *Silent Spring*, Carson describes an American town feeling the results of people's careless use of pesticides. Rachel Carson writes, "There was a strange stillness. The birds, for example, where had they gone? What has happened to silence the voices of spring?"

Rachel Carson made people think about their responsibility to the environment. Her work helped lead to restrictions on the use of pesticides. *See also:* Environmental Protection Agency; Insect Control (Pesticides)

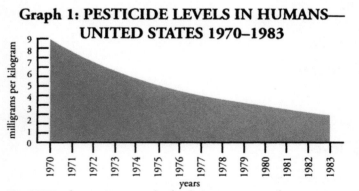

Graph 1: PESTICIDE LEVELS IN HUMANS— UNITED STATES 1970–1983

By 1970, the government had taken more control over pesticide use. Congress passed the Clean Air Acts and set up the Environmental Protection Agency (EPA). Many felt that Carson's Silent Spring *prompted the banning of some dangerous pesticides. The new laws made a difference.*

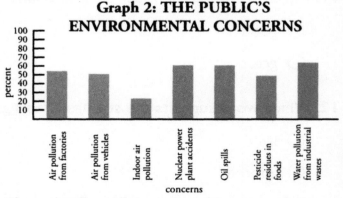

Graph 2: THE PUBLIC'S ENVIRONMENTAL CONCERNS

The graph indicates the percentage of those surveyed who rated the environmental problem "very serious."

Name _____ **TEST 5,** *continued*

Fill in the circle next to the answer to each question.

13. Which of the following are section heads in the encyclopedia entry on Rachel Carson?

○ Carson, Rachel, *Silent Spring*   ○ *Silent Spring, The Sea Around Us*

○ Carson's Life, Writings and Warnings   ○ Marine Biology, Pesticides

14. Which section would you read if you wanted to find the name of a book written by Rachel Carson?

○ Insect Control   ○ Carson's Life   ○ *See also*   ○ Writings and Warnings

15. Which cross-reference would you go to find out about a government agency that regulates pesticide usage?

○ Carson, Rachel   ○ Environmental Protection Agency

○ Pennsylvania College for Women   ○ Marine Biology

16. Between 1970 and 1975, what happened to pesticide levels in Americans?

○ They went steadily down.   ○ They went steadily up.

○ They stayed the same.   ○ The graph does not give that data.

17. Which sentence states a conclusion based on information shown on graph #1?

○ The pesticide levels found in Americans showed no change after the creation of the EPA.

○ The pesticide levels found in Americans has been falling since the EPA was set up in 1970.

○ Pesticide levels in humans have climbed steadily since the EPA was created in 1970.

○ Pesticide levels in humans are much greater in the United States than in Europe.

18. Which statement does graph #2 show to be true?

○ About half of those surveyed were very concerned about pesticide residues in foods.

○ No one worries about pesticide residues in the foods that they eat.

○ People think indoor air pollution is a more serious problem than pesticides in foods.

○ Pesticide residues in food is the public's number one environmental concern.

Comprehension Plus ● **Level F**   **T47**

Read the dictionary entries and the article below. Study the table on the next page. Use details from the three sources to answer questions on page T50.

rapid ► rash

rare (1) (rer) *adj.* 1. not often found or seen; not common; scarce [Black opals are a *rare* gem.] 2. very good, excellent [He told a *rare* joke that made people laugh.] 3. not dense; thin [High atop the mountain the air becomes *rare.*] [from French and Latin *rarus,* meaning "thin" or "scarce."]

rare (2) (rer) *adj.* lightly cooked; partly raw [A *rare* steak will be very pink in middle.] [from Old English *hrere,* meaning "lightly boiled."]

Rare Dog Breeds

"What kind of dog is that?"

Most owners of uncommon dog breeds recognize that question. Explaining the pet's strange appearance is part of the fun of owning a rare dog! While hundreds of breeds are thought of as "rare," this article describes four that are very unusual.

You need not fret about dog hair.
Just choose a dog whose skin is bare!

When people think of dogs, they usually picture hair. Some pet owners choose long-haired dogs like collies or short-haired dogs like beagles. Did you know there are rare breeds that have almost no hair at all? Two such dogs are the Chinese Crested Dog and the Xoloitzcuintli (say *show-low-eats-queen-tlee*), or Xolo *(show-low)* for short. The Chinese Crested has a topknot on its head and a plume on its tail. The Xolo is totally hairless. Both breeds have silk-smooth skin that is amazingly warm to the touch. Through

the ages, owners have actually used these pets as living heating pads. They claim the dogs' natural warmth cures muscle and joint pains.

"What's with your dog?" That's how we're greeted.

Some have not seen a dog who's pleated.

"Is there a dog inside those wrinkles?" "Have you ever tried ironing your dog?" When Shar-Pei owners take their pups for walks, they're likely to get stares and questions. Many folds of loose, wrinkled skin make the Shar-Pei one of the most unusual-looking breeds. Actually, in recent years, a Shar-Pei sighting is less of a rarity as the breed becomes a more popular pet.

The night is filled with eerie sounds
The sad, sweet cries of singing hounds!

A dog you're less likely to meet on city streets is the New Guinea Singing Dog. Ancient tribespeople once valued the singing dog so highly that they built shrines in its honor. If you hear the voice of this unusual breed, you'll understand why many consider the dog special and mysterious. The Singing Dog's natural voice is a high, yodeling howl. In the wild, the dogs' voices unite in a chorus unlike the sound of any other animal. Until recently, Singing Dogs were considered wild. In the United States, they were only seen in zoos. Now people have begun taming and breeding Singing Dogs, finding that they make intelligent pets.

RARE DOG BREEDS

Breed	Country of Origin	Appearance	Positive Traits	Problems
Chinese Crested	China	under 15 pounds; hairless except for topknot and tail plume; warm, smooth skin; large, erect ears; any color, plain or spotted	good house pet; active, graceful, clean, odorless, friendly; well-suited to apartment life	must be protected from cold weather, sun
Xoloitzcuintli (Xolo)	Mexico, Central America	30–50 pounds; hairless; long muzzle; slender neck; warm, sleek, smooth skin; black, dark grey, red, bronze	grooms itself; odorless; good for those with dog allergies; alert; loving with owner; good with children and other dogs; flea resistant; adaptable	needs protection from cold; can have skin problems, including pimples; needs attention and companionship
Shar-Pei	China	35–60 pounds; loose, wrinkled skin; blunt, broad muzzle; compact, muscular body; short, bristly hair; purple tongue	intelligent; loyal; devoted to owner; enjoys human company; seldom wanders; good watchdog	shy, may be unfriendly with strangers; aggressive with other dogs; prone to skin and eye problems
New Guinea Singing Dog	New Guinea	17–25 pounds; fox-like; erect, triangle-shaped ears; bushy tail; small, dark eyes; dense double coat; red, black, or tan	good hunting companion; interesting voice; curious; active; agile and athletic	chases poultry; difficult to train; can easily jump fences; maintains wild instincts

Fill in the circle next to the words that complete the sentence.

1. The guide words on the pictured dictionary page are _____.

   ○ *adj.* and *(rer)*   ○ *rare* and *air*

   ○ *scarce* and *excellent*   ○ *rapid* and *rash*

2. The two entries for *rare* are different from one another because they have _____.

   ○ a different pronunciation   ○ a different part of speech

   ○ a different word history   ○ a different spelling

3. The entry that applies to the article "Rare Dog Breeds" is _____.

   ○ entry number 1, definition number 1   ○ entry number 1, definition number 2

   ○ entry number 1, definition number 3   ○ entry number 2

4. The purpose of the table is to _____.

   ○ identify characteristics of four rare dog breeds

   ○ persuade readers to purchase a certain breed

   ○ discourage readers from owning rare breeds

   ○ present one rare breed as better than three others

5. The Chinese Crested Dog and the Xoloitzcuintli share the unusual trait of _____.

   ○ blue-black tongues   ○ musical howling

   ○ aggressive behavior   ○ hairlessness

6. Imagine that you live in a city neighborhood that has lots of dogs. You have a low fence, want a medium-sized dog, and are allergic to dog hair. A _____ would be a good breed for you.

   ○ Chinese Crested Dog   ○ Xoloitzcuintli

   ○ Shar-Pei   ○ New Guinea Singing Dog

Read the article below and study the map. Then answer the questions on the next page.

The Boston Marathon: Still Running Strong

One April morning each year, runners from around the world gather in the tiny town of Hopkinton, Massachusetts. A sign on Hopkinton Green greets them. It reads: "Welcome to Hopkinton. It all starts here." The "it" that starts in Hopkinton is the famous Boston Marathon, an annual race first run on April 19, 1897.

The first Boston Marathon was organized by the Boston Athletic Association, America's oldest athletic club. Inspired by Olympic marathons, members planned a 24.5-mile course. Its starting point was the rural town of Ashland. Fifteen men ran in that first race. It has since become the world's oldest annual marathon.

Today the road to Boston is paved, but racers follow nearly the same course as those first fifteen men. In 1924, the starting point was moved from Ashland southwest to Hopkinton, adding distance to the route.

Imagine it is the third Monday of April 2001. More than 16,000 men and women stretch their limbs. They attach little time clocks to their shoelaces. They're preparing to tackle the 26.2-mile course from Hopkinton to Boston. Each contestant must be a dedicated marathoner. It takes hard work to qualify for a spot in this race, and most runners take years preparing. To enter, runners must show that they've already raced a qualifying time. Specific rules can be found in library books, magazine articles, and on the Internet.

When the clock on Hopkinton's Main Street reads noon, the racers are off to Boston. The course winds through Massachusetts's countryside and small towns. Then it's on to Wellesley, the halfway point of the race. Scenery changes from rural to urban as racers near Boston. Around mile 17, the hills begin. It's an up-and-down run until the course peaks at Heartbreak Hill. A steady descent leads to the finish in Boston's Back Bay.

After the course is run comes celebration time! There is an awards ceremony and a high-spirited dance party. There is honor in just reaching Boston Back Bay and glory in saying, "I finished the Boston Marathon!"

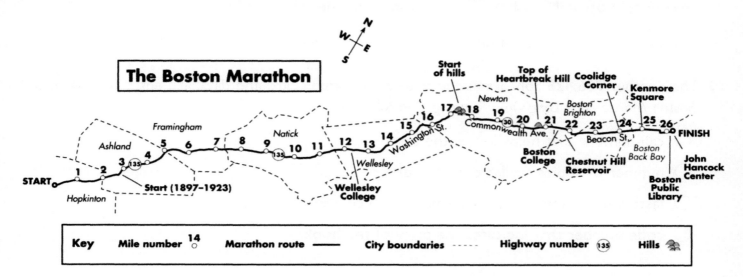

Fill in the circle next to the word or words that answer each question.

7. Through which of these towns do the marathon racers pass between Hopkinton and Framingham?

○ Boston   ○ Wellesley   ○ Natick   ○ Ashland

8. In what direction do the racers run to reach Boston from Hopkinton?

○ directly north   ○ directly south

○ northeast   ○ southwest

9. Just before which mile marker do racers climb to the highest point of the course?

○ mile 2   ○ mile 21   ○ mile 26   ○ mile 17

10. When using the library card catalog or the online database, what keywords would lead someone most directly to information on the first Boston Marathon?

○ Boston Marathon, History   ○ Boston Marathon, Qualifying

○ Boston   ○ Marathons

Fill in the circle next to the word or words that correctly complete each statement.

11. A library or Internet user who wanted to learn more about the big race might use the keywords "Boston Marathon." This person would be searching by _____.

○ title   ○ author   ○ subject   ○ publisher

12. The number 796.425 appears at the top of the catalog card and database entry for the book *Boston Marathon: A Long Time Running.* 796.425 is the _____.

○ call number that helps locate the book

○ number of copies available in the library

○ fastest time in which a racer has run the course

○ code number that indicates the price of the book

Main Idea and Supporting Details (pages 5–10)

Objective: Students can recognize main idea and supporting details.

Teaching TIPS

- Students organize and prioritize information when they identify the main idea and supporting details.

- Students become more critical readers when they learn to recognize both stated and implied main ideas.

Skills Reviewed and Maintained

Comprehension

Drawing Conclusions	See Teach
Cause and Effect	See Checking Comprehension
Making Judgments	See Checking Comprehension

Phonics

Sounds of *th*	See Practicing Vocabulary, Phonics Mini-Lesson

Writing

Paragraph	See Making the Reading and Writing Connection

Teach

Explain to students that in order to fully understand a passage they're reading, they need to recognize its main idea. Display the following paragraph on an overhead projector and read it aloud:

School uniforms are a good idea. They are less expensive than the casual clothes kids usually wear to school. They prevent students from paying too much attention to their clothes. They increase school unity and school spirit. They also save time in the morning because students don't have to think about what to wear.

- Distribute the graphic organizer on page T107 of this Guide. Ask students which sentence in the paragraph presents the main idea. *(the first sentence)* Have them write it in the appropriate place on the organizer.

- Ask which sentences contain details that support the main idea. *(all the other sentences)* Have students write some of the details on the organizer.

- Make sure students realize that the main idea is not always stated directly. Sometimes readers must figure it

out and state it in their own words. To do so, students need to draw conclusions based on details in the text.

- As students read the paragraphs about King Arthur, check for understanding.

 ## Practice

Introducing Vocabulary

Before students read the story, introduce the vocabulary words *(authentic, captivated, chaotic, chivalry, embellished, worthy, legendary)* and discuss their meanings. Have students give examples to clarify the meaning of each word.

Reading the Passage

Ask students to look at the photograph and read the title. Have them predict what the main idea of the article might be. Remind students that the main idea is the most important point made about the topic. Supporting details give facts and information about the main idea.

Checking Comprehension

- Clarify that an effect is something that happens, and a cause is why it happens. Remind students that one effect can have multiple causes. Challenge them to find at least two causes.

- Before students make a judgment, ask them to think about the details in the article. Do these details focus more on real or imaginary people and events?

Practicing Comprehension Skills

Remind students that the main idea is often not stated directly and must be inferred from details in the text. Students can check themselves by asking, *"Does my main idea make sense? Does it cover all the important details?"*

Practicing Vocabulary

- Review the vocabulary words with students. Have them identify the two words containing the letters *th*. *(authentic, worthy)* Talk about what the sound *th* represents in each word.

- Let students complete the vocabulary exercise independently. Review the answers with the group.

Apply

Making the Reading and Writing Connection

Students can read their paragraphs to a partner. The partner should make a chart listing the paragraph's main idea and at least two supporting details.

MEETING INDIVIDUAL NEEDS

Phonics: Sounds of *th*

Draw attention to the two vocabulary words that have the letters *th: authentic, worthy.*

- Write *authentic* on the board. Say the word and have students repeat it. Write the words *thin* and *then.* Ask which word has the same *th* sound as in *authentic.* *(thin)* Repeat the procedure with *worthy. (then)*

- Have students find other words in the article that contain the *th* sound they hear in *authentic* and write them on the board. *(Arthur, fifth, sixth, myth)* Then have stu-

dents find words that contain the *th* sound they hear in *worthy. (other, these, the, they, that, together)*

You may want to use pages 15–16 in *MCP Phonics,* Level F for additional practice with words with *th.*

ESL Strategy

Display simple books from the classroom library. Let groups of three students select a book and read it together, discussing the text and pictures. Then ask them to identify the book's main idea and the details that support it.

Multiple Intelligences: Logical-Mathematical, Visual-Spatial

Have students use the details in "Was There Really a King Arthur?" to make a time line of events connected to the Arthurian legend.

Home-School Connection

Suggest that students talk with family members about a family tradition. They can then write a paragraph explaining what the tradition is *(main idea)* and why the family keeps it *(supporting details).*

Drawing Conclusions (pages 11–14)

LESSON 2

Objective: Students can draw conclusions about characters and events in a story.

Teaching TIPS

- Students synthesize and evaluate information when they draw conclusions.

- Students form logical conclusions based on valid evidence and their own experiences.

Skills Reviewed and Maintained

Comprehension

Main Idea	See Checking Comprehension
Comparing and Contrasting	See Checking Comprehension

Phonics

Vowel Digraph *ie*	See Practicing Vocabulary, Phonics Mini-Lesson

Writing

Story	See Making the Reading and Writing Connection

Teach

Explain to students that they draw conclusions every day. Tell them to imagine they are walking along a sidewalk and notice the following: a broken windshield, a baseball on the ground, a woman with her hands on her hips standing next to the car.

- Ask students what conclusions they can draw from these details. (Most will say that someone hit or threw a baseball that broke the car's windshield and that the car's owner is upset.) Point out how students drew a conclusion by combining the details specified with their own experiences.

- Make sure students understand that a conclusion is a sensible decision or a logical opinion. They can draw good conclusions after thinking about details and facts and putting them together with what they already know.

- Help students understand that they draw conclusions about characters and events as they read stories.

- Have students read the story about Sylvia and Emily. Encourage them to draw conclusions about the characters.

- Invite students to complete the exercise. Then discuss how they drew their conclusions.

 **Practice**

Introducing Vocabulary

Before students read the story, introduce the vocabulary words *(aloof, formally, pried, resentfully, retrieved, shifted, signatures)*. Have students look up the meanings of the words in the Glossary and write sentences with each word.

Reading the Passage

Have students read the title and preview the art. Ask what conclusion they might draw about Tony based on the title. *(He has just moved because he is in a new neighborhood.)*

Checking Comprehension

- To help students determine main idea, have them first think about the story's topic. Then they can decide what the most important idea about this topic is.

- To help students compare and contrast the two meetings, have them think about what Cap expected Joe DiMaggio to be like and what Tony was expecting his new neighborhood to be like.

Practicing Comprehension Skills

Remind students that they will draw many conclusions as they read. Encourage them to cite story evidence as well as personal experiences that support the conclusions that they draw.

Practicing Vocabulary

- Review the vocabulary words. Have students identify the two words with the vowel digraph *ie. (pried, retrieved)*

- Invite students to complete the vocabulary exercise independently. Go over the answers together.

Apply

Making the Reading and Writing Connection

Have partners exchange stories. Tell students to list the details the writer used to draw conclusions. They can then decide if the conclusions are based on good evidence.

MEETING INDIVIDUAL NEEDS

Phonics: Vowel Digraph *ie*

Draw attention to the two words with the vowel digraph *ie: pried, retrieved*. Write them on the board.

- Say both words and have students repeat them. Circle the letters *ie* in each word.

- Ask what sound *ie* makes in the word *pried*. (long *i*) Ask what sound *ie* makes in *retrieved*. (long *e*)

- Challenge students to think of other words with *ie*. List them on the board under the headings *long e* and *long i*. (Possible answers: *receive, believe, deceive, receipt; tried, cries, lied, fried*)

You may want to use pages 39–44 in *MCP Phonics*, Level F for additional practice with vowel digraph *ie*.

ESL Strategy

Show students photographs from newspapers or magazines. Let them study each picture and then draw a conclusion about it. Make sure they can explain the details they used to draw conclusions.

Multiple Intelligences: Bodily-Kinesthetic, Verbal-Linguistic

While one (or more) students read aloud "Tony's New Neighborhood," other students can mime Tony's, Cap's, and Joe's actions.

Home-School Connection

Students and a family member can read a chapter of a fiction book together. Afterward, they can draw conclusions about characters or events.

Identifying Sequence: Order of Events (pages 15–20)

Objective: Students can follow the order of events in a story or article.

Teaching TIPS

- Students learn that following the order of events is essential for understanding both fiction and nonfiction.

- Students pay attention to details to help them follow sequence.

Skills Reviewed and Maintained

Comprehension
Comparing and Contrasting	See Checking Comprehension
Drawing Conclusions	See Checking Comprehension

Phonics
Vowel Digraph *oo*	See Practicing Vocabulary, Phonics Mini-Lesson

Writing
News Article	See Making the Reading and Writing Connection

Teach

Explain to students that following a sequence of events is important when reading newspaper stories, magazine articles, and other nonfiction texts, such as biographies and histories. Copy and distribute the graphic organizer on page T104 of this Guide. Read aloud a newspaper article and help students organize the events sequentially in the organizer.

- Point out dates, times, and clue words that help identify the sequence. Talk about why the sequence is important.

- Remind students that following the sequence of events is just as important when reading a story.

- Together, read the article about the Battle of Lexington.

- To decide on the sequence, students should try to visualize each event and ask themselves what order makes sense. For example, seventy colonists would not have been waiting in Lexington to surprise British troops if the colonists had not been warned before.

- Have students read the story about Isaac and complete the exercise. Discuss the sequence they chose. Make sure students are able to recognize flashbacks.

 Practice

Introducing Vocabulary
Before students read the story, introduce the vocabulary words (*admiration, chided, disguises, footsore, poorly, roaming, somber*) and discuss their meanings. Have volunteers create oral sentences using the words.

Reading the Passage
Have students look at the illustration and read the title. Ask them to predict what they think "Redcoats and Homespun" will be about. You may want to explain that homespun was a plain cloth that people used to make (*spin*) at home. Review clue words students should look for as they read.

Checking Comprehension

- In order to understand the mother's change in attitude, students should compare and contrast her words and actions at the beginning of the story with her words and actions at the end.

- To help students draw conclusions, have them think about their own experiences. What do certain types or styles of clothes suggest about a person?

Practicing Comprehension Skills
Encourage students to reread the story to find the most important events to insert in the chart. They can highlight dates, times, and clue words.

Practicing Vocabulary

- Review the vocabulary words with students. Have them identify the two words containing the vowel digraph *oo*. (*footsore, poorly*)

- Let students complete the vocabulary exercise independently. Review the answers as a group.

Apply

Making the Reading and Writing Connection

Have volunteers read their news articles aloud. Ask the class to identify the clue words that tell when things happen.

MEETING INDIVIDUAL NEEDS

Phonics: Vowel Digraph *oo*

Draw attention to the two vocabulary words that have the vowel digraph *oo: footsore, poorly.*

- Write the words on the board and say them aloud, stressing the different pronunciations of *oo.* Have students repeat the words.

- Explain that in a vowel digraph, two vowels together can make a long or short sound or have a special sound all their own.

- Brainstorm other words with the vowel digraph *oo.*

Have students say each word aloud and tell whether *oo* sounds like it does in *foot* or *poor.*

You may want to use pages 45–46 in *MCP Phonics,* Level F for additional practice with the vowel digraph *oo.*

ESL Strategy

Provide extra practice with clue words such as *first, next, then, after that, before, later,* and *finally.* Have students use at least three of the words to describe a sequence of events.

Multiple Intelligences: Verbal-Linguistic, Interpersonal

Organize students in pairs and have them role-play an interview for a colonial newspaper. One student can play the role of a British spy or a colonial sympathizer. The other student can be a newspaper reporter.

Home-School Connection

Have students watch a television show with a family member. After the show, they can discuss its sequence of events. Were there any flashbacks? If so, how were they handled?

LESSON 4

Identifying Sequence: Steps in a Process
(pages 21–24)

Objective: Students can follow sequence when reading instructions.

Teaching TIPS

- Students realize that being able to follow a set of ordered instructions is an important skill both in and out of school.

- Students use clue words and visualizing to follow sequence.

Skills Reviewed and Maintained

Comprehension
Drawing Conclusions	See Checking Comprehension
Making Judgments	See Checking Comprehension

Phonics
Vowel Pairs *ai, ay*	See Practicing Vocabulary, Phonics Mini-Lesson

Writing
Directions	See Making the Reading and Writing Connection

Teach

Define the word *process* as a series of steps followed in a certain order to get to a certain result. It almost always involves doing or making something in a predictable, unvarying way. For example, getting ready for school each morning is a process. Have students discuss the order of the steps for getting ready for school.

- Write the following steps on the board.

Washing the Dog

_3_ Then, put the dog in the water and get him wet.

_2_ Next, fill the bathtub with warm water.

_4_ Rub shampoo all over the dog.

_1_ First, find the dog hiding under the bed.

_6_ Last, dry the dog with a big towel.

_5_ Rinse the dog.

- Ask students to put these steps in order. Remind them to use clue words to help them follow the sequence. (3, 2, 4, 1, 6, 5)

- Explain that many instructions include illustrations or diagrams. If possible, show examples, such as cookbooks, in which techniques are illustrated.

- Have students read about how to grow carrots, and then have them number the steps in order.

- Check for understanding by having students explain why the order they chose makes sense.

 **Practice**

Introducing Vocabulary

Before students read the recipe, introduce the vocabulary words (*alternate, bisected, delay, devoured, ingredients, obtain, optional*) and discuss their meanings. Ask students to look up the meanings in the Glossary and write a paragraph using as many of the words as they can.

Reading the Passage

Invite students to read the title and list of ingredients and to look at the photograph. Ask them what kind of process they expect to read about. Encourage them to underline phrases to help them remember each step as they read.

Checking Comprehension

- To help students draw conclusions, have them skim the recipe and circle items that are mentioned in the text but are not in the list of ingredients.

- Remind students that a judgment is based on the information they read as well as their own experiences. Ask students to think about a time when they prepared something to eat. What were some of the difficulties they encountered?

Practicing Comprehension Skills

Have students visualize the steps as they put them in order. Encourage students to check their answers by acting out the steps in the sequence in which they labeled them. Does their sequence make sense?

Practicing Vocabulary

- Review vocabulary words with students. Have them identify the two words that contain the long *a* sound, spelled *ai* or *ay*. (obtain, delay)

- Students can complete the vocabulary exercise independently. Review the answers as a class.

Apply

Making the Reading and Writing Connection

Have partners read each other's directions and visualize the process described. They should make sure that the steps are in order and that no important steps are left out.

MEETING INDIVIDUAL NEEDS

Phonics: Vowel Pairs *ai, ay*

Write the long *a* words on the board: *obtain, delay.*

- Point to *delay*, say the word, and have students repeat it. Ask which letters represent the long *a* sound. (ay) Repeat the procedure with *obtain*. (ai)

- Ask students to find other words in the recipe in which /ā/ is spelled *ay*. (may, always, okay, way, days)

- Brainstorm other words in which /ā/ is spelled *ai*. (Possible answers: *bait, fail, maid, nail*)

You may want to use pages 33–34 in *MCP Phonics*, Level F for additional practice with words with vowel pairs *ai, ay*.

ESL Strategy

Photocopy the cupcake instructions, cut them up into paragraphs, and paste each paragraph on a separate index card. Shuffle the cards and have partners put them back in order.

Multiple Intelligences: Musical, Interpersonal

Students can use the recipe for carrot cupcakes as the basis for a rap or other rhyming song. Ask a small group to rephrase the steps in a rap style and rhythm, then perform the song for the class.

Home-School Connection

Students can help a family member follow a recipe to prepare a favorite food. Before they begin to cook, students should read the recipe to make sure that they understand each step in the process.

Predicting Outcomes (pages 25–28)

Objective: Students can make, check, and verify predictions.

Teaching TIPS

- Learning to predict outcomes helps students to become more involved in the story.

- Predicting helps students to understand that a text progresses logically and that it has a recognizable structure.

Skills Reviewed and Maintained

Comprehension
Author's Purpose	See Checking Comprehension
Drawing Conclusions	See Checking Comprehension

Phonics
Vowel Digraph *ea*	See Practicing Vocabulary, Phonics Mini-Lesson

Writing
Journal Entry	See Making the Reading and Writing Connection

Teach

Pantomime some gesture associated with being either hot or cold, such as mopping your brow or shivering. Then walk toward the window. Have students predict what you will do and give reasons for their predictions.

- Give each student a copy of the Graphic Organizer on page T106 of this Guide. Write their responses in a similar chart on the chalkboard.

- Tell students that predicting means using details in the text, visual clues (such as illustrations), and prior knowledge to tell what they think might happen next.

- Have students make predictions about the story on page 25 after they look at the illustration and read the title. Write their predictions and the clues they used in the chart.

- Invite students to read "Ticket to the Future" and to stop after the second paragraph.

- Have students evaluate and refine their predictions in light of what they have just read. Ask them to make additional predictions.

- After students finish reading the story, repeat the previous step.

- As students complete the exercise, check for understanding.

On Your Own Practice

Introducing Vocabulary

Before students read the story, introduce the vocabulary words (*deserted, familiar, liberty, overhead, peal, wispy, wistfully*) and discuss their meanings. Have students use the words in oral sentences.

Reading the Passage

Encourage students to predict what "The New Guy, Ben" may be about by looking at the illustration and thinking about the title of the story. Remind them to use their prior knowledge when making predictions.

Checking Comprehension

- Point out to students that the author doesn't directly say that Ben is Benjamin Franklin. Instead, the author's purpose is to provide several clues and have the reader figure out the identity of the main character.

- Discuss clues, such as the kite string, that made Tom (and the reader) draw the conclusion that the visitor is Benjamin Franklin.

Practicing Comprehension Skills

Discuss how a guess and a prediction differ. A guess is not based on actual knowledge and is not supported by many facts. Encourage students to use their own knowledge as well as the details in the text when they make predictions.

Practicing Vocabulary

Review the vocabulary words and discuss their meanings. Have students identify the two words with the vowel digraph *ea* and note the different sound the digraph makes in each.

Apply

Making the Reading and Writing Connection

Ask volunteers to read aloud their journal entries. Have students figure out what real-life clues each prediction is based on.

MEETING INDIVIDUAL NEEDS

Phonics: Vowel Digraph *ea*

On the chalkboard, write the vocabulary words *overhead* and *peal*.

- Have students say the words aloud. Note the two different sounds of *ea*: /ĕ/ and /ē/.
- Have students look back in the story for more *ea* words, say each word, and listen to the sound of the vowel digraph. (*leather* /ĕ/, *leaving* /ē/, *head* /ĕ/)

See pages 39–40 in *MCP Phonics*, Level F for additional practice with the digraph *ea*.

ESL Strategy

Point out to students that Ben is, like themselves, from another culture. Discuss some of the obstacles he faces or aspects of modern life that confuse him.

Multiple Intelligences: Verbal-Linguistic, Visual-Spatial, Interpersonal

Small groups of students can present the story as readers' theater. Have them review the text and mark the dialogue for each character.

Home-School Connection

Encourage students to watch a television show with a family member. At each commercial break, students should predict what will happen next. At the end of the show, they can verify their predictions.

LESSON 6 Recognizing Cause and Effect (pages 29–32)

Objective: Students can identify relationships between what happened and why.

Teaching TIPS

- Students gain a better understanding of what they read when they understand cause-and-effect relationships.
- Students have better comprehension in all subject areas when they understand cause-and-effect relationships.

Skills Reviewed and Maintained

Comprehension

Main Idea and Details	See Checking Comprehension
Comparing and Contrasting	See Teach, Checking Comprehension

Phonics

Diphthong *ew*	See Practicing Vocabulary, Phonics Mini-Lesson

Writing

Persuasive Paragraph	See Making the Reading and Writing Connection

Teach

Explain to students that in order to understand an event, they need to have some understanding of what caused it.

- Distribute the Graphic Organizer on page T108 of this Guide. Have students brainstorm some things they know about the American Revolution. In each "What happened" section, direct them to write a well-known event from the American Revolution, such as the Boston Tea Party.

- Work with students to identify a cause for the first event and write it in the "Why it happened" section. Have students brainstorm a cause for the second event and write it on the corresponding lines.

> 1. **What happened:** Boston Tea Party
>
>   **Why it happened:** Colonists were angry about high taxes.

- Explain that an effect is something that happens and a cause is why something happens. Point out that clue words such as *because* and *since* can alert readers that a writer is presenting a cause-and-effect relationship.

- Invite students to read the story about a biology student's research paper. Encourage them to look for clue words that suggest why something happened. *(since)*

- Ask students to contrast the narrator's expectations with the actual search results.

- Have students complete the exercise. Check to be sure they can identify causes, effects, and clue words that signal causal relationships.

 ## Practice

Introducing Vocabulary
Before students read the story, introduce the vocabulary words (*brainchild, infancy, Internet, reviewed, shrewd, sites, technology*) and discuss their meanings. Call on volunteers to use the words in oral sentences.

Reading the Passage
Have students preview the title and graphic and then predict what the article might be about. Compare the title word *superhighway* to the familiar word *supermarket*. Explain that a market needs a huge variety of goods to be considered "super"; similarly, the information superhighway contains a huge amount of data.

Checking Comprehension
- Clarify the article's main idea: *The Internet has changed our world in a short period of time.* Discuss supporting details, such as the immense amount of information now quickly available for research.

- Invite students to compare and contrast e-mail and postal mail. Discuss the pros and cons of each method of communication. Have students reread the last paragraph for details about the disadvantages of e-mail.

Practicing Comprehension Skills
Suggest that students identify an effect by asking, "What happened?" and identify a cause by asking, "Why did this happen?" Remind them that a single effect may have multiple causes and a single cause may have multiple effects.

Practicing Vocabulary
- Have students identify the two words that have the *ew* diphthong. *(reviewed, shrewd)* Have them underline the *ew* in each word.

- Invite students to complete the vocabulary exercise independently. Review the answers with the group.

Apply

Making the Reading and Writing Connection
Have partners trade papers. Ask the reader to decide whether a paragraph provides enough details to persuade. Then have the reader identify causes and effects and find any clue words that signal causal relationships.

MEETING INDIVIDUAL NEEDS

Phonics: Diphthong ew
Write *reviewed* and *shrewd* on the board. Have students repeat the words after you read them. Underline the letters *ew* and explain that they blend to make one sound.

- Invite students to find two more words in the article that have the diphthong *ew*. *(few, new)* Point out that *ew* has the same sound wherever it appears in the word.

- Have students think of other words that end with the diphthong *ew*, such as *flew, blew, grew.*

- Ask volunteers to create and recite two-line rhymes. The last word of each line should end in *ew*. For example: *Last year when the final winds blew /The birds said, "It's cold!" and flew.*

You may want to refer to pages 55–56 in *MCP Phonics*, Level F for additional practice with the diphthong *ew*.

ESL Strategy
Discuss with students acquiring English the effects of their learning a new language. Ask them to consider: *What effect has learning English had on your life?*

Multiple Intelligences: Visual-Spatial
Write the cause half of the statements about the Internet on cards of one color. Write the effect half of the statements on cards of another color. Shuffle each set of cards and have students match causes with effects to make complete sentences. Remind them to look for clue words.

Home-School Connection
Encourage students to survey their families about the importance of the Internet. Family members can compare the effects of the Internet on their lives with the effects of other forms of technology, such as videocassette recorders.

Using Context Clues (pages 33–36)

LESSON 7

Objective: Students can use context clues to find the meanings of unfamiliar words.

Teaching TIPS

- Learning to use context clues helps students to understand even complex texts.
- Using context clues helps students become better independent readers.

Skills Reviewed and Maintained

Comprehension

Comparing and Contrasting	See Checking Comprehension
Making Predictions	See Checking Comprehension

Word Study

Prefixes: anti-, counter-	See Practicing Vocabulary, Word Study Mini-Lesson

Writing

Campaign Speech	See Making the Reading and Writing Connection

Teach

Display a page from a science or math book that shows new vocabulary in boldface. Discuss the clues students can use to figure out the meanings of new words. Remind them that context clues may be in the same sentence as the unknown word or in surrounding sentences.

- Point out the chart on page 33. Discuss how using these clues makes reading more pleasurable because readers do not have to stop to consult a dictionary to figure out the meaning of each unfamiliar word.

- Write on the chalkboard these additional context clues and discuss them with students.

Description: At the landfill, mountains of rubbish are buried, not burned.

Multiple-meaning words: The manager was canned for being dishonest.

Homonyms: My junk mail included a catalog offering male clothing for sale.

Specialized/technical words: Bacteria, or microscopic living things, will break down the rubbish.

- Remind students to use dictionaries and glossaries if needed.

- Invite students to read the story. Tell them to use what they know and context clues to figure out the meaning of unfamiliar words.

 Practice

Introducing Vocabulary

Before students read the story, review the vocabulary words (*antisocial, candidate, counterproductive, distributed, platform, tutor, versus*) and discuss their meanings. Have students create sentences using the words.

Reading the Passage

Encourage students to preview the illustration and predict some of the words they may encounter when they read the story. Remind them to use context clues to figure out the meanings of any unfamiliar words.

Checking Comprehension

- Encourage students to list the things that each candidate did and then group the activities to make them easier to compare and contrast.

- Discuss evidence in the story, such as the election results and the discussion of real issues, that might have helped students predict its outcome.

Practicing Comprehension Skills

Encourage students to identify the context clues they used to figure out unfamiliar words in the story. Review why it is important to look for context clues when reading.

Practicing Vocabulary

Review the vocabulary words with students. Have them identify and define the two words that have the prefixes *anti-* and *counter-*. (*antisocial, counterproductive*)

Apply

Making the Reading and Writing Connection

Ask volunteers to give their campaign speeches. Have students listen for context clues that explain the meanings of unfamiliar words.

MEETING INDIVIDUAL NEEDS

Word Study: Prefixes: *anti-*, *counter-*

On the chalkboard, draw a 2-column chart. Write *anti-* and *counter-* at the top of the columns. Write the vocabulary words *antisocial* and *counterproductive* in the appropriate columns.

- Remind students that *anti-* and *counter-* mean *against* or *opposite*.

- Discuss with students how they can use what they know about the prefixes and their meanings to figure out unfamiliar words.

- Have students brainstorm other words with the prefixes to add to the chart.

See pages 71–72 in *MCP Phonics*, Level F for additional practice with the prefixes *anti-* and *counter-*.

ESL Strategy

Help students acquiring English brainstorm and discuss the meanings of expressions such as "running for student government," "student body," and "taking sides."

Multiple Intelligences: Bodily-Kinesthetic, Interpersonal

Have students work in groups to create and perform a play based on the story. Encourage students to include context clues for any unfamiliar words that they use.

Home-School Connection

Encourage students to show family members examples of context clues in a newspaper article and explain how they are used to figure out new words.

LESSON 8

Comparing and Contrasting (pages 37–40)

Objective: Students can recognize likenesses and differences.

Teaching TIPS

- Students better understand new concepts and ideas when they compare and contrast the unknown with the known.

- Students can use comparison and contrast as a method for organizing their own writing.

Skills Reviewed and Maintained

Comprehension

Classifying	See Teach
Drawing Conclusions	See Checking Comprehension
Cause and Effect	See Checking Comprehension

Word Study

Root *spec*	See Practicing Vocabulary, Word Study Mini-Lesson

Writing

Comparison Essay	See Making the Reading and Writing Connection

Teach

Remind students that comparing and contrasting are basic reasoning tools that they use every day, both in and out of school. By using the method of comparison and contrast, a person can explain something unfamiliar by telling how it is similar to and different from something familiar.

- Copy and distribute the Graphic Organizer on page T111 of this Guide. Work with students to use the Venn diagram to compare and contrast a familiar and an unfamiliar food—for example, hot dogs and fajitas.

- Point out that students can use this comparison to help someone understand what a fajita is and decide whether to try one.

- Explain that comparing things and classifying things are closely related skills. Comparing and contrasting concentrate mostly on identifying something's features, particularly pairs of things. Classifying focuses more on groups of things—arranging things into related groups, adding to the groups, labeling the groups.

- Have students read the paragraphs on eyesight. As they read, tell them to look for clue words that signal similarities and differences. (*too long, too short; opposite problem; clearer*)

 **Practice**

Introducing Vocabulary

Before students read the article, introduce the vocabulary words (*aperture, focus, perspective, pupil, retina, spectacularly, visual*) and discuss their meanings. Have students look up each word's meaning in the Glossary and use it in an oral sentence.

Reading the Passage

Ask students to look at the diagrams and read the title. Talk about why the author might have decided to compare and contrast the eye and the camera. Remind students to look for clue words that signal comparisons and contrasts as they read the article.

Checking Comprehension

- To help students draw their conclusions, have them highlight article details that focus on the brain's role.

- Suggest that students complete this sentence to help them identify the cause-and-effect relationship: *The lens of the eye needs to change shape because _____.*

Practicing Comprehension Skills

Encourage students to make comparisons and contrasts themselves. Suggest that they compare what they learn in the article to what they already know about how people see.

Practicing Vocabulary

- Review vocabulary words with students. Help them identify the two words that contain the root *spec*. (*spectacularly, perspective*) Tell students that the root *spec* means "see."

- Have students complete the vocabulary exercise independently. Share the answers as a group.

Apply

Making the Reading and Writing Connection

Have volunteers read their essays aloud. Students can jot down any clue words that they hear. Afterward, list these words on the board and discuss how they make the comparisons and contrasts easier to understand.

MEETING INDIVIDUAL NEEDS

Word Study: Root *spec*

Draw attention to the two vocabulary words that have the root *spec*: *spectacularly, perspective.*

- Write the words on the board. Say the words and have students repeat them. Circle the root *spec* in each.

- Remind students that the root *spec* means "see."

- Ask students how these two words are connected with seeing or sight. (*spectacularly:* describes something that is amazing to look at; *perspective:* how something faraway or nearby appears to the viewer)

- Brainstorm other words that contain the root *spec.* Use a dictionary if necessary. (Possible answers: *respect, spectacle, spectacles, inspect, spectator*)

You may want to use pages 97–98 in *MCP Phonics*, Level F for additional practice with words with the root *spec*.

ESL Strategy

Have partners gather a variety of classroom objects. They can work together to compare and contrast two or more objects. Then they can write a sentence telling how the objects are alike and a sentence telling how they are different. Encourage them to use clue words in their sentences.

Multiple Intelligences: Visual-Spatial, Verbal-Linguistic

Have students do some basic research to find out how the human ear hears. Then they can create Venn diagrams that compare and contrast the ears and the eyes.

Home-School Connection

Each student and a family member can discuss their appearances and/or personalities. Together, they can make a chart or write a paragraph explaining how they are alike and different.

Summarizing (pages 41–46)

Objective: Students can summarize an article or story.

Teaching TIPS

- Summarizing helps students organize and evaluate information.
- Summarizing helps students prepare for tests.

Skills Reviewed and Maintained

Comprehension

Comparing and Contrasting	See Checking Comprehension
Drawing Conclusions	See Checking Comprehension
Outlining	See Practicing Comprehension Skills
Notetaking	See Practicing Comprehension Skills

Word Study

Prefix *de-*	See Practicing Vocabulary, Word Study Mini-Lesson

Writing

Movie Review	See Making the Reading and Writing Connection

Teach

Explain to students that a summary is a short statement—no more than a few sentences—that gives the main ideas of an article or tells what happened in a story. A summary does not include details.

- Tell students the familiar fable of the tortoise and the hare:

  Tortoise and Hare agree to a race. Hare brags that he will win. At first, Hare is ahead because he is faster. He is so far ahead that he decides to stop for a nap. Tortoise is slower, but he keeps trying. He doesn't stop to rest or to look at flowers or to have a snack; he just keeps walking. In time, he walks right past the napping Hare. Tortoise reaches the finish line first and wins the race.

- Distribute the Graphic Organizer on page T105 of this Guide. Have students suggest main ideas or actions in the fable. Write these on the board as students fill out their organizers. Then work together to write a summary using the main ideas.

Main Idea: Hare is ahead of Tortoise in the race, so he stops for a nap.
Main Idea: Tortoise keeps going and reaches the finish line first.

- Invite students to read "Press Release: 'Dr. Nero, Superhero.'" Have them think about how they could summarize the release in two or three sentences.

- As students complete the exercise, check that they have underlined the main ideas.

 Practice

Introducing Vocabulary

Before students read the article, review the vocabulary words (*deflate, descend, electronics, gadgets, facial, comical, remote*) and discuss their meanings. Have students create sentences using the words.

Reading the Passage

Ask students to predict what they will learn in "It Lives!" based on the title and illustrations. As they read, remind them to look for the main ideas that would be included in a summary of the article.

Checking Comprehension

- Ask students why the author compares and contrasts *King Kong* and *Buddy. (to show how much special effects techniques have changed over time)*

- When drawing a conclusion, students should use their own knowledge and details from the text. Discuss how students can draw the following conclusion: *People like special effects that look realistic.*

Practicing Comprehension Skills

Ask students to look at each paragraph in the article and identify the important idea(s) they would include in a summary. Suggest that students take notes or make an outline to help them remember the important ideas.

Practicing Vocabulary

Have students identify the two vocabulary words that begin with the prefix *de-*. *(deflate, descend)* Invite students to complete the vocabulary exercise independently.

Apply

Making the Reading and Writing Connection

Invite volunteers to read aloud their movie reviews. Ask students to discuss whether each summary includes only important information.

MEETING INDIVIDUAL NEEDS

Word Study: Prefix *de-*

On the board, write the two vocabulary words that begin with the prefix *de-*: *deflate, descend*. Have students say each word and ask a volunteer to identify the prefix.

- Tell students that the prefix *de-* can mean "down," "away from," or "the reverse of." Discuss how the meanings of the prefix apply to the vocabulary words.

- Remind students that *de-* at the beginning of a word is not always a prefix. *(deal, dessert)* Have students suggest other words that begin with the prefix *de-*. (possible answers: *decrease, defrost, degrade*)

You may want to use pages 75–76 in *MCP Phonics,* Level F for additional practice with the prefix *de-*.

ESL Strategy

Students can work with partners to select a simple story to read and summarize. Provide help with unfamiliar vocabulary.

Multiple Intelligences: Logical-Mathematical

Have students use the Graphic Organizer on page T111 of this Guide to compare and contrast the two types of special effects described in "It Lives!" *(models and animatronics)*.

Home-School Connection

Suggest that students watch a television show with a family member, and then summarize it in a few sentences.

LESSON 10 Paraphrasing (pages 47–50)

Objective: Students can paraphrase a passage they have read.

Teaching TIPS

- Paraphrasing a text shows that students understand the material.
- Paraphrasing is a valuable tool in the research process.

Skills Reviewed and Maintained

Comprehension

Drawing Conclusions	See Checking Comprehension
Cause and Effect	See Checking Comprehension

Word Study

Prefixes *over-, super-*	See Practicing Vocabulary, Word Study Mini-Lesson

Writing

Descriptive Paragraph   See Making the Reading and Writing Connection

Teach

Point out that paraphrasing is something students do every day without being aware of it. For example, when they relay a phone message, they are paraphrasing.

- Read the following sentences to students.

    Original: On a map, if you draw a line among the volcanoes in the area of the Pacific, you will create a rough circle. Scientists refer to this circular shape as the Ring of Fire.

    Paraphrase: If you draw a line on a map connecting the volcanoes in the Pacific area, you get a circle called the Ring of Fire.

Summary: The volcanoes of the Pacific make a circle called the Ring of Fire.

- Distinguish between paraphrasing and summarizing. The paraphrase and the original are almost the same length because they contain all the same ideas. The summary is shorter because it restates only the main idea.

- Note that the paraphrase is simpler than the original and that no new ideas or opinions have been added.

- As students complete the exercise, check their comprehension.

 Practice

Introducing Vocabulary

Before students read the passage, introduce the vocabulary words *(catapulted, instantaneously, leveled, magnitude, overwhelming, serene, superheated)* and discuss their meanings. Have students use the words in oral sentences.

Reading the Passage

Ask students what they think they will learn from "A Mountain Awakes" by looking at the photos, reading the title, and skimming the text. As they read, remind them to think about synonyms they can use in a paraphrase of the article.

Checking Comprehension

- Ask students what conclusion they can draw from the people not evacuating the area after the earthquakes and explosion in March.

- Use the Graphic Organizer on page T108 of this Guide to relate the chain of causes and effects that led from the March 1980 earthquakes to the eruption on May 18.

Practicing Comprehension Skills

Encourage students to paraphrase the article. Afterward, they can check their paraphrasing by asking themselves, *"Did I use my own words and avoid copying? Does my paraphrase accurately reflect the writer's meaning?"*

Practicing Vocabulary

- Review the vocabulary words and their meanings.

- Have students identify the two words that have the prefixes *over-* and *super-* and distinguish the base word from the prefix. *(overwhelming, superheated)*

Apply

Making the Reading and Writing Connection

Ask partners to read aloud their paragraphs and paraphrases. Have students listen to make sure the meaning and key ideas of the original are included in the paraphrase.

MEETING INDIVIDUAL NEEDS

Word Study: Prefixes

Write the vocabulary words *overwhelming* and *superheated* on the chalkboard.

- Remind students that the prefix *over-* means "too" or "too much." *Super-* means "very," "over," or "greater than."

- Discuss the prefixes and how they affect the meaning of the base word.

- Have students brainstorm other words that have the two prefixes and discuss their meanings.

You may want to use pages 79–80 in *MCP Phonics*, Level F for additional practice with prefixes.

ESL Strategy

Students can make a drawing of the volcano's eruption and label it with key words or information from the text.

Multiple Intelligences: Logical-Mathematical, Visual-Spatial

Have students create an illustrated time line of the Mount St. Helen's eruption from March through May 1980. They can paraphrase sentences from the text to use as labels for the events.

Home-School Connection

Suggest that students read an article from a magazine with a family member and then paraphrase one or two paragraphs from it.

Recognizing Author's Purpose (pages 51–56)

Objective: Students can recognize an author's purpose(s) for writing.

Skills Reviewed and Maintained

Comprehension
Making Generalizations   See Checking Comprehension
Making Judgments   See Checking Comprehension

Phonics
Diphthongs *ou, ow*   See Practicing Vocabulary, Phonics Mini-Lesson

Writing
Eyewitness Account   See Making the Reading and Writing Connection

Teach

Explain to students that the language and style of a piece of writing can help them figure out why the author wrote it.

- Read aloud this imaginary ad:

  There's Never Been a Better Time to See Alaska!

  Enjoy the Beauty and Excitement of the Last Frontier.

  Take Advantage of the Lowest Air Fares in Years.

- Tell students that an author's purpose can be to persuade, inform, entertain, and/or express a feeling. Point out that authors often have more than one reason for writing. Ask why the writer wrote the ad. *(to persuade)*

- Ask volunteers to name familiar examples of writing that tries to persuade, inform, entertain, or express some feelings. (possible answers: *an advertising slogan, a science news report, a short story, a description of a wedding*)

- Invite students to read the article and the passage about the Iditarod race. Tell them to think about the author's purpose(s) for writing each one.

- As students complete the exercise, check for their understanding of the purpose of the article.

 ## Practice

Introducing Vocabulary

Before students read the story, introduce the vocabulary words *(brooded, brutal, captures, classic, confounds, instinct, cowering)* and discuss their meanings. Have small groups of students work together to create a short story using all the words.

Reading the Passage

Ask students to use the title "Recommended Reading: *The Call of the Wild* by Jack London" to predict what the review will be about. As they read, remind them to focus on the author's purpose(s) for writing the review.

Checking Comprehension

- Ask students to make generalizations about why readers like *The Call of the Wild*. Remind them to base their generalizations on a number of comments that the author makes in the review.

- When deciding whether they would like to read *The Call of the Wild*, ask students to make their judgments based on the review, the passage from the novel, and other books they have enjoyed.

Practicing Comprehension Skills

Have students review the four purposes for writing and their definitions, listed on page 51. As they read the review, ask students to judge how well the author's language and style support his or her purpose.

Practicing Vocabulary

- Review the vocabulary words with students.

- Have students identify the two vocabulary words with the diphthongs *ou* or *ow*. *(cowering, confound)*

- Invite students to complete the vocabulary exercise independently.

Apply

Making the Reading and Writing Connection

Ask volunteers to read aloud their eyewitness accounts. Have students identify the author's main purpose for writing and cite evidence from the account that supports that purpose.

MEETING INDIVIDUAL NEEDS

Phonics: Diphthongs *ou, ow*

Say *cowering* and *confound*. Have students repeat the words and listen for the sound that both words have in common.

- Write the words on the board and underline the letters that represent the sound /ou/.

- Ask students to find three other words in the book review that contain the same sound. *(power, allows, sounds)*

You may want to use pages 53–54 in *MCP Phonics*, Level F for additional practice with diphthongs *ou* and *ow*.

ESL Strategy

Students can draw a book cover that would persuade people to read *The Call of the Wild*. Suggest that they write sentences that advertise the book. Make sure their covers include details found in the review.

Multiple Intelligences: Verbal-Linguistic, Interpersonal

Encourage small groups of students to discuss the review and evaluate the author's success in meeting his or her purpose(s). Students should explain why they are or are not persuaded to read *The Call of the Wild*.

Home-School Connection

Have students look at a magazine with a family member and find articles or stories that inform, persuade, entertain, and/or express a feeling. Remind them that an author often has more than one reason for writing.

LESSON 12

Statements of Fact and Opinion (pages 57–60)

Objective: Students can identify statements as fact or opinion.

Teaching TIPS

- Students who can recognize facts and opinions are able to think critically about what they read.

- Students who can distinguish between facts and opinions can avoid being misled.

Skills Reviewed and Maintained

Comprehension

Cause and Effect	See Checking Comprehension
Making Judgments	See Checking Comprehension

Word Study

Roots *pel, pul*	See Practicing Vocabulary, Word Study Mini-Lesson

Writing

Persuasive Paragraph	See Making the Reading and Writing Connection

Teach

Ask students to name their favorite athletes, musicians, or actors and tell the reasons for their choices. Give each student a copy of the Graphic Organizer on page T109 of this Guide. Write their responses in a similar chart on the board.

- Using these examples, discuss the differences between statements of fact and statements of opinion. Remind students that a statement of fact can be proved true or false. A statement of opinion expresses a person's feeling, judgment, or belief about something.

- Have students judge whether their reasons are facts or opinions.

- Call students' attention to the first paragraph of the letter to the editor. Ask them to decide if each sentence is a statement of fact or a statement of opinion. Remind them that sometimes a statement can contain both fact and opinion.

- Ask students to suggest ways of checking whether a factual statement is true or false.

- Distinguish between valid statements of opinion and faulty ones. A valid opinion is supported by facts or by the opinion of an expert.

- As students complete the exercise, check their comprehension.

 **Practice**

Introducing Vocabulary

Before reading the article, introduce the vocabulary words *(attempts, composed, defender, impulsively, propels, recap, superstitious)* and discuss their meanings. Encourage students to look up the words in the Glossary and create oral sentences with the words.

Reading the Passage

Point out that "World Cup '99: The Final Game" is a transcript of a radio or television broadcast. Encourage students to make predictions about the article's content based on their own experiences of listening to sports announcers.

Checking Comprehension

- Clarify the cause and effect relationships in the text. Make sure students understand the cause and effect of the final penalty kick.

- Discuss how students can evaluate statements to make a judgment about the announcer's bias. Have them consider the compliments he pays to the U.S. team and the adjectives he uses to describe each team.

Practicing Comprehension Skills

Remind students that clue words and phrases, such as *best, worst, greatest, I believe, in my opinion,* and *I think,* usually signal an opinion. Encourage them to identify such clues as they read.

Practicing Vocabulary

Review the vocabulary words and their meanings. Have students identify the word that has the root *pel. (propel)* Ask students to complete the vocabulary exercise independently. Review the answers with the group.

Apply

Making the Reading and Writing Connection

Ask volunteers to read aloud their persuasive paragraphs. Have students suggest ways that the facts can be proved true or false and decide whether the opinions are valid or faulty.

MEETING INDIVIDUAL NEEDS

Word Study: Roots *pel, pul*

Write the vocabulary word *propel* on the chalkboard and circle the root.

- Remind students that the roots *pel* and *pul* usually mean "push" or "drive."

- Circle the prefix *pro-* and clarify its meaning in this word, "forward." Discuss how the prefix and the root combine to give the word *propel* its meaning.

- Write the following words on the chalkboard and discuss how the roots *pel* and *pul* affect the meanings: *propulsion, expel, repel, repulse, compel,* and *propeller.*

You may want to use pages 93–94 in *MCP Phonics,* Level F for additional practice with the roots *pel* and *pul.*

ESL Strategy

Have students pantomime some actions and emotions described in the selection, such as *shoulders slumping, scowl, dropping to knees,* and *kick.*

Multiple Intelligences: Verbal-Linguistic, Interpersonal

Small groups of students can write a description of the soccer match from the point of view of a Chinese announcer.

Home-School Connection

Encourage students to read an article from the sports section of the newspaper with a family member, identify the facts and opinions, and decide whether the opinions are valid or faulty.

Making Judgments (pages 61–64)

Objective: Students can make judgments about a nonfiction text.

Teaching TIPS

- When students make and test their judgments about texts, they are better able to gauge their understanding.

- When students judge the accuracy of a text, they are able to decide whether it is reliable.

Skills Reviewed and Maintained

Comprehension
Recognizing Author's Purpose   See Teach
Main Idea and Details   See Checking Comprehension
Cause and Effect   See Checking Comprehension

Word Study
Compound Words   See Practicing Vocabulary, Word Study Mini-Lesson

Writing
Letter   See Making the Reading and Writing Connection

Teach

Display a magazine ad that makes a claim. Ask students whether they believe the claim. Have them explain how they made their judgments. Encourage students to rely on their own experiences as well as "digging" for information from the text and considering the illustrations.

- Have students think about the author's purpose for writing the article about the *Titanic*. Remind them that an author's purpose may be to persuade, inform, entertain, and/or express an opinion.

- Ask students whether they believe everything they read. Discuss how an author's purpose can influence his or her writing and why readers need to question the accuracy of a text.

- Help students establish criteria for making judgments, such as asking if the author considers both sides of an issue.

- After students read the article, have a volunteer read aloud the first sentence. Discuss the claim, have students judge whether it was valid or invalid, and cite details from the text to support their judgment.

- As students complete the exercise, check their comprehension.

On Your Own Practice

Introducing Vocabulary

Before reading the article, introduce the vocabulary words (*estimated, hull, lax, lifeboats, steamship, survivors, vital*) and discuss their meanings. Have pairs of students work together to create a short article using the words.

Reading the Passage

Ask students to look at the photo and read the title "Abandon Ship! To the Lifeboats!," then tell what they expect to learn. Remind them to make judgments as they read, not just at the end.

Checking Comprehension

- Discuss the main idea of the article: *About 1,500 people died unnecessarily when the* Titanic *sank.* Ask students to find details in the article that support the main idea.

- Remind students that the *Titanic* disaster was caused by outdated safety laws and poor planning. In turn, the disaster had many effects, such as prompting changes in shipping laws.

Practicing Comprehension Skills

Encourage students to question the author's objectivity. They should ask themselves, *"Is my judgment based on facts or opinions I found in the text?"*

Practicing Vocabulary

Review the vocabulary words and their meanings. Have students identify the two compound words (*steamship, lifeboats*) and the words that make up each compound word.

Apply

Making the Reading and Writing Connection

Ask volunteers to read aloud their letters. Have students identify the judgments and decide if they are supported by details.

MEETING INDIVIDUAL NEEDS

Word Study: Compound Words

Write the vocabulary words *steamship* and *lifeboats* on the chalkboard.

- Remind students that compound words are words made up of two or more smaller words.

- Discuss how the meanings of the two smaller words work together to create the meaning of the compound word. Have students give the meanings for the smaller words and their compound form.

- Have students identify other compound words in the article and discuss their meanings: *iceberg, good-bye, everyone.*

You may want to use pages 99–100 in *MCP Phonics,* Level F for additional practice with compound words.

ESL Strategy

Nonfiction articles are often difficult for ESL students to understand. Have them work with a more proficient student to read the article and make a time line of the events. Assist with unfamiliar vocabulary as needed.

Multiple Intelligences: Logical-Mathematical

Have students make up math problems using the numbers in the article *(1912; 2,300; 1,178; 11:40 P.M.; and so on).* They can challenge classmates to solve the problems.

Home-School Connection

Urge students to work with all family members to come up with a plan to get out of their home safely in case of a fire. They should rehearse the procedure, judge whether there are any flaws in it, and then refine it.

LESSON 14 — Point of View (pages 65–70)

Objective: Students can identify the narrator's point of view.

Teaching TIPS

- Understanding point of view helps students evaluate information.
- Understanding point of view helps students appreciate an author's style.

Skills Reviewed and Maintained

Comprehension

Main Idea	See Checking Comprehension
Character	See Checking Comprehension

Phonics

Diphthongs *oi, oy*	See Practicing Vocabulary, Phonics Mini-Lesson

Writing

Narrative	See Making the Reading and Writing Connection

Teach

Write the following sentences on the board and ask how they are different:

My parents named me Ben after my grandfather.
Ben's parents named their son after his grandfather.

- Point out that in the first sentence, Ben speaks in the first person, using the pronoun *me.* In the second sentence, an outsider speaks about Ben, using the third person.

- Tell students that authors must decide whether to tell a story from the first-person or the third-person point of view. Third-person point of view can be omniscient *(all-knowing),* limited-omniscient, or dramatic.

- Use this chart to introduce the different points of view.

If the narrator . . .	Then the point of view is . . .
is a story character	first person
is not a story character	third person
tells all characters' thoughts	omniscient
tells one character's thoughts	limited-omniscient
describes only actions	dramatic

- Tell students that if they identify the narrator's point of view in a story, they will better understand the characters and plot.

- Invite students to read the four versions of the story on page 65 and compare the four points of view.

- As students complete the exercise, check for their understanding.

 Practice

Introducing Vocabulary

Before students read the story, introduce the vocabulary words (*conversion, disappointment, overjoyed, solitary, occasionally, illuminate, appalling*) and discuss their meanings. Have students use the Glossary to find the definitions of the words.

Reading the Passage

Ask students to use the title and illustration for "Ben and the Puffins" to predict what the story will be about. As they read, ask them to focus on the narrator's point of view in each section of the story. What thoughts or information does this narrator share with the reader?

Checking Comprehension

- Clarify the story's main idea: *Puffins are interesting and unique birds.* Ask students to cite details from the text that support the main idea.

- Ask students to find things that the character Ben does and says that show he is happy living on the island.

Practicing Comprehension Skills

Suggest that students underline details in each section of the story that reveal its narrative voice. Some pronouns that signal point of view are *I, we* (first person) and *he, she, it, they* (third person).

Practicing Vocabulary

Have students identify the two vocabulary words with the diphthong *oi* or *oy*. (*disappointment, overjoyed*) Invite students to complete the vocabulary exercise independently.

Apply

Making the Reading and Writing Connection

Ask volunteers to read their narratives aloud. Have students identify the narrator's point of view and discuss how they reached their conclusions.

MEETING INDIVIDUAL NEEDS

Phonics: Diphthongs *oi, oy*

Say the vocabulary words *disappointment* and *overjoyed* and write them on the chalkboard.

- Have students repeat the words, listening for the sound they have in common.

- Underline the diphthongs *oi* in *disappointment* and *oy* in *overjoyed*.

- Ask students to name other words that have the *oi* or *oy* diphthong. (possible answers: *boy, coin, destroy, join, oil, point, soil, toy, annoy*)

You may want to use pages 51–52 in *MCP Phonics*, Level F for additional practice with the diphthongs *oi* and *oy*.

ESL Strategy

Students can make illustrated flashcards to help them remember difficult words in the story, such as *lighthouse, lantern, puffins, pufflings*.

Multiple Intelligences: Visual-Spatial

Invite students to create symbols that could be used to represent each point of view. For example, an eye with arrows radiating in all directions might indicate the omniscient point of view.

Home-School Connection

Encourage students to get together with family members and read aloud stories that are narrated from different points of view.

Identifying Text Structure (pages 71–76)

Objective: Students can identify the structure of a text.

Teaching TIPS

- Students are able to choose appropriate reading strategies once they identify the structure of a text.
- Students remember information better when they recognize the pattern of a text.

Skills Reviewed and Maintained

Comprehension
Character   See Checking Comprehension
Drawing Conclusions   See Checking Comprehension

Word Study
Prefixes *im-, em-*   See Practicing Vocabulary,
                             Word Study Mini-Lesson

Writing
Paragraph   See Making the Reading and Writing Connection

Teach

Tell students that each piece of writing, whether it is a memo, a novel, or a science article, has a basic structure or pattern. Recognizing a text's structure will help them read more efficiently and remember what they read.

- Write the types of text structure on the board: *chronological order, cause/effect, compare/contrast, main idea, problem/solution.*
- Then read aloud the following examples of writing and ask students which structure an author might use to organize each one.

    an article on why tornadoes form (*cause and effect*)

    an account of a town that needs a park and how it plans to get one (*problem and solution*)

    a comparison of TV and radio (*compare and contrast*)

    a history of a city (*chronological order*)

    an article about why it is important to wear a bicycle helmet (*main idea*)

- Ask students to read the paragraphs on page 72 and think about each paragraph's text structure.
- As students complete the exercise, check for their understanding.

 Practice

Introducing Vocabulary

Before students read the biography, introduce the vocabulary words (*challenging, composers, emperor, improvise, influence, melodies, urging*) and discuss their meanings. Have students think of synonyms, or descriptions, for as many of the words as possible.

Reading the Passage

Invite students to use the title and illustration for "Mozart: The Wonderchild" to predict what they will learn from the article. As they read, ask them to think about what text structure the author used to organize the information.

Checking Comprehension

- Remind students that understanding the traits of a character can help them understand why a character behaves or reacts a particular way to situations in a story. Ask students if they can find any of these traits in the text.
- Ask students to draw conclusions about young Mozart's life, using information in the article as well as their own experiences of working hard to excel at something.

Practicing Comprehension Skills

After students identify the text structure of "Mozart: The Wonderchild," ask them how else the information might have been organized.

Practicing Vocabulary

Review the vocabulary words with students. Have them identify the two vocabulary words with the prefix *em-* or *im-*. (*emperor, improvise*) Invite students to complete the vocabulary exercise independently. Review their answers with the class.

Apply

Making the Reading and Writing Connection

Invite volunteers to read aloud their paragraphs. Ask students to identify each paragraph's text structure and to give reasons for their choices.

MEETING INDIVIDUAL NEEDS

Word Study: Prefixes *im-*, *em-*

Say the vocabulary words *emperor* and *improvise* and have students listen to the initial sound of each word.

● Have students repeat the words and write them on the board. Underline the *em-* in *emperor* and the *im-* in *improvise* and have students say each prefix.

● Explain that the prefix *im-* means "not." The prefix *im-*, as well as *em-*, can also mean "in," "into," or "on."

● Discuss how the meanings of the prefixes apply to the vocabulary words.

● Ask students to name other words that have the prefix *em-* or *im-*. (possible answers: *embed, emigrate, import, immortal, immobile*)

You may want to use pages 67–68 in *MCP Phonics,* Level F for additional practice with the prefixes *im-* and *em-*.

ESL Strategy

Students acquiring English can work with a more English-proficient student to review the different types of text structure.

Multiple Intelligences: Musical, Interpersonal

Invite a group of students to find recordings of two different works by Mozart. They can play excerpts from each work to the class and then compare and contrast them.

Home-School Connection

Have students read a magazine or newspaper article with a family member. Together they can determine the text structure of the article.

LESSON 16 Understanding Author's Viewpoint (pages 77–80)

Objective: Students can recognize balanced or biased writing.

Teaching TIPS

● Students read more critically when they think about the author's viewpoint.

● Students can evaluate the validity of a text when they recognize the author's viewpoint.

Skills Reviewed and Maintained

Comprehension

Classifying	See Teach, Home-School Connection
Drawing Conclusions	See Reading the Passage, Checking Comprehension
Main Idea	See Checking Comprehension

Word Study

Suffixes *-ous, -al*	See Practicing Vocabulary, Word Study Mini-Lesson

Writing

Letter to the Editor   See Making the Reading and Writing Connection

Teach

Ask students to think about campaign speeches, editorials, and magazine articles they have read or heard. Remind them that author's viewpoint refers to a writer's attitude toward the subject or issues described. Critical readers must judge if the writer has a balanced or biased viewpoint. Balanced writing presents both sides of an issue. Biased writing presents one side more than the other.

● Write the following statements on the board. Have students classify each as biased or not biased.

1. The city's water system is 150 years old.

2. Disgusting rust is in every glass of water the unsuspecting public drinks.

3. Caring, responsible citizens must demand repairs.

4. Funds for repairs might be raised over the next few years.

- Have students point out loaded words (*disgusting, unsuspecting, caring, responsible, must demand*) that signal bias. Be sure they understand that loaded words can be positive or negative. As students read the letter, they should look for loaded words that suggest bias.

- Make sure students understand the terms *balanced* and *biased*, are able to make a judgment about the author's viewpoint, and can support their judgment with evidence from the text.

 **Practice**

Introducing Vocabulary

Before students read the speech, introduce the vocabulary words (*circular, critical, diversions, enthusiasm, experiments, friction, obvious*) and discuss their meanings. Have students brainstorm synonyms for each word.

Reading the Passage

Have students look at the illustration. Ask what conclusions they can draw about the boy based on details in the picture. Have students make predictions about the speech. Have them watch for loaded words and biased writing.

Checking Comprehension

- Help students use the description of the experiments on toys to draw a conclusion about how the lack of gravity affects the way objects move in space.

- Clarify that the main idea of the student's speech is that NASA would benefit by sending kids into space. Have students identify statements that support the main idea.

Practicing Comprehension Skills

Remind students that biased writing presents only one side of an issue, while balanced writing considers both sides. Ask students if the author of the speech presented one side or both sides of the issue.

Practicing Vocabulary

Have students identify the two words that have the suffixes *-ous* and *-al.* (*obvious, critical*) Ask them to underline the suffixes. Ask students to complete the vocabulary exercise independently. Review the answers with the group.

Apply

Making the Reading and Writing Connection

Have volunteers read aloud their letters to the editor. Classmates can judge whether the writing shows a balanced or biased viewpoint and cite evidence to support their judgments.

MEETING INDIVIDUAL NEEDS

Word Study: Suffixes -ous, -al

Say the vocabulary words *obvious* and *critical*. Write the words on the board and underline the suffixes *-ous* and *-al*.

- Explain that the suffix *-ous* means *like, full of,* or *having.* The suffix *-al* means *like* or *having to do with.*

- Write the following words on the board. Ask volunteers to add the suffix *-ous* or *-al* to each to make a new word: *adventure, caution, music, luxury, nature, vary, fury, logic, alphabet.* Tell students that they may have to change the spelling of the base word before they add the suffix.

- Ask students what each new word means. Encourage them to use a dictionary if they aren't sure.

You may want to use pages 117–118 in *MCP Phonics*, Level F for additional practice with the suffixes *-ous* and *-al.*

ESL Strategy

Pair students acquiring English with a classmate who is more English proficient. Partners can scan the passage for loaded words and create a chart that lists the words in English and in the student's first language.

Multiple Intelligences: Logical, Verbal-Linguistic, Interpersonal

Have student groups research the subject of gravity and present their findings to the class. Ask the class to draw conclusions about the effects of the lack of gravity in space.

Home-School Connection

Students and a family member can read a newspaper article, editorial, or letter to the editor. Then they can circle any loaded words and make a two-column chart, classifying the words as either positive or negative. Finally, they can judge if the piece is biased or balanced.

Making Generalizations (pages 81–84)

Objective: Students can recognize and make generalizations.

Teaching TIPS

- Students recognize an author's purpose and viewpoint when they can identify generalizations.
- Students can follow and judge an author's argument when they can make generalizations.

Skills Reviewed and Maintained

Comprehension

Drawing Conclusions	See Checking Comprehension
Making Judgments	See Checking Comprehension

Word Study

Suffixes -er, -ist	See Practicing Vocabulary, Word Study Mini-Lesson

Writing

Advertisement Posters	See Making the Reading and Writing Connection

Teach

Write the following statements on the chalkboard: *There are 20 students in the class. Nine practice sports after school. Five take music lessons. Four do volunteer work. Two have free time after school.*

- Ask what most of these students have in common. Have students answer the question by making a generalization. Suggest they use a clue word such as *most* or *many* in their generalization.

- Help students recognize that this is a valid generalization because it is supported by facts.

- Have students survey their classmates about such things as how they usually spend Saturdays or what types of pets they like. Students can write generalizations based on the information gathered in the surveys.

- Remind students that a person makes a generalization after thinking about a number of examples or facts and what they have in common.

- As students read the paragraphs about smokejumpers, encourage them to find clue words that signal generalizations. *(usually, generally)* Point out that these clue

words make the statements valid by allowing for exceptions to the generalization.

- As students complete the exercise, check for their understanding.

 Practice

Introducing Vocabulary

Before students read the interview, introduce the vocabulary words *(camaraderie, maintaining, mission, parachutist, smokejumper, tenacity, wilderness)* and discuss their meanings. Have students use the Glossary to find the definition of each word.

Reading the Passage

Have students read the title, look at the photograph, and notice the question-answer format. Ask them what they expect to find out as they read the interview. Encourage them to look for clue words that suggest that Mr. Cravens is making generalizations. *(normally, probably)*

Checking Comprehension

- Help students use details about a smokejumper's work to draw conclusions about how the job differs from that of a typical firefighter.

- Remind students to use text details as well as their own reasoning to make judgments. They can ask themselves: *"Why do I think a smokejumper would need this skill?"*

Practicing Comprehension Skills

To identify generalizations in the interview, have students find the clue words *normally* and *probably*. They can test each generalization by asking: *"What details prove that this statement is valid?"*

Practicing Vocabulary

Ask students to identify the words with the suffixes -*er* and -*ist. (smokejumper, parachutist)* Have them underline the base words and circle the suffixes. Have students complete the vocabulary exercise independently. Discuss their answers as a group.

Apply

Making the Reading and Writing Connection

Have students display their posters. Ask the class which generalizations, if any, make smokejumping seem like an interesting career.

MEETING INDIVIDUAL NEEDS

Word Study: Suffixes -er, -ist

On the chalkboard, write the vocabulary words with the suffixes *-er* and *-ist: parachutist, smokejumper.* Say the words and have students repeat them.

- Remind students that a suffix is a word part added to the end of a base word that changes the word's meaning and sometimes its part of speech.

- The suffixes *-er* and *-ist* both mean "someone who does something": A smokejumper jumps into a smoky fire scene; a parachutist uses a parachute. Adding the suffix *-er* changes a verb into a noun.

- Have students find two other words in the article that have the suffix *-er. (firefighter, diver)*
- Brainstorm other words with the suffix *-ist.*

You may want to use pages 113–116 in *MCP Phonics,* Level F for additional practice with the suffixes *-er* and *-ist.*

ESL Strategy

Students can draw a picture showing an activity that most or all smokejumpers do. Point out that the picture makes a generalization about smokejumpers.

Multiple Intelligences: Verbal-Linguistic, Bodily-Kinesthetic, Interpersonal

Have partners role-play the interview with Arlen Cravens. They can read actual passages from the text or paraphrase ideas. Encourage them to include generalizations about smokejumpers in their interview.

Home-School Connection

Have students interview a family member about his or her work and transcribe the interview in a question and answer format. Have students underline any generalizations that are made in the interview.

LESSON 18 Outlining (pages 85–88)

Objective: Students can organize information in outline form.

Teaching TIPS

- Students understand important points and how those points are related to each other when they outline information.
- Students are better able to prepare for tests when they learn to outline information.

Skills Reviewed and Maintained

Comprehension

Main Idea and Details	See Checking Comprehension
Cause and Effect	See Checking Comprehension

Word Study

Prefixes *sub-, mid-*	See Practicing Vocabulary, Word Study Mini-Lesson

Writing

Outline	See Making the Reading and Writing Connection

Teach

Brainstorm a list of outdoor activities students enjoy. Then write the following outline on the board and work together to fill it in, adding details as needed.

Fun for All Seasons

I. Warm weather

   A. Spring

      1. _____

      2. _____

   B. Summer

      1. _____

      2. _____

II. Cool weather

    A. Autumn

      1. _____

      2. _____

    B. Winter

      1. _____

      2. _____

- Review the mechanics of outline style. Remind students that for every Roman numeral I, there must be a Roman numeral II; for every letter A, there must be a letter B; and for every numeral 1, a numeral 2. An outline can have more than two numbers or letters.

- Have students read the passage and study the accompanying outline. Make sure they understand how information was selected and organized for the outline.

 ## Practice

Introducing Vocabulary

Before students read the story, introduce the vocabulary words (*congestion, exhausted, immigrants, merciless, midpoint, repaired, subway*) and discuss their meanings. Have volunteers use the words in oral sentences.

Reading the Passage

Have students read the title and look at the photograph. Discuss main topics they expect "All Aboard" to cover.

Checking Comprehension

- Clarify the main idea of the first paragraph: *At the turn of the century, New York needed a subway system.* Ask students to identify supporting details.

- To help students recognize the cause and effect relationship, have them complete this sentence: *Because New York built a subway system, _____.*

Practicing Comprehension Skills

Assist students in completing their outline of "All Aboard" by pointing out that main topics I through IV correspond in order to paragraphs 1–5. Paragraph 6 provides details for main topic V.

Practicing Vocabulary

- Have students identify the words with the prefixes *sub-*

and *mid-. (subway, midpoint)* Have them write the words and circle the prefixes.

- Invite students to complete the vocabulary exercise independently. Discuss their answers as a group.

Apply

Making the Reading and Writing Connection

After partners have outlined each other's articles, have them compare their outlines. Together, they should decide if each outline includes all the important ideas.

MEETING INDIVIDUAL NEEDS

Word Study: Prefixes *sub-*, *mid-*

On the chalkboard, write the vocabulary words *subway* and *midpoint.* Say the words and have students repeat them.

- Have volunteers underline the prefixes.

- Guide students to see that both prefixes describe place: *sub-* means "under" and *mid-* means "in or near the center."

- To answer the following questions, students should combine the prefix *sub-* or *mid-* with one of these words: *marine, court.*

    What kind of ship goes under water? *(submarine)*

    Where does a basketball game begin? *(midcourt)*

You may want to use pages 83–84 in *MCP Phonics*, Level F for additional practice with the prefixes *sub-* and *mid-*.

ESL Strategy

Have English-proficient students help those acquiring English to outline an encyclopedia article.

Multiple Intelligences: Visual-Spatial, Interpersonal

Ask partners to construct a mobile based on one main topic from the outline for "All Aboard." Have them glue a paper strip across a coat hanger and write the topic on it. They can write subtopics on cards and use string to hang them from the main topic.

Home-School Connection

Have students and a family member imagine that they are going to clean their home and outline what they will do. Roman numerals can be the rooms, letters can be chores, and numbers can be the cleaning supplies.

Persuasive Devices and Propaganda (pages 89–94)

Objective: Students can recognize persuasive devices used in propaganda.

Teaching TIPS

- Students are able to classify evidence as sound or unsound when they recognize specific persuasive devices.
- Students become more critical readers and more astute consumers when they are able to recognize propaganda.

Skills Reviewed and Maintained

Comprehension
Main Idea and Details	See Checking Comprehension
Making Judgments	See Checking Comprehension

Phonics
Words with *ui*	See Practicing Vocabulary, Phonics Mini-Lesson

Writing
Advertisement	See Making the Reading and Writing Connection

Teach

Tell students that to become more critical readers and consumers, they must learn to challenge statements that are presented as fact. This is especially important when reading or hearing propaganda, which is a deliberate effort to persuade people to think or do something. Discuss various forms of propaganda: ads, editorials, political fliers, and speeches.

- Display a magazine advertisement and point out persuasive devices that it contains. Discuss television advertisements students have seen recently. How do advertisers try to convince viewers to buy certain products?

- Read page 89 aloud and complete the exercise together. Ask students to explain their answers. Be sure they understand and can recognize the differences between the persuasive devices.

- Suggest that partners work together to read the pet shop ad and answer the questions on page 90. Review their answers.

 **Practice**

Introducing Vocabulary
Before students read the script, introduce the vocabulary words (*circuit, interior, luxurious, nutrition, pursuit, scrumptious, voice-over*) and discuss their meanings. Use the words in questions and have students supply the answers.

Reading the Passage
Invite students to read the title and look at the photograph. Explain that, since this is a script for a TV commercial, it contains descriptions of scenes as well as actual lines of dialogue. Ask students to highlight persuasive devices as they read.

Checking Comprehension

- To determine the main idea, ask students to answer these two questions: *What is the most important idea the advertiser wants you to know about Nutribeef? What details support this idea?*

- Before students make judgments, have them think about commercials they have seen and reasons they like or dislike them.

Practicing Comprehension Skills
Help students analyze statements of propaganda by asking these questions: *Is this statement always true? What evidence is given to support the statement? Is the statement just one person's opinion? Why is it being made? Who is making it?*

Practicing Vocabulary

- Review the vocabulary words with students. Have them identify the two words containing the letters *ui*. (*circuit, pursuit*)

- Students can complete the vocabulary exercise independently. Review the answers together.

Apply

Making the Reading and Writing Connection

Tell students to be honest but polite when they tell their partners whether the ad was persuasive. They can suggest revisions. Let students present their revised ads.

MEETING INDIVIDUAL NEEDS

Phonics: Words with *ui*

Draw attention to the two vocabulary words that contain the letters *ui: circuit, pursuit.* Write them on the board.

- Say the words aloud, stressing the *ui* sound, and have students repeat them.

- Explain that the vowel digraph *ui* can stand for the short /ĭ/ sound or the /o͞o/ sound.

- Write these words on the board: *biscuits, juicy, nuisance, cruise, guitar.* Have volunteers underline the *ui* in each word and decide the sound the *ui* represents.

You may want to use pages 47–48 in *MCP Phonics*, Level F for additional practice with words with the letters *ui*.

ESL Strategy

Have students find magazine ads that include both pictures and text. Help them circle persuasive devices they see and read. Guide students to talk about specific devices.

Multiple Intelligences: Bodily-Kinesthetic, Interpersonal, Verbal-Linguistic

Groups of three can dramatize the Nutribeef ad. One student can be the dog, one can be the narrator (who also reads the descriptive text), and one can be the woman.

Home-School Connection

Have students watch television with their families and identify persuasive devices they notice in commercials. Afterward, students can work with a family member to write a brief summary of one commercial. They should describe the persuasive devices that were used.

LESSON 20
Literary Elements: Character (pages 95–98)

Objective: Students can use story clues to infer character traits.

Teaching TIPS

- Students practice making inferences when they use story details to make decisions about characters.

- Students gain a better overall understanding of a story when they understand the characters in it.

Skills Reviewed and Maintained

Comprehension

Drawing Conclusions	See Checking Comprehension
Making Predictions	See Checking Comprehension

Word Study

Syllables in Words with Suffixes	See Practicing Vocabulary, Word Study Mini-Lesson

Writing

Character Sketch	See Making the Reading and Writing Connection

Teach

Ask students to imagine they're meeting a new teacher, Mr. Strictly. On an overhead projector, display the following poem. Have three volunteers each read a stanza aloud.

Mr. Strictly marched into the room.
His expression was quite grim.
"I will not stand for tardiness!"
Were the first words out of him.

"What do you think of Strictly?"
"I think he is quite stern.
But I've heard he really knows his stuff,
And there's a lot of stuff to learn!"

We sat up straight and listened
To each word our teacher said.
We raised our hands and called him Sir.
What he assigned, we read!

- Ask students the following questions using details from the poem: *What does Mr. Strictly do? What does he say? What do others say about him? How do others act toward him?* Discuss what each answer suggests about Mr. Strictly's character.

- Invite students to read the story on page 95 and to think about the character traits of Marta and Alex.

- As students complete the exercise, check to be sure they use details as clues to character traits.

On Your Own Practice

Introducing Vocabulary
Before students read the story, introduce the vocabulary words *(ballast, destination, disapproves, exceptional, monotonous, prosperous, tiresome)*. Use the words in questions and have students answer. For example: Which classmate is an *exceptional* artist? What movie was *monotonous*?

Reading the Passage
Have students look at the title, illustration, and format of this passage. Discuss what can be inferred about the characters from this preview.

Checking Comprehension
- Make sure students base their conclusions on story details as well as their own experience. Have them identify specific details that support their conclusions, such as the fact that Pa needed the Kelleys' horse.

- Ask students to think about the characters' words and actions as they predict the boys' future relationship. Remind them that predictions should be based on story details, such as the boys' closeness in age, personality differences, and the absence of other young people.

Practicing Comprehension Skills
Remind students that authors have several ways of revealing character traits. Have them underline a sentence in the diary that suggests something about William's character. Ask if that sentence tells what William does or says, or if it presents James's opinion of William.

Practicing Vocabulary
- Have students identify the two words that have the suffix *-ous. (prosperous, monotonous)* and circle the suffixes.

- Invite students to complete the vocabulary exercise independently. Discuss their answers as a group.

Apply

Making the Reading and Writing Connection
Have partners read their character sketches to each other. Listeners should form an opinion of the character in the sketch and identify details that led to their opinions.

MEETING INDIVIDUAL NEEDS

Word Study: Syllables in Words with Suffixes
On the chalkboard, write the words *prosperous* and *monotonous*. Say the words, emphasizing each syllable, and have students repeat them.

- Divide the words into syllables. Explain that when a word has a suffix, the word is divided into syllables between the base word and the suffix.

- Discuss with students how a suffix added to the end of a base word can change the word's part of speech. Point out that the suffix *-ous* turns the base word *prosper,* a verb, into an adjective. Ask a volunteer to use the word *prosperous* in a sentence.

- Ask students to divide these words from the story: *assistance, properly, careless, tiresome.*

ESL Strategy
Have students choose one character trait to describe either James or William. Have them illustrate the trait by drawing a scene from the story. They can write a caption that describes how the scene exemplifies that character trait.

Multiple Intelligences: Verbal-Linguistic, Bodily-Kinesthetic, Interpersonal
Have small groups create dramatic scenes involving James, William, and family members. Prompt ideas by suggesting that William might convince James to misbehave. Have groups write, rehearse, and present their skits to the class.

Home-School Connection
Have students think of someone their family knows, such as a neighbor or a relative. Students can write a brief description of the person's character.

Literary Elements: Plot (pages 99–102)

Objective: Students can recognize and understand elements of plot structure.

Teaching TIPS

- Students better understand story events when they learn to identify plot structure.
- Students can use plot structure to help them write or give an oral summary of a story.

Skills Reviewed and Maintained

Comprehension
Comparing and Contrasting   See Checking Comprehension
Drawing Conclusions   See Checking Comprehension

Phonics
Sounds of -ear   See Practicing Vocabulary, Phonics Mini-Lesson

Writing
Science Fiction Story   See Making the Reading and Writing Connection

Teach

Tell students that the word *plot* refers to the important events or actions that happen in a story. The plot is an organized pattern of events, and the organization is usually sequential, which means that the plot moves forward in time.

- Draw the following diagram on the board and define the labels:

Problem
Rising Action
Climax
Resolution

- Map the plot of a familiar story, such as "Little Red Riding Hood." As volunteers tell the parts of the plot in sequential order, add them to the diagram. Remind students that details are not part of the plot structure. (Problem: Wolf is hungry and wants to eat. Rising action: Wolf eats Grandmother and then eats Red Riding Hood. Climax: Hunter kills wolf and opens its

stomach. Resolution: Red Riding Hood and grandmother pop out alive.)

- After students read the story, check their understanding of plot structure by asking them to identify the climax.

On Your Own Practice

Introducing Vocabulary

Before students read the play, introduce the vocabulary words (*appears, earthly, helm, hurtles, reusable, unidentified, vaguely*) and discuss their meanings. Have students suggest a synonym for each vocabulary word.

Reading the Passage

Ask students to look at the illustration and read the title. Have them predict what the problem of "Kids in Space" might be. Review the format of a play: The cast of characters is listed at the beginning, the speaker's name is followed by a colon, and actions are written in italics and parentheses.

Checking Comprehension

- Remind students to review what the Captain and Commander say and do before comparing and contrasting the two characters with contemporary kids.

- After answering question 2, ask students whether they think the conclusion the Captain and Commander draw is valid. Have them explain their answers.

Practicing Comprehension Skills

Students might have difficulty recognizing the story's problem. Point out that usually the problem is a conflict between characters. Sometimes, the conflict is between a character and nature. At other times, the conflict is within the character, such as having to make a big decision.

Practicing Vocabulary

- Review the vocabulary words with students. Have them identify the two words containing the letters -ear. (*appears, earthly*)

- Invite students to complete the vocabulary exercise independently. Review the answers together.

Apply

Making the Reading and Writing Connection

Have volunteers explain their plot diagrams to the class. They should identify the four main parts of the plot: problem, rising action, climax, resolution.

MEETING INDIVIDUAL NEEDS

Phonics: Words with -ear

Write the vocabulary words *appears* and *earthly* on the board.

- Say each word aloud and have students repeat it. Help them identify the sound -*ear* represents in each word.

- Explain that the letters -*ear* can stand for the /ear/ sound, the /air/ sound, or the /ur/ sound.

- Brainstorm other words with -*ear*. (Possible answers: *fearless, hearing, nearest, teardrop, heard, learn*) Help students classify the words by the /ear/ sound.

You may want to use pages 21–22 in *MCP Phonics,* Level F for additional practice with words with -*ear.*

ESL Strategy

Bring in newspaper comic strips. Pair students acquiring English with those who are more proficient. Have partners read the cartoons and identify the plot elements.

Multiple Intelligences: Visual-Spatial, Bodily-Kinesthetic

Encourage a group of students to present "Kids in Space" to another class. One student should be the director, while others can make the costumes and scenery and play the roles.

Home-School Connection

Give students a blank plot diagram. They can fill it in as they read a story or watch a TV show with a family member.

 LESSON 22

Literary Elements: Setting (pages 103–106)

Objective: Students can identify and understand the influence of a story's setting.

Teaching TIPS

- Students understand that setting can be an integral part of some stories.

- Students use setting to help them make inferences about story events and characters.

Skills Reviewed and Maintained

Comprehension

Visualizing	See Teach, Reading the Passage
Cause and Effect	See Checking Comprehension
Drawing Conclusions	See Checking Comprehension

Word Study

Possessives	See Practicing Vocabulary, Word Study Mini-Lesson

Writing

Narrative Paragraph   See Making the Reading and Writing Connection

Teach

Remind students that setting is the time and place in which a story occurs. Setting can be stated directly or revealed through details. In some stories the setting is very important, and in others it is less so.

- Ask students to visualize one of the *Star Wars* movies. Ask how the movie would be different if its setting were today in your town. How would the movie's message and outcome be affected?

- Ask students to suggest a movie where the setting is not crucial—the events could take place in any time and place, and the message does not rely on setting.

- Explain that setting also influences a story's mood. For example, most horror movies are set at night, not at noon, since the darkness makes them seem scarier.

- After students read about "Ready Eddie," check their understanding by asking them to identify details that relate to the setting. *(dates, Civil War, Wild West, cowboy, open range)*

Practice

Introducing Vocabulary

Before students read the story, introduce the vocabulary words *(altitude, donned, hikers', huddled, log, nature's, obscuring)* and discuss their meanings. Ask students to suggest synonyms for as many words as they can.

Reading the Passage

Ask students to look at the illustration and read the title. Then ask them to predict when and where "Day Hike" takes place. As they read, have them visualize the setting and think about how it affects the characters and events.

Checking Comprehension

- Remind students that an effect can have more than one cause. Have students complete this sentence: *The hikers were in danger because _____ and _____.*

- Ask students to identify the two details that helped them draw a conclusion about why the patrol was able to rescue the hikers.

Practicing Comprehension Skills

Point out how the setting in "Day Hike" directly affects the story's plot: The setting creates the problem and contributes to the rising action. In this story, the setting—the mountains and weather—also creates a threatening mood.

Practicing Vocabulary

- Review the vocabulary words with students. Have them identify the two words that show possession or ownership. *(hikers', nature's)*

- Students should complete the vocabulary exercise independently. Review the answers together.

Apply

Making the Reading and Writing Connection

Have volunteers read their paragraphs aloud. Then ask listeners to identify setting details.

MEETING INDIVIDUAL NEEDS

Word Study: Possessives

Draw attention to the two vocabulary words that show possession: *hikers', nature's.*

- Write *hikers'* on the board. Say the word and have students repeat it. Ask if the placement of the apostrophe shows that one hiker or more than one hiker owns something. *(more than one)* Ask a volunteer to rewrite the word to refer to only one hiker. *(hiker's)* Then have volunteers use each word in a sentence.

- Write *nature's* on the board and repeat the procedure.

- Write the following words from the story on the board and have volunteers write their possessive forms: *Rosa, lodge, winter, plants, clouds, patrols, snowmobiles, uncle.* Use the possessive words in sentences.

You may want to use pages 101–102 in *MCP Phonics,* Level F for additional practice with possessives.

ESL Strategy

Pair students acquiring English with students who are more proficient in English. Have partners discuss the setting in popular movies and television shows they have seen.

Multiple Intelligences: Visual-Spatial

Ask students to illustrate the setting of their narrative paragraphs. Display the paragraphs and accompanying illustrations on the bulletin board.

Home-School Connection

Have students create a "Setting Yes/Setting No" chart. After they watch television programs or read stories with family members, everyone can vote on whether the setting was very important *(yes)* or not so important *(no)*.

Literary Elements: Theme (pages 107–110)

LESSON 23

Objective: Students can identify major and minor themes in fiction.

Teaching TIPS

- Learning to understand theme helps students see how the components of a story work together to produce some type of message.
- Understanding themes helps students connect a story to their own lives.

Skills Reviewed and Maintained

Comprehension
Drawing Conclusions   See Teach, Checking Comprehension
Character   See Checking Comprehension

Word Study
Suffixes -able, -ible   See Practicing Vocabulary,
                        Word Study Mini-Lesson

Writing
Realistic Story   See Making the Reading and Writing Connection

Teach

Tell students Aesop's fable about the tortoise and the hare. State the moral of the story in the final sentence: *Slow and steady wins the race.*

- Point out that in a fable, the theme is called the moral and is directly stated. While a moral is a "lesson," a theme can be a generalization about life.

- Remind students that most writers do not directly state their theme, or "big idea." More often, it is implied. Readers use clues from the story and draw their own conclusions about its theme.

- After students read the story, discuss how they came to their conclusions about its theme. Ask students to prove their statements of theme by citing evidence from the story.

- Encourage a discussion of how the theme applies to real life.

- As students complete the exercise, check their comprehension.

On Your Own Practice

Introducing Vocabulary
Before students read "Secrets of the Swamp," introduce the vocabulary words (*abruptly, basking, cultivate, encounter, humidity, irritable, miserable*) and discuss their meanings. Have students suggest a synonym for each word.

Reading the Passage
Encourage students to predict what "Secrets of the Swamp" might be about after reading the title, looking at the illustration, and previewing the text. Remind them to look for a theme that stands on its own away from the story.

Checking Comprehension
- Remind students that a character's traits are revealed by the words and interactions with others. Using these clues, what does the reader learn about Leotie?

- Discuss how students can draw a conclusion about leaving the snake alone by using the following evidence from the story: Leotie's dad taught her to identify snakes. He said that harmless snakes should be left alone.

Practicing Comprehension Skills
Remind students that when writing a theme, they should not mention specific events or characters in the story.

Practicing Vocabulary
Review the vocabulary words and their meanings. Have students identify the words that have the suffix *-able*. Have them underline the base words and circle the suffixes. Invite students to complete the vocabulary exercise independently. Discuss their answers as a group.

Apply

Making the Reading and Writing Connection
Ask volunteers to read aloud their stories. Have students suggest a theme. Discuss the evidence students used to draw their conclusions.

Word Study: Suffixes -able, -ible

Write the vocabulary words *irritable* and *miserable* on the chalkboard.

- Tell students that the suffixes *-able* and *-ible* mean "able to be" and "full of."

- Ask volunteers to choose the appropriate meaning of the suffix and to state definitions for *irritable* and *miserable*. *(able to irritate; full of misery)*

- Write the following words on the chalkboard: *enjoyable, fixable, deniable, comfortable, affordable, reversible, collapsible, washable,* and *flexible.* Discuss the meaning of each word.

You may want to use pages 125–126 in *MCP Phonics*, Level F for additional practice.

ESL Strategy

Have pairs of students act out the story. Help them isolate the dialogue and practice it. Point out key words that describe how the characters speak and move.

Multiple Intelligences: Naturalist, Visual-Spatial, Interpersonal

Students can work together to create a mural to illustrate "Secrets of the Swamp." They may want to do some basic research to find out what the plants and animals mentioned in the story look like.

Home-School Connection

Encourage students to read a story with a family member. Together they can write a statement of its theme.

LESSON 24 Synonyms (pages 111–114)

Objective: Students can identify and make distinctions between synonyms.

Teaching TIPS

- Students understand how authors convey shades of meaning and avoid repetition by using synonyms.

- Students can use synonyms as context clues.

Skills Reviewed and Maintained

Comprehension

Visualizing	See Teach
Making Judgments	See Teach, Checking Comprehension
Drawing Conclusions	See Checking Comprehension

Word Study

Doubling the Final Consonant to Add a Suffix	See Practicing Vocabulary, Word Study Mini-Lesson

Writing

Description	See Making the Reading and Writing Connection

Teach

Ask students to picture different people or animals walking. Have them visualize an elderly man, a teenager, a toddler, a duck, and a runway model. Then have the class brainstorm words that are synonymous with *walk*.

- Write *walk* in a circle on the chalkboard. Draw spokes to outer circles and write the synonyms in these outer circles. Point out that the words on this web have similar, but not identical, meanings.

- Discuss the exact meaning of each synonym. Does it have a positive or negative connotation?

- Ask why a writer might use synonyms for *walk*. Prompt students to recognize that the synonyms have more precise meanings and create more vivid pictures. Explain that a writer can avoid being boring or repetitive by using synonyms.

- Explain how authors use synonyms to help readers make judgments about a character. Say: *The teenager strutted down the street.* Ask students what character traits someone who *struts* might have. *(confidence, anger)*

- Have students read the paragraphs about guide dogs and notice where the author uses synonyms.

- As students complete the exercise, check to be sure they have identified the synonyms *obey/follow* and *pair/team/partnership* and recognize the shades of meaning between them.

 **Practice**

Introducing Vocabulary

Before students read the article, introduce the vocabulary words *(adorable, committed, complex, crucial, distractions, exposing, permitting)*. Have students use the Glossary to find the definition of each word.

Reading the Passage

Have students read the title and look at the photo. Ask what they predict "Puppy People" will be about. As they read, encourage them to look for synonyms and to think about why the author chooses specific words.

Checking Comprehension

- Prompt students to draw conclusions about why guide dogs need to be calm and well-behaved by asking: *What could happen if a nervous dog was startled by noises? What could happen if a guide dog was not obedient?*

- Remind students that judgments should be based on their own experiences and knowledge as well as details from the article. Students should consider their own personalities in relation to the training requirements described in the article.

Practicing Comprehension Skills

Remind students that although synonyms have similar meanings, they can suggest very different feelings, ideas, or moods. Discuss the differences between *eat* and *dine*, *valuable* and *useful*, *experience* and *adventure*.

Practicing Vocabulary

- Invite students to identify the two words in which a final consonant was doubled before a suffix was added. *(permitting, committed)* Ask them to underline the doubled letters and circle the suffix.

- Have students complete the vocabulary exercise independently. Discuss their answers as a group.

Apply

Making the Reading and Writing Connection

Have students read each other's descriptions and circle words that are vague. Have them suggest synonyms with a more precise meaning. Invite students to use a thesaurus.

MEETING INDIVIDUAL NEEDS

Word Study: Doubling the Final Consonant to Add a Suffix

On the chalkboard, write *permit + ing = permitting*. Say *permitting* and have students repeat it.

- Underline the two *t*'s and explain that the word's final consonant (*t*) was doubled when adding the suffix.

- Write *commit + ed = _____* on the chalkboard and have a student fill in the blank. *(committed)* Say the final word and have students repeat it.

- Invite students to look for other words in the article in which a consonant was doubled when a suffix was added. *(visually, patting, begging)* Have them circle the suffix and underline the doubled consonant.

You may want to use pages 137–138 in *MCP Phonics*, Level F for additional practice with doubling the final consonant to add a suffix.

ESL Strategy

Give students a key word from the article, such as *dog, guide, train,* or *behave*. Have them create a synonym web that includes English words and words from their native languages. Make sure students know how to use a thesaurus.

Multiple Intelligences: Verbal-Linguistic, Interpersonal

Have partners make flash cards using words from the article. On the front of each card, they should write a word found in the article. On the back, they should list synonyms for the word. They can order the synonyms in one of several ways: by intensity, positive or negative connotations, or specificity.

Home-School Connection

Explain to students that newspaper and magazine advertisements often suggest that a product or service is good. Have students read ads with a family member and circle words that are synonyms for *good*.

LESSON 25 Antonyms (pages 115–118)

Objective: Students can recognize and use antonyms.

Teaching TIPS

- Students better understand the compare and contrast text structure when they recognize antonyms.
- Students recognize and use antonyms as context clues.

Skills Reviewed and Maintained

Comprehension

Cause and Effect	See Checking Comprehension
Drawing Conclusions	See Checking Comprehension
Analogies	See Practicing Comprehension Skills

Word Study

Plural Forms of Words
  Ending in *f* or *fe*   See Practicing Vocabulary, Word Study Mini-Lesson

Writing

Contrast Essay	See Making the Reading and Writing Connection

Teach

Ask students to think about two sports that are very different, such as basketball and swimming.

- Have students suggest antonyms, or words with opposite meanings, that contrast the two sports. (Possible answers: *indoors/outdoors, team/individual, dry/wet*) Write their responses on the chalkboard.

- Present *dis-, un-,* and *im-* as prefixes that mean "not." Explain that adding one of these prefixes to a base word can often form the word's antonym. Demonstrate the procedure for students, using *happy/unhappy* as an example. Invite students to create similar antonym pairs.

- Invite students to look for antonyms as they read the diary entry.

- Make sure students understand that one word can have several antonyms.

- As students complete the exercise, check that they found the antonyms.

On Your Own Practice

Introducing Vocabulary

Before students read the story, introduce the vocabulary words *(cordial, explanation, leisurely, parcel, peculiar, shelves, thieves)* and discuss their meanings. Have students use the words in oral sentences.

Reading the Passage

Have students read the title and look at the picture. Ask what the title suggests about Mr. Franklin. As students read the story, encourage them to look for antonyms and to think about how the author uses them to make contrasts.

Checking Comprehension

- Have students study Mr. Franklin's actions to identify what causes Denise's concern. Prompt them to realize that Mr. Franklin's unusual behavior is affecting Denise.

- Remind students that their conclusions should be based on story details as well as their own experiences. Have them identify details that indicate how Denise feels, such as her smile when she realizes there are two Mr. Franklins. Then ask them to consider how they would feel in such a situation.

Practicing Comprehension Skills

Point out to students that antonyms are often used in analogies—word puzzles with two pairs of words that have the same relationship. Review the structure of analogies. Then model analogies in which words are related by opposite meanings; for example, *big* is to *little* as *up* is to *down*.

Practicing Vocabulary

- Have students identify the two vocabulary words that are plural. *(shelves, thieves)* Ask what letter was changed when the plural ending was added. (*f* to *v*)

- Invite students to complete the vocabulary exercise independently. Discuss their answers as a group.

STRATEGY: Understanding Antonyms • Lesson 25   T89

Apply

Making the Reading and Writing Connection

Have partners read each other's essays and note any antonyms they find. Then each reader should write a sentence that summarizes the contrast in the essay.

MEETING INDIVIDUAL NEEDS

Word Study: Plural Forms of Words Ending in *f* or *fe*

On the board, write *shelf* and *shelves* and say both words. Have students repeat them.

- Explain that the plural form of many words that end in *f* or *fe* is made in an unusual way: the *f* is changed to *v* and *es* is added.

- Draw two columns on the board with the heads *Singular* and *Plural*. Write *thief* in the first column. Ask a volunteer to write the plural form. *(thieves)*

- Brainstorm other singular nouns that end in *f* or *fe*. (Possible answers: *leaf, half, knife*) Work together to form the plurals.

You may want to use pages 147–148 in *MCP Phonics*, Level F for additional practice with the plural forms of words ending in *f* or *fe*.

ESL Strategy

Pair students acquiring English with others who are proficient. Partners can make flashcards with story words on one side and antonyms on the other, and quiz one another.

Multiple Intelligences: Logical-Mathematical

Have students make a Venn diagram to compare and contrast the real Mr. Franklin with the other Mr. Franklin.

Home-School Connection

Have students think about themselves in comparison to a family member. How are they alike and different? Ask students to write a paragraph using the compare/contrast pattern of organization. The paragraph should include several antonyms. Students can then show it to the family member to see if he or she agrees.

LESSON 26 Using Figurative Language (pages 119–122)

Objective: Students can understand and create figures of speech.

Teaching TIPS

- Students gain a better understanding and appreciation of language when they recognize figures of speech.

- Students learn to use figurative language in their own writing.

Skills Reviewed and Maintained

Comprehension

Comparing and Contrasting	See Checking Comprehension
Cause and Effect	See Checking Comprehension

Word Study

Multiple Meaning Words	See Practicing Vocabulary, Word Study Mini-Lesson

Writing

Descriptive Paragraph	See Making the Reading and Writing Connection

Teach

Explain to students that they read, hear, and use figurative language every day. Common figures of speech are a part of everyone's talk. Often, people don't say, "I'm hungry" or "I was tired." Instead, they might say, "I'm starving" (hyperbole) or "I slept like a rock" (simile). They may also "get around to" cleaning their room (idiom) because "it's a dump" (metaphor).

- Ask volunteers to give examples of figures of speech. As prompts, students can fill in the blanks in these phrases: *cold as ___, dry as ___, clear like ___, the garden is a(an) ___, raining ___ and ___, he could eat a(an) ___, thinner than a(an) ___.*

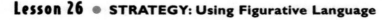

- Ask students to identify the two things that are being compared and explain the comparison.

- Go over the chart on page 119 together. Help students think of other examples of each type of figurative language. Encourage them to avoid clichés.

- Invite students to read the myth and complete the exercise that accompanies it. Check their understanding of figurative language by having them explain their answers.

 ## Practice

Introducing Vocabulary
Before students read the story, introduce the vocabulary words (*culmination, grave, grimaced, placidly, stampeded, succinctly, suspended*) and discuss their meanings. Have students suggest at least one synonym for each word.

Reading the Passage
After students look at the illustration and read the title, ask them to predict what they think "The Labors of Stacy" will be about. Have them study the illustration and suggest figures of speech that might be used to describe it. (Examples: *These two are real workhorses. This room is as messy as a pigpen.*)

Checking Comprehension
- Have students mention at least two story details they used to help them compare and contrast Stacy and Stewart's attitudes toward the play.

- To help students identify the cause-and-effect relationship, have them restate this question: *Because Stewart was injured, ___.*

Practicing Comprehension Skills
One rich source of figurative language is advertisements. Have students bring in ads that contain examples of figures of speech. Display the ads and ask students to identify and explain the types of figurative language used.

Practicing Vocabulary
- Review the vocabulary words with students. Have them identify the two words that have more than one meaning. (*grave, suspended*) Challenge them to use the different meanings of each word in a sentence.

- Let students complete the vocabulary exercise independently. Review the answers together.

Apply

Making the Reading and Writing Connection
Ask volunteers to read their paragraphs aloud. The class can identify the types of figurative language they hear.

MEETING INDIVIDUAL NEEDS

Word Study: Multiple-Meaning Words
Draw attention to the two vocabulary words that have multiple meanings: *grave, suspended*.

- Write *grave* on the board. Say the word and have students repeat it. Ask a volunteer to give the two meanings of the word (*hole where a body is buried; dangerous, serious*) and tell which one is used in "The Labors of Stacy." (*serious*)

- Write *suspended* on the board. Say the word and have students repeat it. Ask which of these meanings for *suspended* is used in "The Labors of Stacy": hung down from above; removed temporarily from a job; stop for a while. (*stop for a while*)

- Challenge students to find other multiple-meaning words in the story. (Possible answers: *part, deal, lines, seconds, rest*)

You may want to use pages 161–162 and 169–170 in *MCP Phonics*, Level F for additional practice with multiple-meaning words.

ESL Strategy
Have students acquiring English work with more proficient students to understand these common idioms from the story: *big deal, by heart, the jitters, clowning around, rolled her eyes*. Partners can read the expressions in context and clarify their meanings by using motions and examples.

Multiple Intelligences: Bodily-Kinesthetic, Visual-Spatial
Have students make the props and paper monsters Stacy and Greg make in the play. Then invite them to perform "The Labors of Stacy" for the class. They might want to add more dialogue.

Home-School Connection
Students can tell a family member about the five types of figurative language. Together they can brainstorm figures of speech to describe objects or events at home. For example, *Our cat is as black as coal; the basement is a gloomy dungeon.*

LESSON 27

Analogies (pages 123–126)

Objective: Students can recognize and make analogies.

Teaching TIP

- Students understand broader relationships, such as compare/contrast and cause/effect, by drawing analogies.

Skills Reviewed and Maintained

Comprehension
Drawing Conclusions   See Checking Comprehension
Making Inferences   See Checking Comprehension

Word Study
Suffix *-ness*   See Practicing Vocabulary, Word Study Mini-Lesson

Writing
Description   See Making the Reading and Writing Connection

Teach

Have students imagine lugging a heavy concrete block up a flight of stairs. Then ask them to visualize the world through an ant's eyes. What object might an ant carry up a flight of stairs that would feel to it like a concrete block feels like to a person? Identify this example as an analogy.

- Explain that an analogy is a comparison. An analogy shows that the relationship between one pair of words is similar to the relationship between another pair.

- Model writing an analogy: *person : concrete block :: ant : pebble.*

- Explain that analogies can show different relationships. Work with the class to complete several analogies.

synonyms	strong : hearty :: weak : (feeble)
antonyms	weak: strong :: feeble : (hearty)
cause and effect	happy : smile :: sad : (frown)
categories	tarantula : spider :: poodle : (dog)
part-to-whole	button: jacket :: (shoelace) : shoe

- As students read the paragraph about tarantulas, have them look for a sentence that presents an analogy.

- Help students write the comparison in analogy form: *tarantula : mouse :: fox : chicken.*

- Ask what is similar about the relationships in the two pairs of words. Prompt students to see that each pair names a hunter and its prey.

- As students complete the exercise, check that their analogies show parallel relationships.

 Practice

Introducing Vocabulary

Before students read the story, introduce the vocabulary words *(acquisition, earnestness, fascination, happiness, hedged, provoked, ushered).* Give synonyms to help students understand word meanings.

Reading the Passage

Have students read the title and look at the illustration. What do they think the "Rain Forest Discoveries" might be? Encourage students to look for an analogy as they read and to think about why the author uses it.

Checking Comprehension

- Have students look for details to help them draw conclusions about why Jason frees the tarantula. What influence did Jason's father have on the boy's decision?

- Students should draw on their prior knowledge to infer why Jason wanted to keep the tarantula as a pet. Suggest that they put themselves in Jason's place and think about the advantages of having an unusual pet.

Practicing Comprehension Skills

To help students get started on the exercise, present the word *normal* and have four students each find a different antonym in the story. Model writing analogies in which word pairs are related by opposite meanings.

Practicing Vocabulary

- Invite students to identify the two words that end with the suffix *-ness.* (*earnestness, happiness*) Ask a volunteer to explain what spelling change occurred when the suffix *-ness* was added to the base word *happy.* (*y changed to i*)

- Have students complete the vocabulary exercise independently. Discuss their answers as a group.

Apply

Making the Reading and Writing Connection

Have volunteers read their descriptions aloud and write their analogies on the chalkboard. Ask classmates to check that each analogy presents a parallel relationship.

MEETING INDIVIDUAL NEEDS

Word Study: Suffix *-ness*

On the board, write *earnest*. Then add the suffix *-ness*, say the word *earnestness*, and have students repeat it.

- Remind students that adding a suffix can change the meaning of the base word as well as its part of speech.

- Ask a volunteer to use *earnest* in a sentence and to identify its part of speech. *(adjective)* Repeat with *earnestness*. *(noun)*

- Write *happy* on the board. Erase the *y*, change it to *i*, and add the suffix *-ness*. Ask a volunteer to explain what happens when the suffix is added. *(y is changed to i)*

- Draw two columns on the board with the heads *Adjective* and *Noun*. Write these words from the story in the first column: *bright, empty, nasty*. Have volunteers create nouns by adding the suffix *-ness* to each word.

You may want to use pages 121–122 in *MCP Phonics*, **Level F for additional practice with the suffix** *-ness*.

ESL Strategy

Present action verbs from the story and help students match each verb with the creature that did the action: *flew/macaw, shrieked/macaw, climbing/spider, crawling/spider*.

Multiple Intelligences: Musical, Interpersonal, Naturalist

Have a small group record an audio reading of the story. Ask them to include background music and sound effects to create a tropical mood.

Home-School Connection

Have students work with a family member to write analogies based on objects found or activities performed in their home. Challenge them to create an analogy for each type of relationship.

 # Connotation and Denotation (pages 127–130)

LESSON 28

Objective: Students can distinguish between a word's denotation and its connotations.

Teaching TIPS

- Students understand that connotations affect the meaning of what they read and hear.
- Students understand that connotations are used in ads and other types of persuasive writing.

Skills Reviewed and Maintained

Comprehension

Cause and Effect — See Checking Comprehension

Setting — See Checking Comprehension

Word Study

Plural Forms of Words Ending in *o* — See Practicing Vocabulary, Word Study Mini-Lesson

Writing

Descriptive Paragraph   See Making the Reading and Writing Connection

Teach

Explain to students that every word has a denotation, which is the word's dictionary meaning. A word may also have connotations—ideas or feelings that are associated with it. A word can have different connotations for different people since these associations are created by personal experiences. Connotations can be either positive or negative.

- Point out that writers of advertisements are aware of words' connotations and use these when they write. As an example, ask students if they would want to buy a soft drink with a "tangy" flavor or one with a "sour" flavor.

- Write the following words on the board: *house, dwelling, residence, home, shack, mansion, cabin, hut, castle.* Point out that the denotation of all these words is basically the same: a place to live.

- Ask students what associations they attach to each of these words. Then ask whether the connotation of each word is generally positive or negative.

- After students read the passage, check their understanding by having them go back through the selection and substitute words that have different connotations.

 **Practice**

Introducing Vocabulary

Before students read the story, introduce the vocabulary words *(aroma, contestants, dismal, heroes, moderator, oration, solos)* and discuss their meanings. Have students tell if each word has a positive or negative connotation.

Reading the Passage

After students look at the illustration and read the title, ask them to predict what "The Quiz Show" will be about. Encourage students to highlight words that have positive or negative connotations as they read the story.

Checking Comprehension

- Remind students to use story details as well as their own experiences to identify the cause(s) of this effect.

- Have students cite story details that helped them identify the setting. Then ask how the setting affects the characters and events of the story.

Practicing Comprehension Skills

Tell students that some words have similar connotations for most people. For example, the word *duty* generally implies something that is required and is a burden. The word *tradition*, though, has different connotations for different people. Ask students what some of these associations are.

Practicing Vocabulary

- Review the vocabulary words with students. Have them identify the two plural words whose singular forms end in *o. (heroes, solos)*

- Have students complete the vocabulary exercise independently. Check the answers together.

Apply

Making the Reading and Writing Connection

Have partners read their paragraphs to each other. The partner can tell if he or she agrees with the writer's decisions about connotations and explain why or why not.

MEETING INDIVIDUAL NEEDS

Word Study: Plural Forms of Words Ending in *o*

Draw attention to the two vocabulary words whose base forms end in o: *heroes, solos.*

- Write *heroes* on the board. Say the word and have students repeat it. Ask students to identify the base word. *(hero)* Then ask what letters were added to make the word plural. *(es)*

- Write *solos* on the board. Say the word and have students repeat it. Ask what letter was added to make the word plural. *(s)*

- Explain that if a word ends in *o*, an *-s* is usually added to make the word plural. However, some words add *-es*.

- Write these words on the board and have volunteers write their plural forms: *photo, piano, radio, buffalo, memo, tornado, video, zero. (photos, pianos, radios, buffaloes, memos, tornadoes, videos, zeroes)*

You may want to use pages 149–150 in *MCP Phonics*, Level F for additional practice with plural forms.

ESL Strategy

Have small groups of students discuss the positive and negative connotations that specific words have in their native cultures.

Multiple Intelligences: Verbal-Linguistic

Have students rewrite their descriptive paragraphs to tell about a game or sport they dislike. Ask them to compare the two paragraphs, paying close attention to how connotations influence the tone of each paragraph.

Home-School Connection

Tell students to pay attention to commercials while watching television with a family member. Have them listen for words that have positive or negative connotations and make a list they can share with the class.

Using a Map (pages 131–134)

Objective: Students can interpret a map and relate it to a text.

Teaching TIPS

- Students can use maps to better understand a text.
- Students can use their knowledge of map reading in many content areas as well as in real-life situations.

Skills Reviewed and Maintained

Comprehension
Drawing Conclusions	See Checking Comprehension
Making Judgments	See Checking Comprehension

Word Study
Adding Suffixes to Words Ending in *y*	See Practicing Vocabulary, Word Study Mini-Lesson

Writing
Journal Entry	See Making the Reading and Writing Connection

Teach

Have students imagine that they've moved to a new town. Ask what graphic aid might help them get around. When they suggest a map, explain that most maps have certain features in common. If students understand these basic features, maps will be easier to read.

- Display a large map of your city or state. Identify the compass rose as a device that shows directions. Have a volunteer identify north, south, east, and west.

- Explain what special symbols in the map key represent. Ask students to name some places they'd want to find in a new town, such as parks or a hospital. Have them draw symbols to represent these places.

- Explain that the scale helps map readers estimate distances. It shows a length on the map as being equal to a set number of miles or kilometers. Model using the scale and then ask a volunteer to measure the distance between two places and calculate the mileage.

- On the road map, have students identify places they read about, such as Main Street and Bristlecone Terrace. Ask them to trace Carlos's route.

- As students complete the exercise, check their proficiency in locating places and recognizing directions on the map.

On Your Own Practice

Introducing Vocabulary

Before students read the story, introduce the vocabulary words (*commanding, grueling, precipitous, qualifying, relatively, scariest, surgery*) and discuss their meanings. Have students use the words in sentences.

Reading the Passage

Have students read the title and preview the map. Ask them to predict what the article might be about. As students read "Against the Odds," remind them to use the map to help clarify details and visualize Lance Armstrong's route.

Checking Comprehension

- Discuss the meaning of the word *odds* as used in the article's title: "differences that favor one side over the other." The odds against Armstrong were his cancer and the difficult treatments for it. Help students conclude that, given these odds, surviving and winning the bike race were incredible accomplishments.

- Students should use article details to make judgments about Armstrong's character. Have them identify specific things Lance does that show him to be courageous, determined, and spirited.

Practicing Comprehension Skills

Have students find and circle the compass rose, key, and scale on the lesson map; highlight the capital city of Paris and the Pyrénées Mountains; and use the map scale to figure the straight-line distance from Paris to Metz.

Practicing Vocabulary

Have students identify the two words with suffixes added to words ending in *y*. (*scariest, qualifying*) Which word's spelling changed when adding the suffix? (*scariest*) Invite students to complete the vocabulary exercise independently. Discuss their answers as a group.

 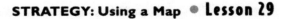

Apply

Making the Reading and Writing Connection

Pairs of students can exchange their journal entries and maps. Partners should trace the race route on the map. Then have partners work together to write questions that can be answered by consulting the maps.

MEETING INDIVIDUAL NEEDS

Word Study: Adding Suffixes to Words Ending in y

On the board, write *qualify* + *ing* = *qualifying*. Say the words and have students repeat them.

- Remind students that a suffix sometimes changes the base word's part of speech. Point out that the base word *qualify* is a verb, but that the word *qualifying* is an adjective.

- Write *scary* on the board. Then add the suffix *-est*.

- Ask a volunteer to explain what happened when the suffix *-est* was added to *scary*. (*y* was changed to *i*)

- Write these base words in a column on the board: *early, victory, enjoy, happy.* Write the following suffixes in a second column: *-ment, -ness, -est, -ous.* Have students match each suffix with a base word to create new words.

You may want to use pages 143–144 in *MCP Phonics*, Level F for additional practice adding suffixes to words ending in *y*.

ESL Strategy

Help students find a map of the city or country in which they were born. Ask them simple questions about places, symbols, and distances on the map.

Multiple Intelligences: Logical-Mathematical, Interpersonal

Have small groups use the map scale to create problems for classmates to solve. For example: Which is a greater distance—Stage 1 or Stage 9? How much farther is it?

Home-School Connection

Have students work with family members to draw maps of their neighborhoods. They can then highlight a route from their home to a favorite place. Instruct them to include a compass rose, a map key, and an approximate scale.

LESSON 30 Understanding Charts and Tables (pages 135–138)

Objective: Students can interpret a timetable and use it to support a text.

Teaching TIPS

- Students recognize that some information is more accessible in tables than in text form.
- Students can use their knowledge of reading timetables in real-life situations.

Skills Reviewed and Maintained

Comprehension

Plot	See Checking Comprehension
Making Judgments	See Checking Comprehension

Word Study

Words with More than One Suffix	See Practicing Vocabulary, Word Study Mini-Lesson

Writing

Story	See Making the Reading and Writing Connection

Teach

Have students talk about occasions when they've used a timetable, such as transportation timetables or movie and TV programming schedules.

- Display the following timetable on the board.

Washington Park Bus #63—Weekday Schedule*			
Stops	**Departures**		
Winter Garden Loop	7:15 A.M.	12:30 P.M.	5:55 P.M.
First and Main	7:55 A.M.	1:10 P.M.	6:36 P.M.
*Mon.–Fri. only. See weekend schedule for holidays.			

- Discuss the information the timetable provides. Point out column heads and abbreviations. Call attention to notes shown by asterisks.

- Model reading the timetable, scanning down columns and across rows to find a specific piece of information.

- Ask questions such as these: *What time does the morning bus leave from First and Main? What time does it reach its next stop? Will this schedule help you travel on Sunday?*

- Explain that a timetable can support a text by showing information visually and by adding details. Have students read the ad and study the timetable. Ask how the schedule adds information to and clarifies details found in the text.

- As students complete the exercise, check to be sure that they are reading the timetable correctly.

 **Practice**

Introducing Vocabulary

Before students read the story, introduce the vocabulary words *(agreeably, compromise, creatively, essential, hastily, terminal, weary)* and discuss their meanings. Have students suggest synonyms for the words.

Reading the Passage

Have students read the title and preview the accompanying chart and timetable. Ask them to predict what "A Day at Westoria" might be about. Remind them to use the timetable in conjunction with the story.

Checking Comprehension

- Help students use story dialogue to determine the plot's conflict or problem: *Family members each want to see a different attraction and are not able to see them all.*

- Encourage students to draw on previous experiences when they judge the family's solution. Suggest that they use the timetable for help in making their judgments.

Practicing Comprehension Skills

Guide students to find information on the timetable by reading heads and scanning across rows and down columns.

Practicing Vocabulary

- Have students identify the two words that have more than one suffix. *(hastily, agreeably)* Ask them to identify the base words and suffixes. *(haste, -y, -ly; agree, -able, -ly)*

- Invite students to complete the vocabulary exercise independently. Discuss their answers as a group.

Apply

Making the Reading and Writing Connection

Have volunteers read their stories and display their tables. They can then ask the class questions based on information in the table.

Word Study: Words With More Than One Suffix

On the board, write the following: *haste + -y = hasty* and *hasty + -ly = hastily.* Say each word and have students repeat it after you. Discuss the spelling changes that occur as the word *hastily* is formed: *e* in *haste* is dropped when *–y* is added; *–y* in *hasty* is changed to *i* when *–ly* is added.

- Repeat the procedure for *agreeably: agree + -able = agreeable; agreeable + -ly = agreeably.*

- Ask students to divide the following words in the same manner: *carefully, pleasantly, studiously.*

You may want to use pages 141–142 in *MCP Phonics,* Level F for additional practice with words with more than one suffix.

ESL Strategy

To familiarize students with timetables, bring in some examples. Discuss the information each schedule provides and let students experiment with finding specific times and places.

Multiple Intelligences: Visual-Spatial, Logical-Mathematical, Interpersonal

Have students work in pairs or small groups to make a simple map of Westoria. They should use the bus timetable to decide where attractions would be in relation to each other and to the bus terminal.

Home-School Connection

Have students find a timetable or schedule at home, such as a TV program guide, sports event schedule, or bus or train timetable. Ask them to show it to a family member and discuss how he/she uses it.

LESSON 31

Using Graphs (pages 139–142)

Objective: Students can understand information presented in line graphs.

Teaching TIPS

- Students realize that some information is easier to understand in graph form.
- Students can use their knowledge of graphs in various contexts and circumstances.

Skills Reviewed and Maintained

Comprehension

Comparing and Contrasting	See Checking Comprehension
Cause and Effect	See Checking Comprehension

Word Study

Suffix -ly	See Practicing Vocabulary, Word Study Mini-Lesson

Writing

News Story	See Making the Reading and Writing Connection

Teach

Remind students that they encounter graphs almost daily, across content areas as well as in their everyday reading. If possible, bring in examples from newspapers and magazines and pass them around.

- Point out that a graph can sometimes present information more quickly than a verbal explanation. Graphs can also show information that is not given in the text.

- Explain that a line graph shows change over time—the average temperature every month for a year or your weight every day for a month.

- Have students look at a line graph in their math or science textbook. Go over it together, pointing out and explaining the parts: title, vertical and horizontal axes, labels for each axis, numbers and dates or times plotted on each axis.

- Point out that the vertical axis usually shows the amount or measurement of something and the horizontal axis shows the time span.

- Have students read about La Niña and El Niño and complete the exercise. Ask them to identify which line shows average monthly rainfall and which line shows rainfall in strong La Niña years.

On Your Own Practice

Introducing Vocabulary

Before students read the selection, introduce the vocabulary words *(confined, disrupts, droughts, easily, phenomenon, probably, pronounced)*. Have groups look up each word's meaning in the Glossary.

Reading the Passage

After students read the title and scan the graph, ask them to predict what the article might be about. Have them think about these questions as they read: *Does the graph support text information by presenting it in visual form? Does it present information that is not in the text?*

Checking Comprehension

- Copy and have students use the Venn diagram on page T111 of this Guide to help them compare and contrast the two weather patterns.

- Students can highlight or underline the sentences that describe the effects El Niño causes in the Northeast and the effects El Niño causes on the West Coast. How are the effects different?

Practicing Comprehension Skills

Point out to students that the graph does not repeat any of the information in the article. Instead, it illustrates and supports the article's main idea: *La Niña and El Niño have a strong impact on the weather.* Ask why the writer might have decided to put this information in a graph.

Practicing Vocabulary

- Review the vocabulary words with students. Have them identify the two words that end with the suffix *-ly. (easily, probably)*

- Invite students to complete the vocabulary exercise independently. Review the answers together.

Apply

Making the Reading and Writing Connection

Have partners exchange their news stories and graphs. Each student should compose three questions that his or her partner can answer by looking at the graph.

MEETING INDIVIDUAL NEEDS

Word Study: Suffix -ly

Draw attention to the two vocabulary words that have the suffix -ly: *easily, probably.*

- Write *easy* and *easily* on the board. Say the words and have students repeat them. Ask how *easy* changed when *-ly* was added. (*y* was changed to *i*)

- Write *probable* and *probably* on the board. Say the words and have students repeat them. Ask how *proba-ble* changed when *-ly* was added. (le *was dropped*)

- Write these words on the board: *lucky, hasty, sleepy, possi-ble, wiggle, noble, feeble.* Ask volunteers to add *-ly* to each. Have them explain any spelling changes.

You may want to use pages 143–146 in *MCP Phonics,* Level F for additional practice with the suffix *-ly.*

ESL Strategy

Have partners compose simple sentences that explain information on the line graph. Review their sentences to check for understanding.

Multiple Intelligences: Verbal-Linguistic, Logical-Mathematical

Students can research a topic they find interesting; for example, the number of students who passed a state exam each year for the last ten years, the average price of a family car for the last twenty years. Then have them create a line graph based on their research.

Home-School Connection

Have students work with a family member to make a line graph showing the time spent on a particular family activity every day for one week—watching TV, reading together, or playing games.

Using a Dictionary (pages 143–146)

Objective: Students can identify and use the parts of a dictionary entry.

Teaching TIPS

- Students recognize that dictionary entries contain more than word meanings.
- Students learn how useful dictionaries are when encountering words with multiple meanings.

Skills Reviewed and Maintained

Comprehension

Main Idea	See Checking Comprehension
Comparing and Contrasting	See Checking Comprehension

Word Study

Suffixes -er, -est	See Practicing Vocabulary, Word Study Mini-Lesson

Writing

Narrative Paragraph   See Making the Reading and Writing Connection

Teach

Ask students what they usually do when they come across an unfamiliar word in their reading. Most will probably say they figure out the meaning of the word from its context. Remind students that a dictionary can also be a useful tool, especially for understanding words with multiple meanings.

- Point out that being able to alphabetize to the second, third, and even fourth letter is very important when using a dictionary. Write these words on the board and have students alphabetize them: *pierce, piece, pie, pick, picnic. (pick, picnic, pie, piece, pierce)*

- Circle the word *pick* and ask students what it means. Prompt students for different meanings; remind them that a word can have several meanings and can also be used as different parts of speech. The context of a sentence helps a reader figure out which meaning or part of speech is the correct one.

- Model using a dictionary to look up the word *pick*. Explain each part of the entry.

- Have students read the dictionary entry for *browse* and complete the exercise. Review their answers to check for understanding.

 **Practice**

Introducing Vocabulary

Before students read the article, introduce the vocabulary words (*commonest, designed, hardier, hazardous, programmed, repetitive, sensor*) and define them. Have students use each word in an oral sentence.

Reading the Passage

After students read the article's title and look at the illustration, ask them to fill in the first two columns of a K-W-L chart. Invite students to share their responses. After students read the article, they can fill in the final column.

What I Know About Robots	What I Want to Know About Robots	What I Learned About Robots

Checking Comprehension

- Remind students that the main idea is the most important idea about the article's topic. Have them think about what robots can do that humans can't.

- Have students make a chart that compares and contrasts sensors and sense organs. To answer the question, they should use the information in the Compare column.

Practicing Comprehension Skills

When students look up a word, encourage them to also look at similar words and their definitions. This will help them realize that a base word is often used to form additional words.

Practicing Vocabulary

- Review vocabulary words with students. Have them identify the two words that end with the suffix *-er* or *-est*. (*hardier, commonest*)

- Let students complete the vocabulary exercise independently. Ask them to explain their answers.

Apply

Making the Reading and Writing Connection

Ask volunteers to read their paragraphs aloud. Have students identify the word, its two meanings, and the different parts of speech.

MEETING INDIVIDUAL NEEDS

Word Study: Suffixes *-er, -est*

On the board, write the words that end with the suffixes *-er* and *-est: hardier, commonest.*

- Write *hardy* under the word *hardier*. Say the two words and have students repeat them. Circle the letters that make *hardier* a comparative form. (*-er*) Explain that the suffix *-er* means "more" and is used to compare two things. Ask volunteers to use each word in a sentence.

- Write *common* under the word *commonest*. Say the words and have students repeat them. Circle the letters that make *commonest* a superlative form. (*-est*) Explain that *-est* means "most" and is used to compare more than two things. Ask volunteers to use each word in a sentence.

You may want to use pages 115–116 in *MCP Phonics*, Level F for additional practice with the suffixes *-er, -est.*

ESL Strategy

Pair students who have the same first language. Partners can practice dictionary skills using a bilingual dictionary. They can look up words in their first language, identify the definition, and then compare the entry to the English.

Multiple Intelligences: Visual-Spatial

Have students each draw or construct their version of a robot, using the dictionary entry for *robot* as a basis for their creation.

Home-School Connection

Every day for a week, students and a family member should use a dictionary to learn a new word. Students can teach the new words to the class.

Using an Encyclopedia (pages 147–150)

Objective: Students can find information in a print or an electronic encyclopedia.

Teaching TIPS

- Students can use encyclopedias to research subjects in different content areas.
- Students gain understanding of organizational strategies, such as headings and cross-referencing, when they use encyclopedias.

Skills Reviewed and Maintained

Comprehension

Comparing and Contrasting	See Teach
Drawing Conclusions	See Checking Comprehension
Making Judgments	See Teach, Checking Comprehension

Word Study

Suffix -*ward*	See Practicing Vocabulary, Word Study Mini-Lesson

Writing

Summary	See Making the Reading and Writing Connection

Teach

Display an encyclopedia set, point out the numbers and letters on the spines, and explain that the volumes are ordered alphabetically. Distribute volumes among pairs of students. Have them look through their volumes and notice that entries are also arranged in alphabetical order.

- Point out that longer entries often have section headings, making it easy to scan the article for specific information. Have students find an example.

- Ask students to look for the cross-reference *See also* at the end of an entry. Explain that this note sends the reader to another entry for more information on the subject.

- Model looking up the subject *bumblebee*. Point out section headings and call attention to cross-references.

- If possible, demonstrate how to use an encyclopedia on the Internet or on a CD-ROM. Have students compare and contrast the features of the electronic and print encyclopedias. Ask them to make a judgment about which version seems easier to use.

- Have students read the excerpt from an encyclopedia article and identify section headings and cross-references.

- As students complete the exercise, make sure they understand the purpose of headings and cross-references and understand how to use them in their own research.

 Practice

Introducing Vocabulary

Before students read the story, introduce the vocabulary words (*committee, defeat, formidable, petitioned, seasoned, toward, upward*). Present synonyms or antonyms as clues to meaning and have students brainstorm others.

Reading the Passage

Have students preview the title, photo, score chart, and cross-references. Have them use the headings to predict specific information the article will provide. What do they expect to learn about the women's ice hockey team?

Checking Comprehension

- Remind students to use article details when drawing their conclusions. Then ask what was special about the women's hockey match at the 1998 Winter Olympics.

- Have students reread the section under the first article heading. Suggest that they underline details to help them judge why the Olympic Committee finally included women's ice hockey in the winter games.

Practicing Comprehension Skills

Have three student groups each research one of the cross-references listed at the end of the article: Winter Olympics; Ice Hockey; Canada (Winter Sports). Groups can look up the entries in a print encyclopedia or in an Internet or CD-ROM version.

Practicing Vocabulary

Review the vocabulary words and their meanings. Ask students to identify the two words with the suffix -*ward* (*upward, toward*) and underline the suffixes. Then have students complete the vocabulary exercise.

Apply

Making the Reading and Writing Connection

Have students share their summaries with a partner. Ask the partner to write down two or three main ideas that might serve as section headings.

MEETING INDIVIDUAL NEEDS

Word Study: Suffix -ward

On the board, write *upward*. Say the word and identify the base word *up* and the suffix *-ward*.

- Explain that *-ward* means "in the direction of," as in "in the direction up" or "in the direction west."

- On the board, write this sentence: *I walked toward the desk.* Underline the suffix *-ward*. Point out that *toward* could be replaced by the phrase "in the direction of."

- Have students scan the encyclopedia article for another word with the suffix *-ward. (forward)* Discuss the word's meaning: "in the direction of the front."

You may want to use pages 119–120 in *MCP Phonics*, Level F for additional practice with the suffix *-ward*.

ESL Strategy

Have students acquiring English work with a more English-proficient student to locate an encyclopedia entry for a sport they enjoy playing or watching. Ask students to read aloud a section of the entry.

Multiple Intelligences: Visual-Linguistic, Bodily-Kinesthetic, Interpersonal

Have the class select an unusual sport to research in encyclopedias. Divide the class into groups. One group can demonstrate how to play. Other groups can tell about the sport's history.

Home-School Connection

Have students scan an encyclopedia volume for a subject they think most people don't know anything about. Have them read the article, noting its main details, and then share what they learn with a family member.

LESSON 34 Using a Library Card Catalog/the Internet

(pages 151–156)

Objective: Students can use a card catalog and the Internet to do research.

Teaching TIPS

- Students learn that there are standard techniques for researching information in a library and on the Internet.

- Students will write better papers, and enjoy the process more, if they know how to locate information.

Skills Reviewed and Maintained

Comprehension

Summarizing	See Checking Comprehension
Making Predictions	See Checking Comprehension

Word Study

Suffixes with Words	See Practicing Vocabulary,
Ending in *e*	Word Study Mini-Lesson

Writing

Summary	See Making the Reading and Writing Connection

Teach

Have students talk about their experiences surfing the Internet or using the library to find information. Sometimes, the amount of information available can be pretty overwhelming and may prolong research because a person must sift through so many sources. Explain that there are several techniques for successful searching.

- Remind students that they have two choices when searching for information. They can look at print material (such as books, magazines, newspapers) or they can look for information on the Internet.

- Read pages 151–152 with students and talk about the techniques people use to conduct research in libraries.

Then read page 153 and discuss how information is found on the Internet.

- Copy and distribute the Graphic Organizer on page T111 in this Guide. Have students think about how finding information in print sources is similar to and different from finding information on the Internet. They should write their ideas in the Venn diagram.

- Have students complete the exercise on page 153. Check for understanding by asking students why it is better to use specific rather than general keywords.

 **Practice**

Introducing Vocabulary

Before students read the article, introduce the vocabulary words (*applications, becoming, environment, galaxies, immersion, introduced, trainees*) and discuss their meanings. Have students use each word in an oral sentence.

Reading the Passage

Ask students if they have heard the term *virtual reality* and, if so, what it means. Discuss students' experiences with virtual reality. As students read, ask them to circle keywords they might use to learn more about this topic.

Checking Comprehension

- To help students answer this question, suggest that they summarize the information in each paragraph.

- Ask students to identify evidence—from the article and their own experiences—that supports their predictions.

Practicing Comprehension Skills

Advise students that, with so much information available, they need to plan carefully before beginning research and allow themselves enough time to skim through all the information they find in a library or on the Internet. Help students practice refining search terms.

Practicing Vocabulary

- Review vocabulary words with students. Have them identify the two words in which the final *e* was dropped before a suffix was added. (*becoming, introduced*)

- Let students complete the vocabulary exercise independently. Review the answers together.

Apply

Making the Reading and Writing Connection

Have small groups of students compare their summaries and combine the best ideas from each one in a new summary of the possible applications of virtual reality.

MEETING INDIVIDUAL NEEDS

Word Study: Suffixes with Words Ending in *e*

Draw attention to the vocabulary words in which the final *e* was dropped before adding a suffix: *becoming, introduced.*

- Write *becoming* on the board. Circle the suffix. Underline the letters *becom* and point out that this is not a word. Ask students how the word *become* changed when the suffix *-ing* was added. (final *e* was dropped)

- Write *introduced* on the board and follow the same procedure.

- Write the following words on the board and have volunteers add *-ing* and *-ed* to each: *describe, complete, immerse, participate, simulate.*

You may want to use pages 139–140 in *MCP Phonics*, Level F for additional practice with adding suffixes to words ending in *e*.

ESL Strategy

Have students acquiring English work with more English-proficient students to narrow one of these broad search terms: *food, animals, sports.* Partners can create word pyramids. The broad search term can be written at the bottom, less general keywords in the middle, and the most specific one at the top.

Multiple Intelligences: Verbal-Linguistic, Visual-Spatial

Have students research virtual reality in the library or on the Internet to find out future plans for its use. Encourage them to create posters that will help them share what they learn with the class.

Home-School Connection

Students should ask a family member to name a topic he or she would like to know more about. The two can work together to refine the topic. At school, students can practice using the library's card catalog to find information on this topic.

Name _____

Story Sequence Chart

Read the story. Answer the questions in each box. Retell the story using what you wrote.

Who?

When?

Where?

What happened? List events in order.

How did it end?

Name _____

Summarizing Chart

Use the title of the story as a clue to the main idea given in the story. Write two or three main ideas. Then write a paragraph that summarizes these ideas.

Main Idea

Main Idea

Main Idea

Summary

Name _____

Prediction Chart

What I predict will happen

_____

_____

_____

_____

**Why I think this will happen—
these are the clues that I used**

_____

_____

_____

_____

What did happen

_____

_____

_____

Name _____

Main Idea and Details Chart

Read the story. Write in the first box the idea that tells what the whole story is about. Then in the other boxes write details that support the main idea.

Main Idea

Detail

Detail

Detail

Name _____

Cause and Effect Chart

1. | What happened

Why it happened

2. | What happened

Why it happened

3. | What happened

Why it happened

Name _____

Fact and Opinion Chart

Read the story. Identify three statements of fact or opinion from the story. Write why they are statements of fact or opinion.

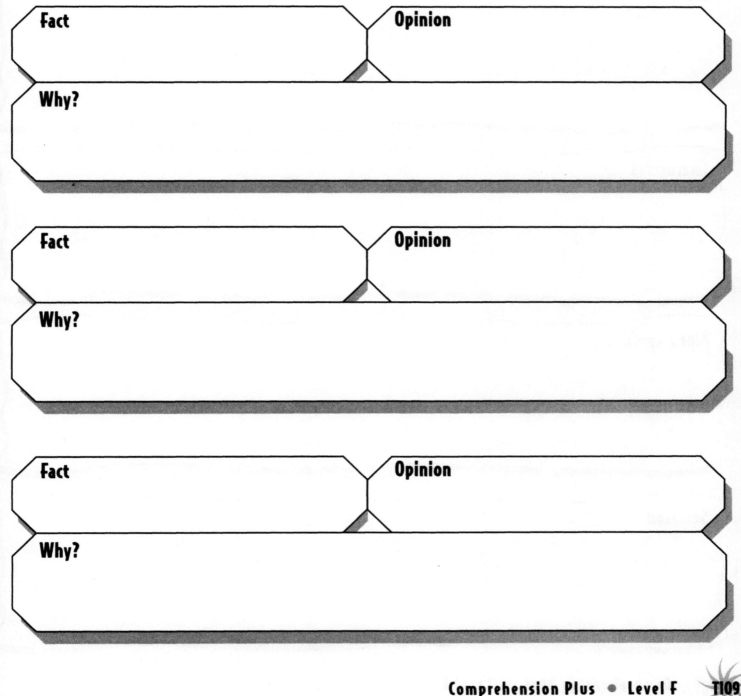

Name _____

Story Elements

Title _____

Setting

Characters

Plot / Conflict

Solution

Name _____

Venn Diagram for Comparing and Contrasting

Read the selection. Compare and contrast the two main items of the selection by writing the differentiating features in the outside circles. Write the common features in the middle part.

_____   _____

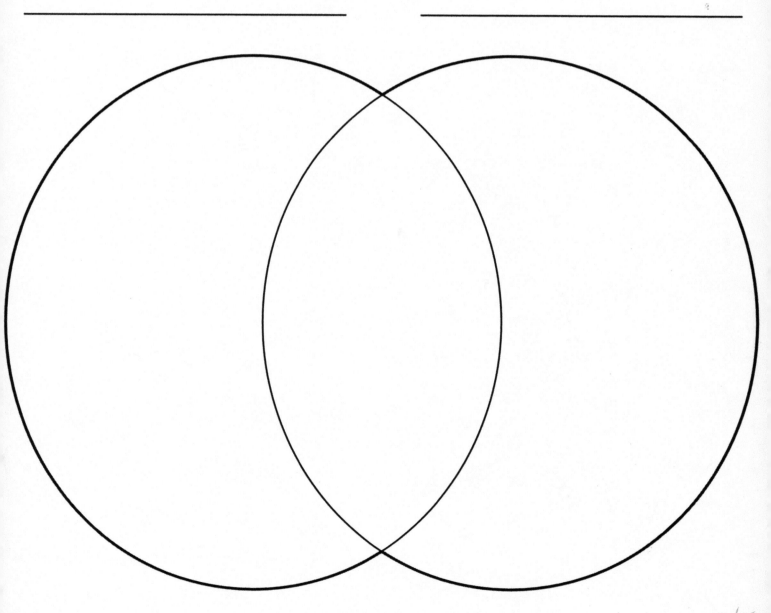

Comprehension

PLUS

LEVEL F

Dr. Diane Lapp
Dr. James Flood

Modern Curriculum Press

Photographs:
1: Adam Woolfitt/NGS Image Collection. 29: Kwangshin Kim/Photo Researchers. 42(t): Photofest. 42(b): Photofest. 43(t): Archive Photo. 43(b): Photofest. 46: Gene Trind/MPTV. 47: Bernhard Edmaier/Science Photo Library Photo Researchers. 48(l): R.G. Everts/ Photo Researchers. 48(r): Harvey Lyode/FPG International. 51: Jeff Schultz/Alaska Stock/PNI. 52: Associated Press/AP. 53: Archive Photo. 57: Neal Preston/CORBIS. 58: AFP/CORBIS. 60: Najlah Feanny/Stock Boston. 61: Archive Photo. 62: Photofest. 64: Express Newspaper/ Archive Photo. 72: Michael Lutch for WGBH/Everett Collection. 81: CORBIS. 82: 2000 Redding Crew/USDA Forest Service. 85: Danny Kirst/Uniphoto. 86(t): Courtesy of New York Transit Museum Archives. Brooklyn. 86(b): Gail Mooney/ CORBIS. 108: M.P. Kahl/Photo Researchers. 111: S. McBrady/PhotoEdit. 112: Cate Myrleen/PhotoEdit. 123: Sharon and Ray Baily/Uniphoto Picture Agency. 132: AFP/ CORBIS. 134: Manfred Mehlig/Stone. 144(t): Lowell Georgia/ CORBIS. 144(m): Kevin R. Morris/ CORBIS. 144(b); Lowell Georgia/ CORBIS. 146: Jim Sugar Photography/CORBIS. 147: Associated Press/AP. 148: Associated Press/AP. 154(l): Virtual Reality Lab/University of Michigan. 154(r): Virtual Reality Lab/University of Michigan.

Illustrations:
5, 6, 9: Judy Love. 11, 12, 14: John Nez. 15, 16, 17: Judy Love. 25, 26, 28: Wallace E. Keller. 33, 34, 35: John Nez. 41: Wallace E. Keller. 53, 56: Gershom Griffith. 65, 67, 67: Gershom Griffith. 73, 75, 76: Judy Love. 77, 78, 80: Michael Rex. 95, 96: Judy Love. 107, 108, 110: Michael Rex. 115, 116, 118: Michael Rex. 124, 125, 136, 138: Kathleen Kuchera.

Cover art: Photo montage: Wendy Wax. Background: Doug Bowles.

Design development: MKR Design, Inc. New York: Manuela Paul, Deirdre Newman, Marta Ruliffson.

Modern Curriculum Press
An imprint of Pearson Learning
299 Jefferson Road, P.O. Box 480
Parsippany, NJ 07054-0480
www.pearsonlearning.com

ISBN: 0-7652-2185-3

7 8 9 10 BAM 09 08 07 06 05

Table of Contents

Comprehending Text

Lesson 1: Main Idea and Details 5

Lesson 2: Drawing Conclusions 11

Lesson 3: Sequence: Order of Events 15

Lesson 4: Sequence: Steps in a Process 21

Lesson 5: Predicting Outcomes 25

Lesson 6: Recognizing Cause and Effect 29

Lesson 7: Using Context Clues 33

Lesson 8: Comparing and Contrasting 37

Lesson 9: Summarizing 41

Lesson 10: Paraphrasing 47

Lesson 11: Author's Purpose 51

Lesson 12: Statements of Fact and Opinion 57

Lesson 13: Making Judgments 61

Lesson 14: Point of View 65

Lesson 15: Text Structure 71

Lesson 16: Author's Viewpoint 77

Lesson 17: Making Generalizations 81

Lesson 18: Outlining. 85

Lesson 19: Persuasive Devices and Propaganda . . . 89

Story Structure

Lesson 20:   Literary Elements: Character 95

Lesson 21:   Literary Elements: Plot 99

Lesson 22:   Literary Elements: Setting 103

Lesson 23:   Literary Elements: Theme 107

Word Study

Lesson 24:   Synonyms 111

Lesson 25:   Antonyms 115

Lesson 26:   Using Figurative Language 119

Lesson 27:   Analogies 123

Lesson 28:   Connotation and Denotation 127

Document Reading

Lesson 29:   Using a Map 131

Lesson 30:   Understanding Charts and Tables 135

Lesson 31:   Using Graphs 139

Lesson 32:   Using a Dictionary 143

Lesson 33:   Using an Encyclopedia 147

Lesson 34:   Using a Library Card Catalog/
the Internet 151

Glossary 157

Main Idea and Supporting Details

The **main idea** of a story or an article is the most important idea about the topic—the point the writer wants you to understand and remember. In some paragraphs and articles, the main idea is stated in a topic sentence. The topic sentence often, but not always, appears at the beginning of a piece of writing. When you know the main idea, you are much more likely to remember what you have read.

The **supporting details** in a paragraph or article are sentences that tell about or support the main idea. Supporting details are small pieces of information that help you better understand the main idea.

Read the following paragraph. As you read, look for the main idea.

The King Arthur legends are often remembered for their large cast of memorable characters. First is Arthur himself. He was the wise, brave ruler of the Knights of the Round Table. His beautiful queen, Guinevere, is also a favorite of many people. The daughter of a king, she helped Arthur to rule Camelot. Of course, the Arthur legends would not be complete without the brave knights themselves. These noble men give the legends such great heroic characters as Lancelot, who was famous for his skill in combat. Another famous knight, Gawain, was known for his great courtesy.

Underline the sentence that is the main idea of this paragraph.

The King Arthur legends are often remembered for their large cast of memorable characters.

First is Arthur himself.

Of course, the Arthur legends would not be complete without the brave knights themselves.

What details support this main idea?

Possible answer: The other sentences in the paragraph talk about different characters in the

legend and give information about them.

The main idea of a paragraph or article is not always stated directly. In those cases, you can figure it out. First study the supporting details. Then think of a topic sentence that summarizes the important information in the supporting details.

Read the following legend about King Arthur. As you read, look for the main idea and supporting details.

The king of England had died, and many powerful nobles wanted to be the next king. These lords of the region rode from far and wide to meet in the great city of London. Each was sure he would be the next king. At an inn, the nobles were startled to find a giant stone with a sword embedded in it. Writing on the stone announced that whoever could pull the sword from the stone would be king. One by one, the lords tried, but the sword held firmly. Then Arthur, a boy who had traveled with one of the nobles, stepped forward. In Arthur's hands, the great sword slid out easily! Arthur was crowned king, and he vowed to be a wise and fair ruler.

If the main idea is stated in the paragraph alone, write the word *stated* on the lines provided and circle the topic sentence. If the main idea is unstated, write the word *unstated*. Then write a topic sentence of your own on the lines.

Possible answer: unstated. Arthur became king of England by

pulling a sword out of a stone.

_____

Write two supporting details that helped you figure out the main idea.

1. Possible answer: Writing on the stone announced that whoever

   could pull the sword from the stone would be king.

2. In Arthur's hands, the great sword slid out easily.

   _____

Tip

A writer does not always state the main idea of a story or article. You can figure out the main idea by summarizing the information given in the supporting details.

Read the following article about King Arthur of England. As you read, look for the main idea and supporting details.

Was There Really a King Arthur?

by Lou Ann Walker

Did a king named Arthur really live in the late fifth or early sixth century? Did he invent the Round Table? Were Guinevere, Lancelot, and the other characters in Arthur's story real people? These questions have captivated historians and writers for centuries. Worthy proof is hard to come by. The events described in legends about King Arthur took place in the Dark Ages. Little was written down during that time. Most of what we know about Arthur comes from poets and storytellers.

Ruins of Cadbury Castle in Somerset, England

When the Romans ruled Britain, beginning in the first century, they built roads and kept order. After they departed early in the fifth century, European invaders arrived. In such chaotic times, people needed inspiration. If the figure of Arthur is purely legendary, it is easy to see why the myth sprang up—and continued growing.

In the 1130s, Geoffrey of Monmouth wrote *History of the Kings of Britain*. Arthur's fame spread. A fanciful writer, Geoffrey said that Arthur fought the Saxons with a sword called "Caliburn." After marrying Guinevere, he brought together knights from every corner of the earth. Later writers further embellished the tale. Sir Thomas Malory, who wrote about Arthur in the late 1400s, was one of the authors who added his own ideas to the story.

In building the case for a real-life Arthur, some people point to the writings of early Welsh historians. A sixth-century writer told of a leader named Ambrosius Aurelianus. This leader fought against the Anglo-Saxons in the fifth century. In the 800s, a Welsh monk wrote of "Artorius." This means "Arthur" in Latin. The monk called Artorius a "leader of battles." Other people who might have been Arthur include a Scottish prince and a Welsh king. One scholar claims that Arthur is Riothamus, a Briton who led an army in A.D. 470. The name means "supreme king." It might have been given to Arthur.

What about Camelot? In the 1960s, archaeologists were studying the ruins of Cadbury Castle in Somerset, England. They uncovered a large hall with a fifth-century gatehouse. The owner must have been extremely powerful, and the site fits in with the area storytellers claim is Camelot.

Is Arthur a historical figure around whom legends grew? Or is he a legendary figure we've tried to make real? We will probably never know for certain. We do know that some of the details of our fantasies, such as knights in armor roaming a grand palace, could not be authentic. Arthur's story comes from the Dark Ages, before armor was invented. More certain is that the Arthurian legend, with all its intrigue, bravery, and chivalry, will continue to fascinate people for centuries to come.

Checking Comprehension

1. What reason might people have had for inventing the stories of the legendary king named Arthur? [Cause and Effect/Inferential]

   The people were living in chaotic times. It may have been inspiring to believe in a leader of

   great character and courage.

   [Making Judgments/Inferential]

2. Was Arthur a real figure or an imaginary one? Explain your answer.

   Possible answer: There may have been a real king around whom the legends of Arthur arose.

   However, many of the details surrounding his life are probably legendary. Some are impossible

   and others can't be proved.

Practicing Comprehension Skills

3. Was the main idea of "Was There Really a King Arthur?" stated or unstated?

   unstated

4. Write the main idea of "Was There Really a King Arthur?" in the top box.
   Write a supporting detail in each of the other boxes. Possible answers are shown.

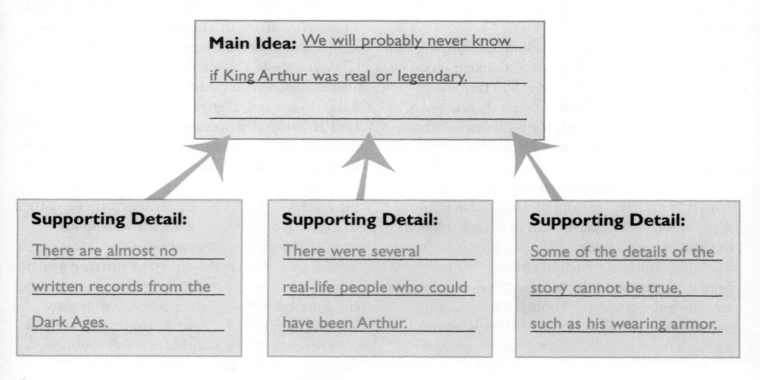

Main Idea: We will probably never know
if King Arthur was real or legendary.

Supporting Detail:
There are almost no
written records from the
Dark Ages.

Supporting Detail:
There were several
real-life people who could
have been Arthur.

Supporting Detail:
Some of the details of the
story cannot be true,
such as his wearing armor.

Fill in the circle before the correct answer or answers.

5. Which statement supports the idea that Arthur might have existed?

 ● A Welsh monk wrote of a great leader, Artorius, which is Latin for "Arthur."

 ○ There are many movies about the knights of the Round Table.

 ○ Everyone has heard of King Arthur.

 ○ Romans ruled Britain in the first century.

6. What if the following statement had been the main idea of this passage: "King Arthur was an authentic figure of history"? What kinds of details would the author have needed to include to support this statement?

Possible answer: The author would have needed to include supporting details that give definite

evidence of Arthur's existence. For example, the author might have showed that several

historians wrote about him, or that there is proof of Arthur's birth and death.

Read the following passage.

During the past century, the King Arthur legend has been retold in numerous books, films, TV shows, and even a major musical. In 1917, *The Boy's King Arthur*, a version of Sir Thomas Malory's tales, was illustrated by artist N. C. Wyeth. T. H. White's *The Once and Future King*, a collection of four novels published together in 1958, brought the Arthur legend to a new generation.

In 1960, the musical *Camelot*, based on White's novel, opened on Broadway. A movie version followed in 1967. Another movie, 1981's *Excalibur*, adapted Sir Thomas Malory's tales, and a television show retelling the legend was the highest rated miniseries in 1998.

7. If the main idea of the paragraph is stated, underline it. If the main idea is unstated, write it on these lines.

_____

_____

8. Fill in the circle next to the best title for the passage.

 ○ The Books Inspired by the King Arthur Legend

 ○ Stage and Screen Versions of the Arthur Legend

 ● The Legend of King Arthur Lives On in Numerous Retellings

 ○ The Story of Arthur and Guinevere

List three details that support the main idea you identified for the passage on page 9.

9. Books such as *The Boy's King Arthur* were published. _____

10. The musical *Camelot* opened in 1960. _____

11. The movie *Excalibur* adapted Sir Thomas Malory's tales. _____

Practicing Vocabulary

12. Choose the word from the box that best fills each blank in the paragraph.

authentic	captivated	chaotic	chivalry	embellished	legendary	worthy

I just saw the new movie about King Arthur, and I was _____captivated_____ !

It was truly a _____worthy_____ way to spend a rainy afternoon. The movie showed

how confused and _____chaotic_____ the Dark Ages were. The costumes

looked very real and _____authentic_____ for the time period. The movie added

some original touches that _____embellished_____ the stories about Arthur's knights.

Since the characters might be _____legendary_____ figures rather than real ones from history,

the additions didn't bother me. The movie captured the heroism, bravery, and

_____chivalry_____ of the knights of the Round Table.

Writing a Paragraph
Think of a legendary character from a book or folktale. On a separate sheet of paper, write a paragraph telling what you know about this character. State your main idea clearly in a topic sentence. Then use supporting details to tell more about the character.

Drawing Conclusions

When you read, you often have to draw conclusions about people, places, things, and events. A **conclusion** is a sensible opinion you have or a decision you reach after thinking over the facts or details you've read.

Drawing a conclusion is a two-step process. First, you note the facts and details you have read about a person, place, thing, or event. Then you put that information together with what you know from your own experiences. Asking yourself questions like these will help you draw conclusions:

- What do these details suggest?
- What do these facts mean?
- What do this character's appearance, words, and behavior reveal about him or her?

Read the following story. Then draw some conclusions of your own.

Sylvia stopped in surprise in the doorway of the classroom. Someone new was sitting at the desk right behind hers. The classroom rang with chatter and activity, but the new girl sat alone, quiet and still. She was startled when Sylvia thumped her books down and smiled a greeting. "I'm Sylvia. What's your name?" she asked.

"I'm Emily Ozawa," answered the classmate, smiling back.

"Come meet my friends," urged Sylvia. "I think you'll like them!" She led Emily over to a lively group. By the time the bell rang, Emily felt as if she'd known Sylvia and her friends for years.

What conclusion can you draw about Sylvia after reading the story?

She is friendly, kind, and outgoing.

_____

What details support your conclusion?

Sylvia smiles, introduces herself, and invites Emily

to join her and her friends.

Tip

Back up your conclusions with information from the text as well as your own experiences with people and events.

Read the following story about an unlikely friendship. As you read, draw conclusions about the characters and events in the story.

Tony's New Neighborhood

Tony shut the front door gently but then stomped down the front steps. He looked around at his new block. Two rows of small, red brick houses faced each other across a narrow city street. Except for an older man sitting on his front steps with a dog at his feet, the block was deserted. "Why did we have to move here?" Tony thought resentfully.

Tony wondered what Sean, Michelle, and José were doing this morning. He looked at the going-away present they'd given him—a baseball signed by several New York Yankees. "I'll never find new friends like them," he thought sadly.

Tony wandered down the street, throwing the ball in the air and catching it. When he missed a catch, the dog sprang up, retrieved the ball, and came running back. The man stood up slowly, leaning on his cane. He wore jeans, a baseball cap, and a faded red shirt. He gently pried the ball from the dog's jaws, grinned at Tony, and glanced at the signatures on the ball as he handed it back. "New York Yankees," he said.

"You like baseball–" Tony hesitated, "sir?"

"Friends call me Cap," answered the man. He sat down again, stretching out his long legs. "I used to play. Then one day I ripped a leg muscle sliding into second base, and it never healed. I had to quit. Are you a pitcher?"

Tony grinned. "I can't hit, so I had to learn to throw. I'm Tony."

"I'm pleased to make your acquaintance, Tony," Cap said formally, shaking hands.

"Just as if I were a grown-up, too," thought Tony. "What's your dog's name?" he asked.

"He's called Joe," Cap answered, "for the day I shook hands with Joe DiMaggio." Joe thumped his tail at the sound of his name.

"You met Joe DiMaggio?" Tony's eyes grew round with wonder.

Cap shifted over on the stoop and Tony sat down, taking off his glove and pushing his hair back. "It was July 1947. My brother Esteban and I had saved our money for a Yankees–Red Sox game. We sat just behind the right field wall.

"When Joe DiMaggio came up in the seventh inning, he smacked the prettiest line drive home run you ever saw—right into my glove! Esteban and I waited after the game and asked Joe to sign the ball for us. I'd heard he was aloof around people, but he was kind to us."

Tony looked at his own prized ball. "My friends saved their money to buy this for me."

Cap took the ball again, turning it around slowly to read all the signatures. Joe pressed his head against Tony's knee. Tony patted the dog. "How about a game of catch?" he asked Cap.

Cap's slow smile wrinkled up the corners of his eyes. "I was just waiting for an invitation."

Checking Comprehension

1. What do you think Tony learned about friendship? [Main Idea/Critical]

   Possible answer: Tony is used to friends his own age, but he

   learned that people of different ages can be friends, too.

2. How is Tony's meeting with Cap like young Cap's [Comparing and Contrasting/Inferential]
   meeting with Joe DiMaggio?

   Possible answer: Tony respects and likes Cap; Cap recalls his respect

   and liking for DiMaggio. In both stories, a baseball establishes the contact.

Practicing Comprehension Skills

Read the questions. Then fill in the circle next to the best answer.

3. How does Tony feel when Cap shakes his hand?

   ○ Tony is angry that he moved away from his friends.

   ○ Tony is afraid of Cap.

   ● Tony is pleased that Cap shows him respect.

   ○ Tony feels as though he's known Cap for years.

4. Fill in the circle next to the detail that helped you draw the conclusion you did in item 3.

   ● Tony thinks to himself that Cap is treating him just like a grown-up.

   ○ Cap tells Tony that he shook hands with Joe DiMaggio.

   ○ Tony's eyes grow round with wonder.

   ○ Cap and Tony play catch.

5. How does Tony feel about the going-away present his friends gave him?
   List some details from the story and something you know from your own experiences that helped you draw this conclusion.

   Answers will vary, but may include: Tony treasures the ball; it reminds him

   of his friends. The story says it's prized. It is signed by players from a baseball

On the chart below, write a conclusion you drew about Cap and Tony's relationship after reading this story. Then list three details from the story that helped you draw that conclusion. Answers will vary, but may include:

CONCLUSION

6. <u>Cap and Tony will</u>

<u>become friends.</u>

_____

DETAILS

7. <u>They both like baseball.</u>

8. <u>They treat each other well.</u>

9. <u>They both seem lonely.</u>

Practicing Vocabulary

Write a word from the box to complete each sentence.

| aloof | formally | pried | resentfully | retrieved | shifted | signatures |

10. The catcher _____ shifted _____ his position slightly as he waited for the pitch.

11. Fans complained about the player's _____ aloof _____ manner.

12. The ball sailed over the fielder's head, but he soon _____ retrieved _____ it.

13. The girl _____ pried _____ the ball loose from where it had lodged under the bleachers.

14. Instead of being good sports, the losing team walked _____ resentfully _____ off the field.

15. Some autograph collectors get the _____ signatures _____ of famous sports stars.

16. The managers of both teams _____ formally _____ shook hands before the game.

Write a Story
On a separate sheet of paper, write a short story about a friend. Describe your first meeting. What did you conclude about this person? Try to include specific details about things your friend did or said that helped you draw these conclusions.

Identifying Sequence: Order of Events

Thinking about the order in which events happen helps you understand what you read. The **sequence of events** can be important to the meaning of a story or an article. In many cases, an outcome would change if events had occurred in a different order.

References to dates and times of day are clues to the sequence of events. Words that suggest time order, such as *first, then, meanwhile,* and *next,* or *yesterday, today,* and *afterward,* are also clues.

As you read the following article, look for words that are clues to the sequence of events.

In the American colonies of 1775, no war with England had been officially declared. Massachusetts husbands, fathers, and sons were gathering their weapons anyway. They were preparing to fight for their freedom.

Meanwhile, the British were preparing, too. On April 18, about 700 British soldiers moved toward the town of Concord. They planned to take the colonists' weapons. That same night signal lights flashed in a Boston church. The lights told the colonists that the British were on the move! A few moments later, colonist Paul Revere raced across the countryside. He warned people that the soldiers had been sent to Concord.

The next morning the British were in for a surprise. At the village of Lexington, near Concord, a group of about 70 colonists were waiting.

The events below are out of sequence.
Write numbers from 1 to 5 to show the correct order.

___4___ Paul Revere spreads word of the British soldiers' movement.

___1___ Colonists store weapons.

___3___ Colonists flash signal lights in a Boston church.

___5___ An army of colonists surprises the British at Lexington.

___2___ British soldiers begin moving toward Concord.

Usually, an author starts a story at the beginning and tells events in the order in which they occurred. Sometimes, however, an author will interrupt the order of events to tell about something that happened before the main action began. This interruption is called a **flashback**.

How can readers tell when a flashback begins? Often an author will use phrases such as *"I remember when . . ."* or *"She thought of the time months ago when . . ."* Such phrases alert readers to the change in time that signals a flashback.

Read this story and look for flashbacks as you read.

The loud knocking woke Isaac from a deep sleep. Who would be out in Lexington at this time of night? Downstairs, Isaac's father opened the door. "The Regulars are out! Be ready!" the stranger announced.

Isaac was thrilled by the news, but not surprised. He remembered how his father had trained with the other patriots last summer. Though father was usually quick with a smile or a witty word, he had taken his training very seriously. Isaac also recalled how, just last week, Father had argued with Sam Collins about the supplies at Concord. "Those weapons will spell trouble for us all," Sam had warned.

Father's boots thumped up the stairs to Isaac's room. "The militia is gathering on the Green, Isaac," he said. "You'll need to take charge at home for a little while."

Read these events from the story. If the incident is part of the main action, write **M** on the line to the left. If the incident is told in a flashback, write **F**. Then, on the lines to the right, number the statements from 1 to 4 to show the order in which they occurred.

F	Isaac's father trained with other patriots	1
M	Isaac's father told Isaac to take charge at home for a while.	4
M	A stranger came to Isaac's house late at night.	3
F	Sam Collins and Isaac's father argued about the supplies.	2

Tip

As you read, try to picture in your mind what is happening. After reading, ask yourself, "Would the outcome have changed if the events had happened in a different order, or if a certain event had not happened?"

Picture events in your mind as you read the following story. Use clue words to keep track of the order in which the events happen.

Redcoats and Homespun

BY BETSY STERMAN

The sound of drums drew Rebecca to the window. Redcoats again, marching out from Philadelphia. What a fine sight!

Rebecca sighed. She ought not to admire the enemy's red jackets, but she couldn't help herself. She looked down at her somber clothes: gray homespun dress, brown shoes laced up over gray stockings. No bright color anywhere—not in this room, and nowhere in the November countryside.

"Rebecca, come away from the window!" her mother called. "'Tis traitorous to look with admiration at the enemy."

"Just their uniforms," Rebecca protested. "They're as fancy as Lucy Wheeler's new shawl."

"Lucy Wheeler is a vain, foolish girl, and the splendid uniforms you so admire are worn by men who war against us."

"I know," Rebecca said, "but I can't help—"

"Can't help giving more notice to what folks wear than to who they are," Mother chided her. "No good will come of such a habit. Now look to your knitting, for Father will need those stockings soon enough."

Rebecca took up her needles. Dear Father. Just yesterday they had received a message from him. He was camped with General Washington's footsore troops northeast of Philadelphia.

A knock sounded at the door. When Mother opened it, there stood a man in farm clothes.

"Looking to join Gen'ral Washington," he said. "Could you spare me something to eat?"

"I can give you some of today's loaf," Mother told him. Rebecca stiffened. Since Washington's defeat at Brandywine, he had moved his troops constantly, hoping to save his poorly equipped men from another battle. Each day, redcoats marched out, searching for him. Spies were busy too, roaming the countryside in various disguises.

She peered closely at the farmer. His knee breeches and jacket were of homespun, his stockings knitted of the familiar gray yarn. A plain countryman, surely welcome in General Washington's weakened army. Still...something about his clothing was wrong. What was it?

As the man leaned back in his chair and stretched his feet toward the hearth, Rebecca's heart jumped. There it was—proof he was no rough countryman, but a spy!

He stood to leave. "Thankee," he said. "Could ye steer me toward Gen'ral Washington...?"

Mother hesitated, but Rebecca blurted, "He's southwest of Philadelphia! Father sent us word!"

After the man was gone, Mother said, "How clever to mislead him, Rebecca. What made you think he was not a simple farmer?"

"Farmers don't wear buckles on their shoes," Rebecca explained.

"Nor did he," Mother said, puzzled. "Plain scuffed shoes he had."

"But with smooth, unscuffed leather where the buckles had been removed!" Rebecca said.

Mother smiled. "Good *does* come of minding what folks wear," she said. Rebecca smiled too. Let Lucy Wheeler have her elegant shawl. Today's adventure made the world bright enough!

Checking Comprehension

1. How does Mother's attitude toward Rebecca and her interest in clothes change from the beginning of the story to the end? [Comparing and Contrasting/Inferential]

   <u>Possible answer: At the beginning of the story, Rebecca's mother thinks it's bad to care so much</u>

   <u>about clothes. By the end, she sees that Rebecca's interest in clothes was a good thing.</u>

   [Drawing Conclusions/Inferential]

2. What causes Rebecca to suspect that the visitor is a British spy?

   <u>Rebecca notices smooth, unscuffed spots on his shoes where buckles used to be. Most farmers</u>

   <u>didn't wear fancy buckled shoes, so Rebecca suspects that the visitor is a spy in disguise.</u>

Practicing Comprehension Skills

3. Think about the sequence of events in this story. Write one or two sentences in each box to tell what happened at the beginning, middle, and end of the story. Possible answers are given.

   Beginning

   <u>Rebecca thinks her life is plain and somber and admires the redcoats'</u>

   <u>fancy uniforms. Her mother tells her she pays too much attention</u>

   <u>to clothes.</u>

   Middle

   <u>A stranger dressed like a farmer comes to the house. He asks</u>

   <u>Rebecca and her mother questions about the location of General</u>

   <u>Washington's army.</u>

   End

   <u>Rebecca notices that the stranger's shoes once had buckles and realizes</u>

   <u>he is not a farmer. Suspecting he's a British spy, she gives him the</u>

   <u>wrong information.</u>

Write answers to the questions on the lines.

4. What are three clue words the writer uses to suggest the time an event occurred?

   Possible answers: November, yesterday, after, today's

5. Read the following events from the story. If the event is part of the main action occurring in the present, write M on the line to the left. If the incident occurred earlier and is told in a flashback, write F on the line.

   _M_ Rebecca gives wrong information to the stranger.

   _F_ Rebecca's family receives a letter from Father.

   _M_ A stranger appears at Rebecca's door.

   _F_ Washington's army is defeated at Brandywine.

   _F_ Mother bakes a loaf of bread.

   _M_ Rebecca admires the uniforms of the British soldiers.

6. Reread the six events listed in question 5. Think about the time order in which they occurred. On the time line below, write the events in time order from earliest to latest. Write one event on each set of lines.

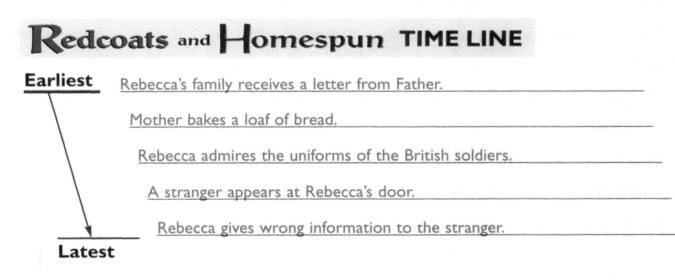

Redcoats and Homespun TIME LINE

Earliest   Rebecca's family receives a letter from Father.

   Mother bakes a loaf of bread.

   Rebecca admires the uniforms of the British soldiers.

   A stranger appears at Rebecca's door.

   Rebecca gives wrong information to the stranger.

Latest

7. Which event on the time line is the least important to the story's outcome? Which event is the most important?

   The least important event is that Rebecca's mother bakes bread. The most important event

   is that Rebecca gives wrong information to the stranger.

8. How would the outcome of this story have changed if Rebecca had answered the stranger's question about General Washington *before* she noticed his shoes?

Possible answers: Rebecca or her mother might have given valuable information to a spy if Rebecca had not noticed the buckle marks and decided the visitor could not be trusted. The entire course of the Revolution might have changed if the spy had had correct information.

Practicing Vocabulary

Circle the word or phrase that means the same as the underlined word or words in the sentence.

9. A spy's closet is likely to hold many <u>disguises</u>.
    a. dishes   b. costumes   c. shoes

10. Dark colors are more <u>somber</u> than bright ones.
    a. dull   b. sad   c. simple

11. The stranger seemed to be <u>roaming</u> from one farm to another.
    a. running   b. wandering   c. riding

12. The soldier <u>was footsore</u> after marching 30 miles.
    a. had tired feet   b. was wounded   c. was barefoot

13. Mother <u>chided</u> Rebecca for neglecting her chores.
    a. praised   b. punished   c. scolded

14. After fooling the spy, Rebecca won her mother's <u>admiration</u>.
    a. approval   b. anger   c. surprise

15. The Minutemen were <u>poorly</u> equipped compared to the redcoats.
    a. expensively   b. properly   c. badly

admiration
chided
disguises
footsore
poorly
roaming
somber

MAKING THE
Reading
AND
Writing
CONNECTION

Writing a News Article
Imagine that you are a reporter covering an important news event. On a separate sheet of paper, write a news story that identifies the events in the order in which they occurred. Use at least two clue words to help your readers keep track of the sequence of events.

Sequence: Steps in a Process

What do a recipe, a model airplane, and a new VCR have in common? All of them come with an organized set of instructions for completing a process. Once you recognize the **steps in a process**, you can use the order of the steps to complete an action.

Before you begin to follow steps in a process, read all the steps carefully. Then you'll have an idea of what you will need to do, and you can gather any necessary materials. Looking carefully at illustrations or diagrams will also make it easier to follow the steps.

Read the following paragraphs. As you read, think about the steps required in the process of planting and growing carrots.

If you're interested in growing carrots, it's important to begin by selecting a bright, sunny spot in your garden. Then you'll need to loosen the soil with a tool called a trowel, which looks like a small shovel. Check to be certain that the soil drains well.

After that, you're ready to plant the seeds. You'll have to be careful as you're planting because carrot seeds are extremely small. Plant them about 1/4 inch deep and 3 inches apart. Gently pat down the soil after each seed is in the ground.

Carrots prefer moist soil. Because of that, it is very important that the soil stays damp until the seeds sprout in 12 to 18 days. As the carrots grow, be careful to keep the soil weed-free. In approximately 60 to 80 days, you can pick the carrots for part of a delicious dinner.

Write these steps in order from 1 to 6:

__3__ Plant the seeds.   __1__ Locate a sunny spot.

__6__ Pick the carrots.   __2__ Loosen the soil.

__5__ Weed the garden.   __4__ Water the seeds.

Write at least three words or phrases that helped you identify the sequence of these steps.

begin, then, after, as, in . . . days _____

_____

Tip

Some instructions use numbers to order the steps. Others use clue words, such as *first, second, later, next, then,* and *last*. If there are no numbers or clue words, use common sense to figure out the order of the steps.

As you read the following recipe, try to visualize what happens at each step and what the final result will look like.

Carrot Cupcakes
by Ann Hodgman

Ingredients

1 1/4 cups corn or canola oil
2 cups sugar
2 cups all-purpose flour
2 teaspoons cinnamon
2 teaspoons baking powder
1 teaspoon baking soda
1 teaspoon salt
4 large eggs, well-beaten
1 pound carrots
1 cup chopped pecans (optional)

If you've been living in an alternate universe and have never tried carrot cake, you may not know how delicious it is. Carrot cupcakes are just as good.

Preheat the oven to 350 degrees. Take 36 cupcake papers and put them into muffin pans. (You may not need all 36, but you can always put the unused ones back.)

In a large bowl, whisk together the oil and the sugar until they're combined. The sugar won't dissolve, but that's okay. In another large bowl, sift together the flour, cinnamon, baking powder, baking soda, and salt.

Now you have to grate the carrots. This is sort of a boring job, so you might want to listen to some music while you're working. Wash the carrots, cut off the ends, and peel them with a vegetable peeler. Then grate them on the smallest side of a metal grater. (Be careful! You want to shred the carrots—not your skin.) Sift half the dry-ingredients mixture into the oil-sugar mixture and beat well. Sift in the second half, beat well again, and then beat in the eggs. Now stir in the grated carrots and the optional pecans, and mix thoroughly.

Using a large spoon, carefully fill the cupcake papers 2/3 to 3/4 of the way. (The batter needs room to rise.) Bake the cupcakes on the middle rack of the oven for 10 minutes. Then—using potholders, of course—rotate the cupcake pans until the back of each is facing front. This will help the cupcakes bake evenly. Bake for 10 more minutes.

Next, choose the most lopsided cupcake and carefully lift it out of the pan onto a plate. Peel off the paper and cut the cupcake in half to see whether it's done. If it is done, take the cupcakes out of the oven. If your test cupcake seems mushy, bake the rest of the cupcakes for another 5 to 7 minutes. (You can't continue baking the bisected cupcake, so if it's done baking, eat it without delay.)

You can ice the cupcakes with your favorite frosting if desired—but let the cupcakes cool *completely* before you ice them. The icing will melt if you put it on while the cupcakes are still hot!

This recipe makes 2 to 3 dozen cupcakes, which you should cover with plastic wrap. The cupcakes will keep at room temperature for at least 3 days. After that, you'll obtain the best results by putting them in the freezer and thawing them as needed—if your family hasn't already devoured them.

Checking Comprehension

1. Aside from the ingredients listed in the recipe, what other things do you need to have on hand in order to make carrot cupcakes? [Drawing Conclusions/Critical]

   You need an oven, cupcake papers, muffin pans, 2 large bowls, a whisk or other mixing spoon,

   a sifter, a metal grater, a vegetable peeler, measuring cups and spoons, a large spoon,

   potholders, a knife, frosting if desired, plastic wrap   [Making Judgments/Critical]
2. What do you think is the most difficult part about making carrot cupcakes?

   Possible answer: judging how long to cook the cupcakes so that they are completely baked

Practicing Comprehension Skills

Write your answer on the line.

3. Order these steps to show what happens after you put the cupcakes in the oven. Write the numbers 1–6 to show the correct order.

   _5_ Then you can eat them.

   _3_ When they are done, take the cupcakes out of the oven to cool.

   _1_ After 10 minutes, rotate the pans.

   _4_ When they are cool, frost them if you wish.

   _6_ Cover any remaining cupcakes with plastic wrap.

   _2_ Then, after another 10 minutes, test one cupcake to see if it is done.

4. Between which two steps do you beat in the eggs?

   You beat in the eggs after you have beaten the second half of the dry ingredients and the

   oil-sugar mixture, and before you add the grated carrots and the optional pecans.

5. Do all of the steps in the recipe have to be completed in the order in which they are listed in the recipe, or can some be switched around? Support your answer with an example.

   All of the steps do not have to be completed in the order listed. For example, you could peel

   and grate the carrots before doing anything else.

6. As you read this recipe for frosting, underline all the clue words that help you determine the order of the steps.

First, allow two sticks of unsalted butter and eight ounces of cream cheese to reach room temperature. Then, with an electric mixer, beat the butter and cream cheese together. Next, gradually add four cups of confectioners' sugar, beating well after each addition until the icing is smooth and fluffy. Add one teaspoon of vanilla extract and a pinch of salt, then beat the icing one more time. Finally, spread the icing on the cool cupcakes.

7. Write numbers to show the order of these steps for making icing.

___2___ Beat the butter and cream cheese together.

___1___ Allow the butter and cream cheese to reach room temperature.

___5___ Beat the icing for the last time.

___6___ Spread the icing on the cupcakes.

___4___ Add vanilla extract and salt.

___3___ Gradually add 4 cups of confectioners' sugar and beat after each addition.

Practicing Vocabulary

8. Choose the word from the box that best fills each blank in the paragraph.

| alternate | bisected | delay | devoured | ingredients | obtain | optional |

I decided to make carrot cupcakes, but first I had to _____obtain_____ the necessary ___ingredients___ . Searching for the cinnamon caused a _____delay_____ before I could start to bake. I decided to skip the ___optional___ pecans and substitute an ___alternate___ nut, walnuts. The first cupcake I ___bisected___ was mushy, so I baked the rest for five more minutes. My family ___devoured___ the cupcakes before I could frost them!

Writing Directions
On a separate sheet of paper, write directions that tell how to prepare something you like to eat. Organize the steps in sequential order and make sure there are at least six steps. Number each step, or use clue words *such as first, next,* and *last.*

Predicting Outcomes

When you read a story or article, you are likely to find yourself making predictions—thinking about what will happen next. Try **predicting outcomes** at several points in your reading. Before you begin, preview the title and pictures to make predictions about what you will read. As you read, use details and your own experiences to predict what might happen next. After reading, check the accuracy of your predictions and think about the clues that helped you predict.

Look at the title and the picture below. Predict what the passage will be about. As you read, use details to predict what will happen next.

Ticket to the Future

Bartholomew had ten $20 bills in his pocket and a nervous rumbling in his stomach. He had worked hard to save for the trip to the future. He planned to return home for school in September.

The departure dock was deserted except for the ticket master. Bartholomew bought a ticket printed "For forward travel." The other side had gotten wet, and the lines were blurred. He could make out CAU ON. The word *one* appeared in one line, the word *no* in another.

"All aboard!" cried the ticket master. "Departure time! Now or never!" Bartholomew hurried to the platform.

Once the craft left the station, Bartholomew focused again on the ticket. "Caution!" the heading said. Then, in much smaller print, "For one-way travel only. No return trip."

How did the title or the illustration help you predict what this story would be about?

Possible answer: The title "Ticket to the Future" suggests that a character

is going to travel to the future. The picture shows a boy who is going to

time travel into the future.

What clues helped you predict the outcome of this story?

Possible answers: Bartholomew is nervous even before he buys his

ticket; he can't make out all the words on his ticket; the ticket says

"For forward travel."

Tip

As you read, look for clues that will help you predict what might happen next. Think about your own experiences and things you have read or heard about.

The New Guy, Ben

The locker swung open, and a boy stepped out and stretched. He smoothed his leather printer's apron, leaving a dark ink splotch.

"It worked," the boy whispered. He moved down the hall, staring intently at the overhead lights. Spying his image in a window, the boy stopped. He straightened his wire-rimmed glasses and smoothed his long, wispy hair as he tucked a kite string back into his pocket.

The boy jumped as a bell sounded. The students of Colonial Heights Middle School swarmed out into the halls.

"Who's the new guy?" asked Patrick.

"Check out the knee pants," said Betsy. "Is he in a rock band? He looks familiar."

One student held out his hand. "I'm Thomas," he said. "And you are . . . ?"

"I'm Ben." When the two shook hands, Thomas was surprised to feel a small electric shock.

As Thomas showed the mysterious visitor around school, the boys discovered they had much in common. Both enjoyed swimming and sailing.

"You would like the place I come from," Ben said, "but I doubt you would enjoy my after-school job."

"I baby-sit after school sometimes so I can buy CDs," said Thomas.

"CDs?" Ben puzzled. "Candle dippers? Copper doorstops?" He said, "I'm saving my wages. After all, a penny saved is a penny earned!"

When Thomas pointed out the library computers, Ben was surprised, but then he got busy at a keyboard. At first he didn't notice the thunder. Then a flash of lightning caught Ben's attention. "Perfect travel conditions," he said, looking wistfully at the computer screen.

Thomas watched Ben from the next computer. On Thomas's screen an encyclopedia entry showed a man with small wire-rimmed glasses. Although the man was balding on top, wispy hair flowed to his shoulders. Dates in the entry read 1706–1790.

"Benjamin," Thomas said gently, "you have to go." He nodded at the flag above the door. "You have things to do. Remind George and Tom J. that we're all created equal. Don't forget the life, liberty, and happiness part."

"It *is* time to go." Ben smiled. "Both fish and visitors smell in three days."

Thomas shook his head. Someone should write a book of this guy's sayings!

A peal of thunder sounded as the boys entered the deserted hall. "Ben," Thomas said, "how did you get here?"

"It's all in the lightning," Ben said. He opened a locker, pushed a kite to the back, and climbed in.

Just one flash glowed from behind the locker door. Thomas knew Ben Franklin was gone.

Checking Comprehension

1. Why does the writer give so many details about Ben, such as his glasses, the kite string in his pocket, and the fact that he comes and goes with lightning? [Author's Purpose/Critical]

   Possible response: The writer wants readers to figure out that the visitor is really Ben Franklin.

2. Thomas tells Ben, "You have to go. You have things to do." What do you think he means? [Drawing Conclusions/Critical]

   Answers will vary. Students may say that at this point Thomas realizes who Ben is.

   He wants Ben to return to his own time in order to keep history on course.

Practicing Comprehension Skills

List three clues from the picture, title, and/or text that helped you predict that Ben was actually the famous Benjamin Franklin from American history.

3. Possible answers: the name Ben; wire-rimmed glasses; hair style, clothing style

4. mention of working in a print shop; kites; interest in electric lights and lightning

5. the names Colonial Heights Middle School, references to George (George Washington) and Tom J. (Thomas Jefferson), mention of lines from the Declaration of Independence

Complete the following chart by writing on the lines.

What I Already Knew About Benjamin Franklin	What I Predicted Would Happen	What Actually Happened
6. Possible answers: He experimented with electricity and kites. He lived during Colonial times.	7. Possible answer: Ben had come from the past and would eventually return to his own time.	8. Possible answer: My prediction was right. Ben was a time traveler and did return home.

The following are predictions you might have made as you read the story. On the line after the prediction, write A if the prediction was accurate and NA if it was not accurate. List the clues you could use to check the prediction.

9. **The story would involve someone traveling from the past to the future.**

   A. Possible clues: Ben's clothing did not belong in a modern school;

   Ben did not understand what CDs and computers were.

10. **Ben would bring Thomas back to colonial times.**

   NA. Possible clues: Ben does say, "You would like the place I come from."

   However, he returns to the past alone.

Practicing Vocabulary

Write a word from the box to complete each sentence.

deserted	familiar	liberty	overhead	peal	wispy	wistfully

11. The school was _____deserted_____ before the students arrived at 8:00 a.m.

12. We viewed the picture of Ben Franklin on an _____overhead_____ projector.

13. The thin, _____wispy_____ clouds were replaced by thick, dark ones.

14. Ben sighed _____wistfully_____ , wishing he could stay a little longer.

15. Ben was used to the musical _____peal_____ of bells, but the school bell was a harsh buzz.

16. Ben Franklin helped create the Declaration of Independence, which called for _____liberty_____ .

17. The name Ben Franklin is _____familiar_____ to most Americans.

Writing a Journal Entry
Imagine that you are a time traveler visiting America 100 or 200 years in the future. On another sheet of paper, write a travel journal entry describing what you find. Base your predictions about the future on clues you see in the world today.

Recognizing Cause and Effect

Did you ever work hard to make something happen? Maybe you practiced hard in order to perform well at a sport. If so, then you saw **cause and effect** in action. An **effect** is something that happens. A **cause** is the reason it happened. Sometimes one cause can lead to many effects. A bad storm could cause a game to be postponed and also damage homes and flood roads. In the same way, one effect can have many causes. If your team wins, the win may be the result of hard work from you, your teammates, and your coach.

When you read stories and articles, you may stop to think about what happened and why it happened. Clue words such as *because, since, thus,* or *as a result* often signal a cause and effect relationship. If an author doesn't use clue words, ask yourself, "What happened? Why did it happen?"

Read the following story. Think about the cause-and-effect relationships that occur.

"Class, please don't forget that your research paper is due Monday," my science teacher said.

"Uh-oh," I thought. "Research paper! I completely forgot! Okay, don't panic. There's plenty of time before Monday."

As soon as I got home, I logged on the Internet and started a search. I typed B-I-O-L-O-G-Y in the search window. Wow—it returned thousands of Web sites with the word *biology*! Since that didn't work, I tried to narrow my search. That was a much better idea! We'd been studying germs, so I typed B-A-C-T-E-R-I-A in the search window. Then I got a list that was a lot shorter, but still had several thousand hits! This was going to be harder than I thought.

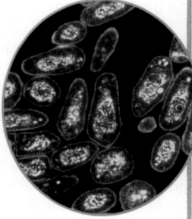

Fill in the missing causes and effects below.

Cause	Effect
The teacher reminded the class about the research paper assignment.	The student began an Internet search.
The student did a search on the word *bacteria*.	Thousands of Web sites were returned.

Tip

Clue words such as *because* or *as a result* signal cause-and-effect relationships. When an author does not use clue words, you should ask yourself, "What happened? Why did it happen?"

STRATEGY: Recognizing Cause-and-Effect Relationships   29

Traveling on The Information Superhighway

In the early 1990s, few people outside of governments and universities had ever heard the term *Internet*. The World Wide Web was in its infancy. Back then if you said to someone, "Send me an e-mail with directions to your house," all you would have received is a puzzled look. Technology has come a long way since those days. Today, the Internet connects millions of computers around the globe, making a worldwide exchange of information possible.

The Internet is often called the "information superhighway." That's because vast amounts of information travel over it. If you searched the word *grasshopper*, for instance, you would have thousands of sites to look at. Some sites would give information on these insects. Other sites would be companies with "grasshopper" in their names. Still other sites might want to sell you books about grasshoppers.

In addition to information, the Internet also offers one of the greatest inventions in communications: electronic mail, or e-mail for short. E-mail is the brainchild of a shrewd man named Ray Tomlinson. He developed the program and sent himself the first e-mail in 1971. He isn't sure, but he thinks his first message was QWERTYUIOP (the top row of letters on a keyboard). As a result of Tomlinson's invention of e-mail, the way in which the world communicates has changed.

Thanks to e-mail, you can communicate with a student in London and find out how his weather experiment is going. E-mail has also changed the speed with which we exchange information. In minutes, you can contact another person who shares your love of kites or stamps. Your aunt and uncle can send you pictures of their new puppy without ever leaving their home. If you're sick and can't attend school, your teacher can e-mail you the assignments you have missed. You can even send e-mail to a grasshopper expert and ask questions for a research paper.

However, if you're going to use e-mail, you need to follow some simple rules of "Netiquette." Netiquette is the good manners, or etiquette, you should remember when using the Internet. This is especially important when using e-mail. For example, it's rude to shout your e-mail message. How do you shout e-mail? TYPING YOUR MESSAGE IN ALL CAPITAL LETTERS is shouting. It may offend the person you send the message to.

There is one big disadvantage to using e-mail. Unlike a letter you send through the mail, e-mail is NOT private. It can be reviewed by anyone with access to your receiver's computer. Your receiver could also forward it to other people—so be careful. Do not say anything in an e-mail that you wouldn't say in front of a crowd!

Mail Folder "Inbox"		
Subject	**From**	**Received**
Math Homework	surfer@xyz.com	7:00 P.M.
My Party	raffles@sunshine.net	5:01 P.M.
Hi From Grandma	ericapatrick@anytown.com	11:46 A.M.

Checking Comprehension

1. How has the Internet changed our world? [Main Idea/Critical]

    Possible answers: People all around the world can communicate at a much faster pace.

    People can find vast amounts of information on any topic very quickly.

                                                            [Comparing and Contrasting/Critical]
2. How is e-mail similar to and different from the postal service?

    Both e-mail and the postal service allow people to communicate in writing with others.

    E-mail is much faster, but it is not as private.

Practicing Comprehension Skills

This article presents several cause-and-effect relationships. Think about the article
as you look at the chart below. Where there is a cause listed, write the effect.
Where an effect is listed, write what caused it to happen.

Cause	Effect
3. The Internet connects millions of computers around the globe.	A worldwide exchange of information is possible.
4. Search the word *grasshopper*	Find thousands of Web sites
5. Type an e-mail message in all capital letters	You may offend the receiver.
6. Send an e-mail with private information	Find yourself embarrassed by an e-mail you sent.

7. What is the cause in this sentence? What is the effect? What clue words helped
    you to identify the cause and effect relationship?

    As a result of Tomlinson's invention of e-mail, the way in which the world
    communicates has changed.

    Cause: Tomlinson's invention

    Effect: The way in which the world communicates has changed.

    Clue word or words: as a result

Complete this cause/effect sentence.

8. The Internet is often called the "information superhighway" because
so much information travels over it.

List three effects of the invention of e-mail.

9. _People who are far away from each other can communicate with each other._

10. _People can communicate quickly._

11. _People can send pictures without ever leaving their home._

Practicing Vocabulary

Write the word from the box that answers each question.

brainchild	infancy	Internet	reviewed	shrewd	sites	technology

12. What are the places on the Internet that have information on a given subject?
_____ _sites_ _____

13. In what category could you group computers, cell phones, pagers, and VCRs?
_____ _technology_ _____

14. What do you call it when you have looked at something again? _____ _reviewed_ _____

15. What is the name for the "information superhighway" we have today? _____ _Internet_ _____

16. What is another name for someone's idea, invention, or discovery? _____ _brainchild_ _____

17. How can you describe an early stage of childhood? _____ _infancy_ _____

18. When someone is very clever, what might you say he or she is? _____ _shrewd_ _____

Writing a Persuasive Paragraph
Imagine that your local library does not have enough computers to meet its Internet access needs. On another sheet of paper, write a paragraph to persuade the library to invest in more computers. Be sure to include some convincing cause-and-effect relationships in your paragraph.

Using Context Clues

When you come to an unfamiliar word in your reading, you can use **context clues** to help you figure out its meaning. Context clues may be in the same sentence as the unknown word, or in surrounding sentences. This chart gives examples of four types of context clues.

Definition or Explanation	Example	Synonym	Description
The *slate*, or list of candidates, includes students from every class.	Our president has many fine *characteristics*, such as confidence and friendliness.	The students called for *reforms*. They said changes were needed.	The *incumbent* president had already been in office for a full term.
• The meaning of the word *slate* is explained with a definition.	• *Confidence* and *friendliness* are examples of characteristics.	• The words *reforms* and *changes* are synonyms.	• Context clues describe *incumbent* as someone who is already in an elected position.

Read the following passage. Use context clues to figure out the meanings of the underlined words.

Tanya frowned as her father tossed a tuna can into the trash. She believed everyone ought to <u>recycle</u>, or put items back into use.

Tanya began a family campaign. She made posters and wrote <u>slogans</u> such as, "Use it once, use it twice. Please help make this planet nice!" No one listened, so Tanya quietly began collecting her family's recyclables in a storage closet. A few weeks later Tanya's mother pulled the closet door <u>ajar</u> and gasped. "Where are our suitcases?" she asked.

"They're buried in all this <u>rubbish</u>," Tanya said. "If we don't start recycling, *we're* going to be buried in garbage, too!"

Find each word below in the passage. On the line next to the word, write its meaning. Then write *definition*, *example*, *synonym*, or *description* to name the type of context clue given in the passage.

recycle: <u>put items back into use; definition</u>

slogans: <u>catchy phrases and sayings; example</u>

rubbish: <u>garbage; synonym</u>

ajar: <u>slightly open; description</u>

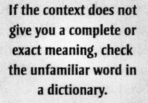

Tip

If the context does not give you a complete or exact meaning, check the unfamiliar word in a dictionary.

Read the following story. Use context clues to figure out the meaning of unfamiliar words.

The Cookie Campaign

The students at Lincoln Middle School looked forward to election time. It meant free stuff! Last year a candidate handed out pens. Another office seeker gave away yo-yos. It was no surprise that the students showed little interest in *who* was running for student government but a lot of interest in *what* a candidate was giving out!

A week before election day, Andy pulled cookies from the oven. Each one had an "A+" formed from chocolate chips. That was Andy's logo, the symbol of his campaign for president. His motto was, "Lincoln gets an A+ with Andy!" He had made chocolate chip cookies, fudge cookies, and brownies. Anyone who loved chocolate would surely vote for Andy.

The same day, Connie left the bakery with boxes full of sugar crinkles and snickerdoodles. She'd spent her savings, but it would be worth it when she was elected student body president.

All that week, Connie and Andy distributed treats. By Friday, the cookie campaign had reached the whole student body. Students were arguing about cookie flavors. They were taking sides—chocolate versus vanilla!

Election day arrived, and just in time! The students had gained a combined total of 500 pounds. Three candidates sat on the stage that day. Few students had realized there was a third student in the race for president. While Andy and Connie had been busy with cookies, Harrison had quietly built his campaign platform. This list of plans was all that Harrison had to offer.

Andy spoke first. He called for a larger dessert selection at lunch. Then his campaign manager served brownies.

Connie moved to the podium. Speaking from the stand, she promised a bigger budget for party refreshments. "We'll have more money available to buy baked goods!" she said.

Finally, Harrison stood. He had no cookies—no gifts at all. "Fellow students," he began, "this cookie campaign has been counterproductive. Rather than producing real ideas, it has led us nowhere. Now, don't think I'm antisocial. I like parties, treats, and good times as much as anyone else does, but there are more important issues for our school to tackle."

The audience put down their cookies and listened as Harrison suggested new programs. He said students could tutor, or teach, classmates after school. Work parties could clean up the ball fields. Harrison had no cookies, but he had ideas.

That election day was a turning point. Oh, everyone still enjoyed a good cookie once in a while, but now the students had advantages such as clean school grounds and volunteer tutors. Led by Harrison, their new president, the chocolate lovers and vanilla fans set aside their differences and addressed real issues. They joined forces to make Lincoln Middle School a better place for all.

Checking Comprehension

1. How was Harrison's campaign different from those run by Andy and Connie? [Comparing and Contrasting/Inferential]

   Harrison presented important ideas for improving the school. Connie and Andy

   tried to get votes by giving away food.

2. How do you think Lincoln Middle School's presidential campaign might be different next year? [Making Predictions/Critical]

   Answers will vary, but may include: Students will not be interested in treats and gifts.

   They will want to know how a candidate plans to help the school.

Practicing Comprehension Skills

Find each word in the passage. Use context clues to figure out the meaning. Then fill in the circle before the correct meaning.

3. A logo is a

   ○ catchy saying.   ○ campaign promise.   ● special symbol.   ○ list of candidates.

4. A podium is a

   ○ candidate.   ○ type of cookie.   ○ voting booth.   ● speaker's stand.

5. Counterproductive means

   ● leading nowhere.   ○ making a product.   ○ a counter for cookies.   ○ producing results.

6. Antisocial means

   ○ against dancing.   ● against the company of others.   ○ against food   ○ against the issues.

Find each word in the passage. Use context clues to understand the word's meaning. Then write an original sentence that includes the type of context clue requested (definition, synonym, example, or description).

7. motto (definition)

   Possible answer: My favorite motto, or saying, is "Never say never."

8. addressed (synonym)

   Possible answer: Harrison addressed the problem with the school grounds,

   and he also dealt with the issue of tutoring.

9. advantages (example)

   Possible answer: There are many advantages to volunteer work,

   such as meeting new people and gaining experience.

10. budget (description)

    Possible answer: With a bigger budget, the students would have more money

    to spend on class trips.

Practicing Vocabulary

Write a word from the box to complete each sentence.

antisocial	candidate	counterproductive	distributed	platform	tutor	versus

11. The race was Andy _____versus_____ Connie until Harrison appeared on the scene.

12. The homeroom teachers _____distributed_____ ballots to the students.

13. "Complaining can be _____counterproductive_____," said the president, "so let's take action and improve our school."

14. That student has an interesting _____platform_____ that includes exciting new programs.

15. Although Harrison enjoys time alone, he is very friendly and not at all _____antisocial_____.

16. The math _____tutor_____ helped Connie prepare for the final test.

17. The _____candidate_____ with the best ideas is likely to win the election.

Writing a Campaign Speech

Imagine that you are running for president of your class, school, club, or other organization. Write a short speech giving reasons voters should elect you. Be sure to check your speech and provide context clues for any words that might be unfamiliar.

Comparing and Contrasting

When you read, you'll find that authors often make **comparisons** that tell how two or more things are alike. They also make **contrasts** that point out differences between the things. Authors compare and contrast so that readers can understand ideas clearly. Sometimes, though not always, authors use clue words such as *like, similar to*, or *also* to compare. Clue words such as *but, different from, however, in contrast*, or *unlike* may be used to show contrasts.

As you read, look for the author's comparisons and contrasts. Also look for ways to make comparisons and contrasts on your own.

Read the following paragraphs. Find comparisons and contrasts.

In normal eyes, light rays focus on the back of the eye. This part of the eye is called the retina (RET-in-uh). If your eyes are either nearsighted or farsighted, however, then the light rays do not meet where they should.

Nearsightedness means that close things appear clear but faraway ones look fuzzy and unclear. The eye tends to be too long. The light rays meet before they reach the retina. The image on the retina is then out of focus.

Farsightedness is the opposite problem. Faraway things appear clearer than close ones. The eye is too short, so light rays from close objects are not yet focused when they reach the retina.

Wearing glasses or contact lenses can solve both of these problems.

On the chart below write two ways that nearsightedness and farsightedness are alike and two ways in which they are different.

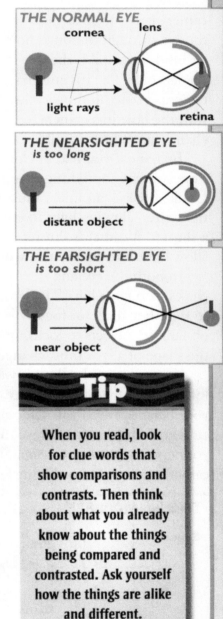

THE NORMAL EYE
cornea   lens
light rays
retina

THE NEARSIGHTED EYE
is too long
distant object

THE FARSIGHTED EYE
is too short
near object

Nearsightedness and Farsightedness

Alike	Different
1. Both nearsighted and farsighted eyes have a problem focusing.	1. A nearsighted eye is too long. A farsighted eye is too short.
2. Both nearsighted and farsighted eyes can be corrected with glasses or contact lenses.	2. In a nearsighted eye, distant objects appear unclear. In a farsighted eye, objects close up aren't as clear.

Tip

When you read, look for clue words that show comparisons and contrasts. Then think about what you already know about the things being compared and contrasted. Ask yourself how the things are alike and different.

Read the following article. Think about what is being compared and contrasted, and why.

The Eye and the Camera

How does the human eye see? In some ways, the way you see can be compared to the way a camera takes a picture.

The first thing that an eye needs to see, and a camera needs to take pictures, is light. Light enters the eye through the small hole called the pupil. Around the pupil is the iris, the ring that gives your eye its color. The iris automatically opens or closes the pupil to let in more or less light. In the same way, the hole in a camera, called the aperture, can change size automatically.

Imagine if you had to close your eyes every time you saw something new. A camera is like that. Unlike the eye, a camera must return to darkness right after allowing light to enter. That's why it has a shutter. A camera's shutter acts like a curtain to allow light into the camera when a picture is taken.

In both the eye and the camera, light then passes through a lens. The lens bends the light rays so that they meet, or focus. To shift from focusing on faraway objects to focusing on nearby objects, the shape of a lens must change.

Your eye muscles do this work for you. Try looking at something far away. Quickly change your perspective so you're looking at something close up. Thanks to your eye muscles, the lens of your eye just became thicker. Similarly, the lens of a camera can be changed. One lens might be used for a close-up photograph and another for a distant view. However, a photographer must decide to change a lens. Your eye muscles change the lens's shape automatically.

The light rays inside the camera focus on a chemical layer on film. The points of light change the chemical, forming a pattern. Then the film goes through the developing process. The patterns of light and darkness turn into a photograph.

Inside the eye, the light also forms a pattern on a light-sensitive layer. This layer, at the back of the eye, is called the retina (RET-in-uh). The cells of the retina respond to light. In contrast to a camera with film, the eye processes its images instantly. The cells of the retina send electrical impulses speeding along the optic nerve. When the impulses reach the brain, it makes sense of the image.

The images on film and on the retina are not the same as in real life. Because of the way light rays travel, the image is upside down. To look at a photograph, you must turn it right-side up. To look at the words on this page, however, you don't have to turn the book. Your brain turns the visual image around for you.

A fine camera can be a marvel of engineering. Even the best camera, though, is nowhere near as spectacularly complex as the eye-brain connections you are using right now.

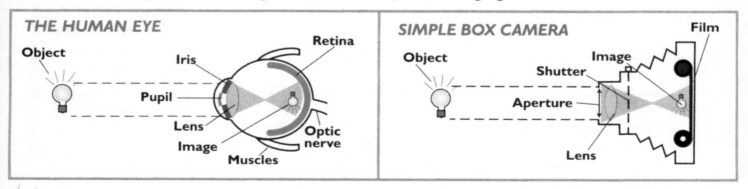

THE HUMAN EYE

Object, Iris, Retina, Pupil, Lens, Image, Muscles, Optic nerve

SIMPLE BOX CAMERA

Object, Shutter, Aperture, Lens, Image, Film

Checking Comprehension

1. Why do you think the brain is so important in the way the eye sees?

   Possible answer: The brain makes sense of visual images. It also turns around the upside-

   down images sent from the retina.

2. What is the purpose of a lens, and why does it need to change shape?

   Possible answer: A lens bends light rays so that they focus. It changes shape for close-up and

   distant views.

Practicing Comprehension Skills

Write the answer to each question on the lines.

3. Why does a camera need a shutter when an eye does not? What clue word
   or words signal this difference?

   A camera needs to return to darkness after taking a picture. An eye doesn't need to do

   this; "unlike the eye"

4. How is the retina of the eye like the film in a camera? What clue word
   signals this similarity?

   Possible answer: Both the retina and a camera's film are layers that are sensitive to light; "also"

5. Which can process an image more quickly: the eye or a camera? Explain your answer.

   The eye. It can process a picture instantly because it works together with the brain.

   A camera's film must be developed.

6. Fill in the circle before the correct answer.

   Why can people see right-side up?

   ○ Unlike a camera, the eye has no shutter.

   ○ Like a lens, light rays are focused.

   ● Unlike a camera and photograph, the brain turns upside-down images around for us.

   ○ Like a camera, light enters the eye through a small hole.

Use the Venn diagram below to compare and contrast the eye and the camera.

The Eye

7. Doesn't need to close after seeing an image.

8. Eye muscles change shape of lens.

Processes its images instantly. Images turn right-side up automatically.

Both

9. Light is needed to see and take pictures.

10. Light enters through a small hole that changes size.

Light passes through a lens.

Camera

11. Must return to darkness right after light enters.

12. Has a shutter.

Photographs must be turned right-side up.

Practicing Vocabulary

Write a word from the box to match each definition.

aperture	focus	perspective	pupil	retina	spectacularly	visual

13. ___aperture___   hole in a camera that changes size to let in light

14. ___perspective___   point of view in judging what you see

15. ___pupil___   small hole in eye through which light enters

16. ___retina___   layer of light-sensitive cells at the back of the eye

17. ___focus___   to cause light rays to meet in order to make an image clear

18. ___visual___   having to do with sight

19. ___spectacularly___   in an amazing way

MAKING THE
Reading
AND
Writing
CONNECTION

Writing a Compare and Contrast Essay
How is the heart like a pump? How is the brain like a computer? On another sheet of paper, write one or two paragraphs to answer either of those questions or a similar question you make up. Use clue words such as *like*, *also*, *different from*, and *but* to make your comparisons and contrasts clearer.

Summarizing

Writing a summary can help you when you do research or study for a test. A **summary** is a short statement that tells the main ideas and most important details of an article or the main events in a story. These are the same main ideas and important details you would include in notes or in an outline, but they are written in paragraph form. Before you summarize a selection, read it carefully. Look for topic sentences to help you determine the main idea or ideas. Since a summary should be brief, you must choose only the most important information from the events, details, or examples you are given.

The more important information there is in a selection, the longer your summary will be. The summary of a TV show may be two or three sentences. The summary of a book or chapter in a social studies book may be several paragraphs long.

Read the following press release announcing a new TV show. Underline the most important ideas. One paragraph has been done for you. On the lines below, finish writing a summary of the piece that uses only 2-3 sentences.

PRESS RELEASE:

DR. NERO, SUPERHERO

MCP-TV Broadcasting proudly announces a new action-adventure show called "Dr. Nero, Superhero," which will air every Sunday from 9:00 to 9:30 P.M.

Who is Dr. Nero? She's the most thrilling action character ever! A former principal, Dr. Nero gained X-ray vision and the ability to fly after she was accidentally exposed to radioactive isotopes in the school lab. She decided to become . . . Dr. Nero, Superhero! Each Sunday at 9:00 P.M., Dr. Nero helps a student in need to overcome problems ranging from a lost library book to a missed football practice. Watch "Dr. Nero, Superhero," the hottest new show around!

Summary:

MCP-TV is announcing a new action-adventure show called "Dr. Nero, Superhero," which will air on Sundays from 9:00 – 9:30 P.M. Possible answers may include: Dr. Nero, a former principal, uses X-ray vision and the ability to fly to help students overcome their problems.

Read the following selection. As you read, underline main ideas that you would include in a summary of the selection. The main ideas in the first paragraph have been underlined for you.

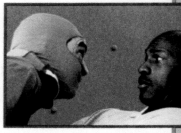

A camera crew wants to shoot a scene in which an actor talks to a cartoon character against an animated background. How can this be done? Many film makers would use the "blue screen" or "green screen" technique. With this process, a character can be shown against any background.

The star would first be filmed in front of a solid blue or green screen. An actor clothed in blue or green might play the cartoon character's part. Cameras would shoot this scene. Then a special computer system would filter the blue or green out of the film. It would be replaced with animation footage.

This technique has many uses in feature films and television shows. It is also used in television weather forecasting, where the weather map replaces the blue or green screen.

Which sentence presents a main idea from the passage that *should* be included in a summary?

○ A camera crew wants to shoot a scene with an actor and a cartoon character.

○ An actor clothed in blue or green might play the cartoon character's part.

● With this process, a character can be shown against any background.

○ The weather map replaces the blue or green screen.

Which of the following sentences gives the best summary of the third paragraph from the passage?

● The technique has many uses in movies and television.

○ TV weather forecasting also uses the blue or green screen technique.

○ You have probably seen this technique before.

○ The screen can be blue or green.

On the lines below, write a summary using only three or four sentences. Include the main ideas you underlined.

Possible answer: The blue or green screen technique can place a character against any background. First, the actor is filmed in front of a blue or green screen. Computers filter out the blue or green, replacing it with the new background. The technique has many uses in movies and television.

Tip

A summary tells the most important ideas in as few words as possible. Summarizing helps you to understand, remember, and review information you read or hear.

Read the following article. As you read, think about the main ideas you would include in a summary.

It Lives!

How do filmmakers bring an imaginary creature, such as a dragon or sea monster, to life? How do they turn an ape into a movie star? They use "special effects," techniques referred to as *SFX*.

In the 1930s, a special effects pioneer, Willis O'Brien, made film history with the movie *King Kong*. O'Brien studied the movements of gorillas in zoos to develop small skeletons of a giant ape. He designed eighteen-inch frames and padded them with foam rubber and cotton. Then he covered them with rabbit fur. O'Brien filmed the model using a stop-action camera, which would take one picture, or frame, at a time. He would position the model, take a picture with the camera, then move the model slightly and take another picture. It took hundreds of shots to make the model move for thirty seconds on the screen!

Three large models were used. One was a giant gorilla arm and hand used to hold a frightened actress. Another was a gorilla foot that could descend upon the streets of New York. Finally there was a life-sized model of King Kong built of wood, wire, cloth, and metal. It was covered with bearskins. Three levers controlled Kong's facial movements. King Kong may not look very

realistic to audiences today, but the film terrified people in 1933.

One SFX method is "animatronics," the art of bringing creatures to life by using electronics and remote control. In the 1997 movie *Buddy*, animatronics put another gorilla in a starring role. Artists used puppets and special gadgets to build life-sized models of a gorilla in four stages of life. They also built a gorilla head for a human actor to wear. They punched in each hair by hand. The fake skin and teeth made the head look very realistic. Buddy's movements were what made the special effects so special.

Inside Buddy were control systems made of rods and cables. These were run by a computer to create Buddy's arm, leg, and facial movements. Eyebrows could twitch to show emotion. An air tube would puff to inflate and deflate Buddy's cheeks so that the gorilla seemed to breathe. Buddy's movements were far more realistic than King Kong's. Most people in the audience accepted Buddy as a real gorilla.

Thanks to models and technology, animals can appear on screen today with no need for animal handlers or retakes and with no risk of injuring the animal. Aliens, dinosaurs, and monsters can co-star with humans—and each other! When an audience accepts a creature as real, whether it's terrifying or comical, SFX have done their job.

Checking Comprehension

1. How were the special effects in *King Kong* similar to those in the movie *Buddy*?
How were they different? [Comparing and Contrasting/Inferential]

Answers will vary, but may include: Similarities: Both films used models of gorillas. Both used a

type of remote control. Differences: Both small and large models were used in *King Kong*,

and they were brought to life by film animation. Life-sized models were used in *Buddy*. Kong's

remote devices were mechanical, but Buddy's were electronic and run by a computer.

2. Why do you think filmmakers would rather use animatronic models
than real animals? [Drawing Conclusions/Critical]

Answers will vary, but may include: Models do not require special handlers. Models are

predictable, and there is no risk to an animal. Models can be made to do things a real

animal would not or could not do.

Practicing Comprehension Skills

Write one sentence to summarize each set of details from the article.
An example is completed for you.

3. Willis O'Brien made film history with the movie *King Kong*.
O'Brien studied the movements of gorillas in zoos to develop the models he used.
O'Brien filmed the models using the technique of a stop-action camera.

   Summary: Willis O'Brien made film history with *King Kong* by using special models

   and a stop-action camera.

4. O'Brien used three large models: a giant gorilla arm and hand, a gorilla foot,
and a life-sized model.
Three levers controlled Kong's facial movements.
The film terrified people in 1933.

   Summary: Possible answer: O'Brien's use of three large models and levers that controlled

   Kong's facial movements helped make the 1933 film terrifying.

5. One SFX method is "animatronics," the art of bringing creatures to life
    by using electronics and remote control.
   In the 1997 movie *Buddy*, animatronics put another gorilla in a starring role.
   Artists used puppets and gadgets to build life-sized models of a gorilla.

   Summary: Possible answer: In the 1997 movie *Buddy*, models of a gorilla were brought to life

   with an SFX method called "animatronics," which uses electronics and remote control.

6. Artists built a gorilla head for a human actor to wear in the film *Buddy*.
   The artists punched in each hair of the gorilla head by hand.
   Facial features, such as fake skin and teeth, made the head look very realistic.

   Summary: Possible answer: In the film *Buddy*, a human actor wore a gorilla head with

   realistic-looking hair and facial features.

7. Inside Buddy were control systems made of rods and cables.
   The control systems were run by a computer to create Buddy's arm, leg, and facial movements.
   Buddy's movements were far more realistic than King Kong's.

   Summary: Possible answer: The use of control systems run by a computer made Buddy's

   movements seem far more realistic than King Kong's.

Read the following statements. Write **Yes** next to each idea that should be included in a
summary of "It Lives!" Write **No** next to ideas that would not be included in a summary.

8. __No__ The letters SFX are an abbreviation for "special effects."

9. __Yes__ The art of animatronics uses electronics and remote control.

10. __No__ The small model in King Kong was covered with rabbit fur.

11. __Yes__ In the 1930s, Willis O'Brien made film history with *King Kong*.

12. __Yes__ O'Brien used a stop-action camera to bring King Kong to life.

13. __No__ The actress in *King Kong* was frightened.

14. __Yes__ The 1997 movie *Buddy* used animatronics to make a gorilla's
        movements seem realistic.

15. __No__ Buddy's eyebrows could twitch to show emotion.

16. Review the article "It Lives!" Are all the main ideas from the article listed in items 8-15? Explain your answer.

    No. The main idea that filmmakers use special effects to bring an imaginary creature to

    life is not listed.

17. Write a summary of the passage "It Lives!" Be sure you include only the most important information.

    Summaries will vary, but may include: Filmmakers use special effects to bring imaginary

    creatures to life. In the 1930s, Willis O'Brien made film history by using models and a

    stop-action camera to create the gorilla King Kong. In 1997, animatronics, which uses

    electronics and remote control, made the gorilla Buddy seem real.

Practicing Vocabulary

Write the word from the box that matches each clue.

comical	deflate	descend	electronics	facial	gadgets	remote

18. _____deflate_____ let the air out

19. _____facial_____ has to do with the face

20. _____descend_____ move downward

21. _____comical_____ humorous

22. _____gadgets_____ small devices

23. _____remote_____ distant

24. _____electronics_____ a science that deals with technology

MAKING THE Reading AND Writing CONNECTION

Writing a Movie Review

Think about a movie you have seen recently. On another sheet of paper, write the title of the movie, a summary of the plot, and whether or not you would recommend that others see it. Be sure to include only the most important information in your summary.

Paraphrasing

Paraphrasing is useful when you take notes in class, study for a test, or research a topic for a report. To **paraphrase** means to restate or explain something in your own words. It is not the same as summarizing. When you summarize, you state the most important points of a piece of writing. When you paraphrase, you restate all the information—not just the important points. A paraphrase should be simpler to read than the original piece.

Read the following article. As you read, think how you could paraphrase the information.

The word *volcano* comes from a story the ancient Romans told about Vulcan, their god of metalworking and fire. They said that Vulcan's workshop was underneath a "fire-breathing" mountain off the coast of Italy. In honor of this god, they gave the name "Vulcano" to the island. Since then, all such mountains have come to be called volcanoes.

Today, we know that a volcano is an opening in the earth's crust. Through this opening, melted red-hot rock is pushed out, often violently. The pressure that pushes the molten rock out is caused by movement of huge slabs of rock that form Earth's shell. As these plates collide, they create friction and pressure that open holes in the crust.

Decide whether the following is a paraphrase or a summary of the first paragraph of the article. On the line, write "paraphrase" or "summary" and explain your choice.

Volcanoes are named for Vulcan, the Roman god of metalworking and fire. Today, all "fire-breathing" mountains are called volcanoes.

Summary; it only states the most important pieces of information.

Paraphrase the second paragraph.

Possible answer: A volcano is really a hole in the surface of Earth.

Through the hole, molten rock is pushed out because of pressures

inside Earth. The movement of rock slabs causes the pressure

that forces the melted rock out.

Tip

When you paraphrase, you can use synonyms for words in the original piece, change word order in sentences, rearrange phrases and clauses, and combine sentences.

As you read the following passage about Mount St. Helens, think about how you would paraphrase the information.

A Mountain Awakes

To some Native people of the Pacific Northwest, the peak was known as "Smoking Mountain." The name Mount St. Helens was given to the mountain in 1792. People thought of it as a serene location for hiking, camping, and other outdoor pleasures. The volcano had been active in the mid-1800s, but its last eruption was in 1857. It had been quiet for over a century.

In March 1980, a number of small earthquakes signaled that the mountain was waking up. On March 20, a "minor" earthquake (4.2 on the Richter scale) occurred. People who lived near Mount St. Helens could feel some of the quakes. Hundreds of small earthquakes followed. Then, on March 27, there was an overwhelming explosion. Ash and steam catapulted 6,000 feet into the air.

Soon an odd bulge developed on one side of the mountain. That bulge was caused by steam and superheated rock gushing from inside the earth. Many people began to feel uneasy.

On May 18, 1980, David A. Johnston, a scientist, was stationed on a post six miles from the volcano. He had just taken some measurements. Two geologists, Keith and Dorothy Stoffel, were flying over the mountain's crater in a small plane. At 8:32 in the morning, an earthquake with a magnitude of 5.1 on the Richter scale loosened the bulge.

"Within a matter of seconds," the Stoffels recall, "the whole north side of the crater began to move instantaneously." Tons of rock and ice began sliding down the mountain in the biggest landslide in recorded history. The earthquake triggered a violent sideways blast of gas, steam, and earth. The blast of superheated material swept across the land at speeds of up to 670 miles per hour, while a cloud of ash shot twelve miles into the air. The pilot of the Stoffels' plane was able to escape the deadly blast, but 57 other people, including David Johnston, were not as lucky.

In addition to the 57 dead, more than 200 homes were leveled by the blast as it raced over the landscape. Thousands of acres of forest were destroyed. Camping grounds, bridges, trails, and miles of highways and railway lines disappeared. About 7,000 large animals died. The birds and smaller animals in the blast area perished.

On May 18, 1983, a ceremony declared the mountain and surrounding land to be the "Mount St. Helens National Volcanic Monument." Since that time, visitors, animals, and plant life have returned, but never again will people take "Smoking Mountain" for granted. Scientists at an observatory named for David Johnston now watch the volcano to help prevent another disaster.

Checking Comprehension

1. Why is it that before the spring of 1980, Washington residents were not concerned about a Mount St. Helens eruption? [Drawing Conclusions/Critical]

   Possible answer: The volcano had not erupted in more than 100 years. They must have assumed

   it would not erupt again.

2. What final events caused the devastation and destruction that occurred on May 18, 1980? [Cause and Effect/Inferential]

   Possible answer: An earthquake caused a huge landslide. Then a blast of superheated material

   came out of the side of the mountain, destroying everything in its path.

Practicing Comprehension Skills

Which of the following is the best paraphrase of these sentences?
Fill in the circle next to the correct answer.

3. Soon an odd bulge developed on one side of the mountain. That bulge was caused by steam and superheated rock gushing from inside the earth. Many people began to feel uneasy.

   ○ The bulge on the mountain's side was odd.

   ● A strange swelling grew out of one side of the mountain. The swelling, which was created by steam and very hot rock, made many people nervous.

   ○ Many people wondered what was causing the side of the mountain to bulge out.

   ○ Steam and superheated rock could explode at any time. People now thought that the mountain was very dangerous.

4. On May 18, 1980, David A. Johnston, a scientist, was stationed on a post six miles from the volcano. He had just taken some measurements. Two geologists, Keith and Dorothy Stoffel, were flying over the mountain's crater in a small plane.

   ○ The events of May 18, 1980 interested all the scientists in the area.

   ○ Two geologists as well as scientist David A. Johnston were near the volcano on May 18, 1980. All these people were aware that they would be in great danger if an earthquake occurred.

   ○ On May 18, 1980, the safest place to be was an airplane.

   ● Scientist David A. Johnston was measuring the volcano's activity on May 18, 1980, from a post six miles away. Geologists Keith and Dorothy Stoffel were flying above the crater.

5. Read this paraphrase of the second paragraph of "A Mountain Awakes."
Tell why it is or is not a good paraphrase.

In early spring, 1980, a number of small earthquakes signaled a change.
On March 20 a "minor" earthquake occurred.

Students should say it is not a good paraphrase. It uses some of the writer's original words,

it doesn't include all of the ideas, and it is much shorter than the original.

6. Write a paraphrase of the last paragraph.

Paraphrases will vary, but should resemble this: Three years after the eruption,

the mountain and the area nearby was declared a national monument.

As time passed, visitors, plants, and animals returned, but scientists now

watch the volcano in case it erupts again.

Practicing Vocabulary

Write the word from the box that belongs with each group.

7. red-hot, melting, _____ superheated _____

8. thrown, hurled, _____ catapulted _____

9. destroyed, demolished, _____ leveled _____

10. right away, now, _____ instantaneously _____

11. strength, enormity, _____ magnitude _____

12. quiet, peaceful, _____ serene _____

13. awesome, breathtaking, _____ overwhelming _____

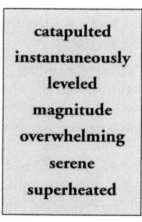

| catapulted |
| instantaneously |
| leveled |
| magnitude |
| overwhelming |
| serene |
| superheated |

Writing a Descriptive Paragraph
Write a short paragraph describing a time you were a witness to an "act of nature," such as a thunderstorm, blizzard, or tornado. Pay close attention to your description of what happened. Then exchange papers with a classmate and paraphrase each other's descriptions.

Recognizing Author's Purpose

When authors write, they usually have a purpose in mind. Four common reasons for writing are:

- To **persuade**: to convince readers to think or act a certain way
- To **inform**: to explain something or give information or directions
- To **entertain**: to amuse or scare readers, or make them feel sadness or joy
- To **express**: to create a mood or feeling through description, to help readers visualize a scene

Sometimes an author has more than one purpose for writing. If you can identify the author's purposes, you will better understand what you read. Knowing the author's purposes can also influence the way you read. When you read a selection that is meant to inform, such as a textbook chapter, you may need to read slowly and carefully. When you read a selection that is meant to entertain, you might want to read more quickly. The author's language and style of writing can help you determine his or her reasons for writing.

Read the following article. Think about the author's purposes for writing.

In Alaska, a dogsled race of over 1,100 miles known as the Iditarod is held annually. Many people wonder how the dogs that participate in this grueling event are trained.

Sled dogs usually begin their training as puppies at around three months of age. They begin by running behind a team of dogs. Some common commands that sled dogs have to learn are *hike* (which means to go) and *easy* (which means to slow down). They also practice pulling light weights with a harness, learning to keep the tug line tight. Trainers quickly weed out dogs that are not intelligent enough or that lack self-control.

Fill in the circle next to the correct answer.

What purpose or purposes do you think the author had for writing this article?

○ to persuade   ○ to entertain   ○ to express   ● to inform

Think about the way you read this passage. Which of the following selections would you be likely to read in a similar way?

○ a mystery story   ○ a book of jokes   ● a news article   ○ a poem about dogs

Read the following passage. Think about the author's purposes for writing.

It was my first Iditarod. I didn't expect to win, but I did want to complete the race. Not every musher makes it to the finish line. I wanted that bronze belt buckle stamped with the indelible words, "Iditarod Finisher." I wanted to get my personal police escort down Nome's Main Street to the sound of cheering crowds. Most of all, I wanted to finish for my dogs. I'd been warned about winds that blew snow into solid sheets of blinding whiteness. I'd heard about the moose that blocked your trail like big, shaggy mountains. Yet I knew I had to brave it all for the sake of my beautiful, hard-working team of champions.

What purpose or purposes do you think the author had for writing this article? Explain your answer.

<u>Answers will vary, but should include "to express": The author uses descriptive language to</u>

<u>help us visualize the experience of finishing the Iditarod. Students may also perceive the</u>

<u>passage as written to inform, to entertain, or both. It gives some information about the</u>

<u>Iditarod and evokes some of the challenges of the trail.</u>

Fill in the circle next to the correct answer or answers.

Which of the following selections would you be likely to read in the same way?

- ● a first-person article by an athlete
- ○ a chapter in a history book
- ○ a novel about a dog
- ○ a poem

Which of these phrases did the author use to express—to evoke a mood and help you visualize a scene?

- ● winds that blew snow into solid sheets of blinding whiteness
- ○ I did want to complete the race
- ● moose that blocked your trail like big, shaggy mountains
- ○ I didn't expect to win

Tip

As you read, think about the author's reasons for writing the selection. Often the words the author chooses and the style of writing will help you determine the author's purpose.

Jack London's
The Call of the Wild

Jack London's *The Call of the Wild* delivers all the thrills and adventure you could possibly want in a book. In this classic novel, you'll follow the journey of Buck, a proud dog whose power, intelligence, and courage make him a hero. Buck's adventure begins as a greedy gardener steals him from a comfortable California home. Buck has never known anything but love and easy living. Now he is beaten and starved, and his new life confounds him. Buck soon finds himself in the brutal setting of the 1897 Alaska gold rush. There, uncaring masters with gold fever put him to work as a sled dog.

The great dog uses every instinct to survive. Buck learns to sleep in snow. Rather than cowering, he fights to be top dog. He wins the respect of every person and beast he meets. Each test Buck faces brings out the best in him.

The Call of the Wild is clearly Buck's story. The only human character London allows the reader to know is John Thornton. Through Buck's eyes, you see Thornton's respect for his dogs and his fitness for life in the wild Yukon. You see love grow as Buck grasps Thornton's hand in his teeth and Thornton playfully shakes the dog's head. However, John Thornton never engages the reader's emotions the way Buck does. It is Buck for whom most readers fear as ice cracks during a river crossing. It is Buck we follow to the very end of the journey.

Jack London

London clearly describes the sights, sounds, and smells of the frozen North: "Over the whiteness and silence brooded a ghostly calm. There was not the faintest whisper of air—nothing moved, not a leaf quivered, the visible breath of the dogs rising slowly and lingering in the frosty air."

If you've ever loved an animal, *The Call of the Wild* will be a special joy for you. Jack London captures the bond between a human and a dog as no other author has. Yet London insists that every dog is, first, an animal. He reminds us that every animal hears the call of the wild and longs to answer. You will never again look at your family pet in quite the same way after you have read the book.

The Call of the Wild was published in 1903 and has never been out of print. With its gripping scenes and the portrait of an unforgettable dog, the book will keep you on the edge of your seat right up to the last page.

Checking Comprehension

1. Write a sentence that summarizes the author's attitude toward *The Call of the Wild*.

    Answers will vary, but may include: The author is impressed with the book and touched by

    the character of Buck.

2. Based on this review, tell whether or not you would want to read *The Call of the Wild*.
    Include one or more details to support your point of view. [Making Judgments/Critical]

    Answers will vary, but may include: I would like to read this book because I enjoy stories

    about animals.

    .

Practicing Comprehension Skills

3. Fill in the blanks in the chart below. In the blank line on the left, write a purpose
    that could be described with the sentence provided. In the blank lines on the right,
    write a sentence that could show the purpose "to inform."

Author's Purpose	Sentence That Shows the Purpose
a. to persuade	Jack London's *The Call of the Wild* delivers all the thrills and adventure you could possibly want in a book.
b. to inform	Possible answer: *The Call of the Wild* was published in 1903 and has never been out of print.

4. In your opinion, does the author of this review succeed in meeting the purposes
    listed above? In two sentences, tell why or why not.

    Most students will say that the author does meet the purposes. They might say that the review

    made them want to read the book and told them what *The Call of the Wild* was about.

Read this passage from *The Call of the Wild* describing a scene in which Buck rescues Thornton from the rapids. Think about author Jack London's purposes for writing.

Buck had sprung in on the instant; and at the end of three hundred yards, amid a mad swirl of water, he overhauled Thornton. When he felt him grasp his tail, Buck headed for the bank, swimming with all his splendid strength. But the progress shoreward was slow; the progress downstream amazingly rapid. From below came the fatal roaring where the wild current went wilder and was rent in shreds and spray by the rocks which thrust through like the teeth of an enormous comb. The suck of the water as it took the beginning of the last steep pitch was frightful, and Thornton knew that the shore was impossible. He scraped furiously over a rock, bruised across a second, and struck a third with crushing force. He clutched its slippery top with both hands, releasing Buck, and above the roar of the churning water shouted: "Go, Buck! Go!"

5. Based on the author's language and style, what do you think his purpose or purposes might have been in writing this scene? Explain your answer.

Possible answer: The author wants to entertain and to express. He is describing an exciting

moment in the story and evoking the feeling of danger from the rocks and the water.

6. On the lines below, write the author's purpose or purposes that you identified for the passage. Then give a sentence or phrase from the passage that shows the purpose.

Author's purpose: To entertain. Examples may include: He scraped furiously over a rock,

bruised across a second, and struck a third with crushing force.

Author's purpose: To express. Examples may include: rocks which thrust through like the teeth

of an enormous comb.

7. In your opinion, did the author succeed in meeting the purpose or purposes you listed above? In two sentences, tell why or why not.

Answers will vary. Students might say that the action and description made them want to

know how the scene turned out.

8. Which of the following selections would you be likely to read in the same way as the passage from *The Call of the Wild?*

   ○ a chapter in a social studies book   ● an exciting adventure story

   ○ a poem about a river   ○ a newspaper article

Practicing Vocabulary

Choose the word from the box that best replaces the underlined word or words. Write the word on the line to the left.

brooded	brutal	captures	classic	confounds	cowering	instinct

9. _____instinct_____ Buck's <u>natural behavior</u> often warned him when danger was near.

10. _____captures_____ *The Call of the Wild* <u>catches</u> the emotions of the canine hero.

11. _____classic_____ The book, like the movie version, is a <u>timeless work</u> that people have enjoyed for generations.

12. _____brooded_____ Buck never <u>dwelled gloomily</u> over the difficulties of his new life.

13. _____cowering_____ Rather than <u>hanging back in fear</u>, the brave dog led others forward.

14. _____brutal_____ The book tells of dogs and humans facing danger in the <u>harsh</u> climate of Alaska and northern Canada.

15. _____confounds_____ A sudden attack by the other dogs <u>puzzles</u> Buck.

Writing an Eyewitness Account

Think about a memorable animal you have known or one you saw in a zoo or park. What do you know about the animal? How did the animal affect you? Determine a purpose or purposes for writing about this animal: to persuade, inform, entertain, or express. Then write an eyewitness account of your experience with the animal. Be sure to think about your purpose or purposes as you write. Write your paragraph on another sheet of paper.

Statements of Fact and Opinion

When you read, you will often come across statements of fact and statements of opinion. There are important differences between these types of statements.

A statement of fact can be checked and proved true or false. Even if it is false, it is still considered a statement of fact.

- Tony Meola holds the U.S. National team record for appearances by a goalkeeper.

⬇

You can check whether the statement is true or false by looking up the information or by verifying it yourself.

A statement of opinion presents ideas and feelings. It cannot be checked, but it can be supported. Words that signal statements of opinion include *I believe* and *seems to.*

- Tony Meola is one of the best soccer players in the world today.

⬇ ⬇

Valid opinion: Supported by facts or opinions of experts in the field.

Faulty opinion: Either not supported, or supported only by opinions of nonexperts.

As you read the following editorial letter, try to distinguish statements of fact from statements that present the writer's opinions.

Dear Editor,

I like your soccer articles, but I am unhappy about one thing. Your paper never seems to give any attention to goalkeepers. Please print some articles that feature goalkeepers such as Tony Meola.

Tony Meola holds the U.S. National team record for most appearances by a goalkeeper. He played in the Major League Soccer All-Star game three years in a row. I believe Meola is one of the best players in soccer today. Just look at the records he set for saves and shutouts.

Write one sentence from the letter that is a statement of fact. Then name a source you might use to check the fact.

"He played in the Major League Soccer All-Star game three years in a row." The fact could be checked by looking up articles in sports magazines.

Write one sentence from the letter that is a statement of opinion. Then tell if the opinion is supported with details.

"I believe Meola is one of the best players in soccer today." This opinion is supported by references to Tony Meola's records and his appearances in All-Star games.

Tip

As you read, pay attention to words or phrases that signal statements of opinion such as *I believe, seems to,* or *in my opinion.*

STRATEGY: Recognizing Statements of Fact and Opinion

Read a sports announcer's comments during the last minutes of the 1999 Women's World Cup final soccer match. As you read, identify statements of fact and statements of opinion.

WORLD CUP 99
THE FINAL GAME

Welcome back, soccer fans! We rejoin the 1999 World Cup final between women of the United States and China. More than 90,000 spectators have gathered at the Pasadena, California, Rose Bowl. It is the largest stadium crowd ever to see a women's sporting event.

We've got a scorching day here in Pasadena. The temperature on the field is more than 100 degrees! Michelle Akers has already fallen victim to the heat. The U.S. defender collapsed after ninety minutes of play. What a loss for team U.S.A.! I believe the U.S. would have scored had Akers remained on the field.

Let me recap the action. After 120 minutes of play, the U.S. and China are tied 0–0. Penalty kicks will settle this game. Each team will have five kick attempts.

China prepares to make its first attempt. Team captain Sun Wen looks nervous.

China's first kick finds the net! Four attempts to go . . . and number two is good! Now midfielder Liu Ying steps to the twelve-yard mark. I don't think she really wants to kick this one! Her shoulders are slumping. She appears tired. U.S. goalkeeper Briana Scurry seems to pick up on Liu Ying's discomfort. Scurry's scowl tells me she's ready for action.

Liu Ying kicks! Briana Scurry dives to her left! She blocks the kick! What a play! China's third attempt has failed! This may well be the turning point of the game! Go, U.S.A.!

China prepares for a fourth penalty kick. The kick is good. Here comes number five. It's in the net.

Four of China's five shots have hit home. That leaves room for the U.S. to win. If there was ever a team to do it, it is this group of warriors. In my mind, they're number one!

The U.S. lines up to kick. A superstitious Briana Scurry impulsively turns her back as her teammate takes the first shot. "I can't look," Scurry's motion seems to say. Yes! The first kick is good! The fans go wild! Surely you listeners can hear them.

Kicks number two, three, four—they are all good! The shoot-out is tied at China 4, U.S. 4. This moment will go down in history!

Now Brandi Chastain is at the mark. The thirty-year-old defender looks composed. The woman has nerves of steel! Chastain's kick propels the ball into the net! She has dropped to her knees. Her teammates are crowding around her. Today Brandi Chastain is America's hero! This must be the greatest moment of her life!

The U.S. women's soccer team has won the World Cup! Remember this moment, sports fans! In my opinion, this victory will change women's athletics forever.

Checking Comprehension

[Cause and Effect/Inferential]

1. Why was the U.S. Women's team able to win the 1999 Women's World Cup?

   Briana Scurry blocked the shot of China's third kicker, Liu Ying. The U.S. team

   successfully completed its five attempts.

[Making Judgments/Critical]

2. Which team do you think the sports announcer favored? What makes you think so?

   The announcer favored the United States. The announcer's cheers of "Go U.S.A.!", compliments

   for the U.S. players, and excitement at the outcome all point to this conclusion.

Practicing Comprehension Skills

Find three statements of fact and three statements of opinion
in "World Cup 99: The Final Game." Write them below.

Statements of fact: Answers will vary, but may include:

3. More than 90,000 spectators have gathered at the Pasadena, California, Rose Bowl.

4. It is the largest stadium crowd ever to see a women's sporting event.

5. The temperature on the field is more than 100 degrees!

Statements of opinion:

6. I believe the U.S. would have scored had Akers remained on the field.

7. I don't think she really wants to kick this one!

8. The woman has nerves of steel!

Find at least five clue words or phrases in the passage that point to a
statement of opinion. Write the clue words or phrases on the lines.

9. Possible answers: I believe, I don't think, seems to, may well be, in my mind,

   surely, must be, in my opinion

10. The following statements were made in the announcer's post-game commentary. On the line before each statement, write **F** if it is a statement of fact and **O** if it is a statement of opinion.

_F_ In the first overtime, midfielder Kristine Lilly contributed to the Americans' victory by blocking a headed ball from reaching the goal.

_O_ Surely those penalty kicks offered some of the most exciting minutes in sports this year.

_F_ Remember, the 1994 Men's World Cup final was also decided on penalty kicks.

_O_ Never again will a women's soccer team be as popular as this one!

Practicing Vocabulary

Write a word from the box to match each definition.

attempts	composed	defender	impulsively	propels	recap	superstitious

11. _____recap_____ a summary of highlights

12. _____impulsively_____ driven by a sudden decision

13. _____attempts_____ tries

14. _____defender_____ one who plays a defensive position

15. _____composed_____ calm

16. _____propels_____ pushes or drives something forward

17. _____superstitious_____ influenced by fearful beliefs

Writing a Persuasive Paragraph
On another sheet of paper write a paragraph persuading readers that one of your favorite sports teams or stars is the best. Include three statements of fact that could convince your readers. Reread the completed paragraph and underline any statements of opinion.

Making Judgments

When you read, you make **judgments**, or form opinions, about the people, events, and ideas in the text. To make a judgment, think about your own experiences, the information presented in the text, and the author's purposes for writing.

As you make a judgment, ask yourself, "What made me think this way?" Look for facts that support your opinions. A **valid judgment**, or judgment that is sound, must be based on details in the text. An **invalid judgment** is one that has no support in the text.

As you read the following passage about the *Titanic*, think about judgments you can make about the writer's ideas.

The *Titanic* was called the safest ship ever built. Many said it was "unsinkable." The world's largest ocean liner had the newest safety features. They included a double-layered steel bottom. The hull had sixteen watertight compartments.

The ship also had a wireless radio and a crow's nest with two lookouts. On April 14, 1912, during the ship's first voyage, the lookouts spotted a huge iceberg. They alerted the ship's officers, but it was too late. The iceberg damaged the hull and filled five compartments with water. In the early hours of April 15, the "unsinkable" *Titanic* sank.

Tip

Stop to make judgments as you read. Do not wait until you finish the selection. Question your own judgments as you make them and look for proof in the text.

Which of the following statements is a valid judgment you might make after reading the article? Fill in the circle next to the correct answer.

○ The newest safety features made the *Titanic* unsinkable.

● The newest safety features could not prevent the *Titanic's* disaster.

○ The crow's nest lookouts were not doing their job.

○ The *Titanic* was the worst disaster ever.

Which of the following statements is not a valid judgment? Fill in the circle before the correct answer.

○ The watertight compartments could not keep the *Titanic* afloat.

○ The author believes people were overly confident about the *Titanic's* safety.

● The author believes the *Titanic* was unsinkable.

○ The *Titanic* was not "unsinkable."

STRATEGY: Making Judgments About Ideas and Text

Abandon Ship!
TO THE LIFEBOATS

In 1912, the *Titanic* sank after striking an iceberg in the North Atlantic. There were about 2,300 people on board. An estimated 1,503 were lost at sea. Did so many people need to die?

At 11:40 P.M. on April 14, passengers felt a jolt. Few knew that anything serious had happened, but the giant steamship had hit an iceberg. For many on board, the next hours would be their last.

Captain E. J. Smith knew that the problem was grave. His crew below deck fought to keep water from rushing in through the damaged hull. At 12:30 P.M., Captain Smith ordered all passengers to gather on deck.

As the crew began loading women and children onto the lifeboats, a frightful truth became clear. If the lifeboats were fully loaded, they would hold only 1,178 passengers. More than 1,000 people had no way to escape the sinking ship! Few could survive in the icy water.

There were more problems. The crew of the "unsinkable" ship had little practice with the new equipment. It took them too long to lower the lifeboats. They also worried that the wooden crafts could not hold much weight. Crew members lowered some of the boats when they were half full.

The passengers, too, were poorly prepared. Many did not understand what was happening. They were slow to board the boats. There had been no emergency drill. Captain Smith, an experienced commander who had sailed for 38 years, seems to have been lax about that vital detail.

Boat after boat left the ship partly filled. There was, by most reports, little panic as women and children said good-bye to the men. Most seemed to expect to be together again soon.

At around 4:00 A.M., the *Carpathia* arrived to rescue the passengers in the lifeboats. On board the rescue ship, many survivors learned the truth. Their husbands and fathers had gone down with the *Titanic*.

Many of the passengers had been famous, wealthy Americans. The public wanted answers. U.S. Senate hearings uncovered outdated safety laws meant for smaller ships. The *Titanic* was 50 percent larger than any other ship afloat. It could carry as many as 3,547 people. Naval laws required it to provide lifeboats for only 1,000. Reports also showed that owners knew there were too few lifeboats on the *Titanic*. It seems that they wanted to keep deck space open for strolling.

Both American and British agencies looked into the sinking. Their findings led to laws that made sea travel safer. In a matter of days, steamship companies were providing enough lifeboats for everyone on board all ships. New rules called for lifeboat drills and crew training. It is unfortunate that it took a tragedy to spur the safety measures.

Checking Comprehension

1. How might the belief that the *Titanic* was "unsinkable" have contributed to the disaster? [Main idea/Inferential]

   <u>Possible answer: There weren't enough lifeboats, the crew had little practice with the</u>

   <u>equipment and lowered some boats before they were full, and the passengers hadn't had</u>

   <u>an emergency drill.</u>

2. How did the *Titanic* disaster influence international shipping laws? [Cause and Effect/Inferential]

   <u>New laws required all steamships to provide lifeboat space for every person on board,</u>

   <u>along with lifeboat drills and crew training.</u>

Practicing Comprehension Skills

In the first paragraph, the following sentence asks the reader to make a judgment: "Did so many need to die?" Write your judgment about the question on the lines below. Then write three details from the article that support your judgment.

Your Judgment:

3. <u>No, so many did not need to die.</u>

Supporting details:

4. <u>The crew was not familiar with the equipment.</u>

5. <u>There were not enough lifeboats.</u>

6. <u>Not all lifeboats were filled.</u>

7. Read the last sentence of the passage. Does the author draw a valid conclusion based on the evidence in the passage? Give evidence to support your judgment.

   <u>Yes. The last two paragraphs give evidence that the sinking caused the shipping industry to</u>

   <u>create safety measures. Also, most people would agree that it is unfortunate that it took</u>

   <u>so many deaths to result in these new procedures.</u>

8. On the lines before the following judgments, write V if you think the judgment is a valid one. Write I if you think the judgment is invalid.

__V__ Safety rules for sea travel were not as strict in 1912 as they are today.

__I__ The *Titanic* disaster was all Captain E. J. Smith's fault.

__I__ The *Carpathia* could have rescued the survivors more quickly.

__V__ Even if the lifeboats had been fully loaded, many passengers would have died.

__V__ The public wanted to know why the disaster occurred.

Practicing Vocabulary

Choose a word from the box that best matches each clue.

estimated	hull	lax	lifeboats	steamship	survivors	vital

9. ____steamship____ ship operated by steam

10. ____estimated____ roughly figured

11. ____survivors____ those who live though a catastrophe

12. ____lifeboats____ crafts for saving lives at sea

13. ____lax____ lacking in firmness

14. ____hull____ outer frame of a ship

15. ____vital____ extremely important

MAKING THE Reading AND Writing CONNECTION

Writing a Letter
Think about a family vacation or class field trip you've taken recently. Was it enjoyable? Did it turn out the way you expected it to? What judgments can you make about the experience? Write a letter about your trip, supporting the judgments you make with details. Use another sheet of paper for your letter.

Point of View

What is the difference between these statements?

On Sunday, November 15, 1987, I was born.

Pamela Elizabeth Jones was born on Sunday, November 15, 1987.

Before beginning to write, an author must decide whether the story will be told by one of the characters, as in the first sentence, or by an outsider, as in the second sentence. The perspective from which a story is told is called the **point of view**. An author has several choices for a narrator, or speaker, as the following four versions of the same story show. Each version uses a different point of view. The amount of information given about each character depends on the point of view used.

Version 1

As I climbed the winding staircase, I began to wonder why the thought of reaching the top of the lighthouse had seemed so appealing. Behind me, I could hear my brother Max puffing and his footsteps slowing. Then I arrived at the next window and paused to look out. Gazing open-mouthed at the view below me, I knew why I had made the effort.

Version 2

Growing increasingly short of breath as she climbed the winding lighthouse staircase, Pam couldn't remember why she had wanted to reach the top. When she arrived at the next window, she looked out and thought, "What a gorgeous view! It was certainly worth the effort." Still trudging up the stairs, Max was wondering, "Why did Pam drag me up here, anyway?"

Version 3

Pam had lost count of the stairs as she steadily climbed the winding lighthouse staircase. "Why on earth did I want to reach the top?" she asked herself. Then she reached the next window. Pam gazed out the window and caught her breath. "What a beautiful view!" she told herself. "I'm glad I came after all." She could hear her brother Max's puffing and panting as he trudged up the stairs.

Version 4

Pam climbed the lighthouse stairs steadily, her breath coming more rapidly with each step. When she reached the next window and paused to look out, her eyebrows arched and her mouth dropped. Max was trudging up the stairs behind her.

Answer the following questions about each version of the story by writing **Yes** or **No** on the line in the appropriate column.

	STORY VERSION			
	1	2	3	4
Is the narrator a character in the story?	Yes	No	No	No
Is the narrator an outsider?	No	Yes	Yes	Yes
Do you know what Pam is doing?	Yes	Yes	Yes	Yes
Do you know what Pam is thinking?	Yes	Yes	Yes	No
Do you know what Max is doing?	Yes	Yes	Yes	Yes
Do you know what Max is thinking?	No	Yes	No	No

First Person Point of View: The narrator is a character in the story. In telling the story from a personal point of view, the "I" narrator, or first person, tells us only her thoughts. She cannot enter the minds of other characters. **Version 1** is told from a first-person point of view.

Third Person Point of View: The narrator is not a character in the story. The narrator uses third-person pronouns such as *he*, *she*, *it*, and *they*. **Version 2, 3, and 4** are told from a third-person point of view. Third-person point of view can be omniscient (all-knowing), limited-omniscient, or dramatic:

Omniscient:
The narrator is an all-knowing outsider who knows the thoughts of all the characters. In the versions of the story, only one gives us both Pam's and Max's thoughts: **Version 2**. This has an **omniscient** point of view.

Limited-omniscient:
A narrator tells the story through the eyes of one character. The narrator is outside the story, but can see into the mind and thinking of one of the characters. **Version 3** has a **limited-omniscient** point of view.

Dramatic:
The narrator describes only what can be seen and heard, like a news reporter. The narrator does not know the thoughts of any of the characters. **Version 4** has a **dramatic** point of view.

Tip

As you read a story, ask yourself, "Who is doing the talking?" Is it an outside observer, or is it someone involved in the story? Whose thoughts does the narrator reveal? The answers to these questions will help you determine the point of view.

The following story is told in four sections, each with a different point of view. As you read, think about how your understanding of the story changes based on the point of view used.

Ben and the Puffins

Section 1

Benjamin Shaw lived with his parents on a light station off Maine's coast. His father, the lighthouse keeper, faithfully climbed the winding lighthouse stairs to illuminate the lantern that warned ships away from the rocky shore. By 1901, when Ben was twelve, some lighthouses had begun the conversion to electric power.

Ben was glad his father's light was still powered by oil. When he helped his father fill the lantern, he thought proudly, "Maybe I'll be the keeper here someday."

Section 2

My favorite time on the island was spring, when the puffins came. I never tired of looking at their colorful, grooved beaks and bright orange feet. I was overjoyed as hundreds of them arrived, returning to the place where they had been born.

Father occasionally viewed the birds with me, though he didn't have much time for bird-watching. First, they would meet at their nesting site from the previous year, for the puffins, while mated for life, were solitary creatures for most of the year.

Section 3

Once the single egg was laid, the parents would take turns incubating it until the little puffling was born. After about two months in the nest, the young pufflings were ready to leave the breeding colony. They would return to the island as adults.

In the spring of 1901, however, only four puffins returned to the island.

"What's wrong, Dad?" Ben asked. "Where are the rest of the puffins?"

"Maybe hunters got them," his father replied. "Some folks eat them, you know. People kill them for their feathers, too."

Section 4

"But that's appalling!" Ben cried.

Ben's father couldn't bear to see his son's disappointment. "Maybe they got caught in a storm," he said quickly.

"Well," Ben replied hotly, "I'm going to protect those four birds. I won't let anyone disturb them while they're nesting. I can—" he paused and thought about what else he could do. "I can make sure no seagulls threaten the pufflings, too!" he said.

"Ben is so much like his grandfather!" thought his father. Aloud, he said, "That's a good plan, son."

Checking Comprehension

1. What are some interesting and unique characteristics of puffins? [Main Idea/Inferential]

   Possible answers: They return to the place where they were born to breed. They mate for life

   but do not spend the year together. They lay one egg only. Both parents incubate the egg.

2. What did Ben enjoy about living on the light station? [Character/Inferential]

   Possible answers: He liked helping his father with the light and watching the puffins.

Practicing Comprehension Skills

Fill in the blanks with the correct letter choice:

   a. dramatic   b. first   c. limited-omniscient   d. omniscient

3. Third-person __c__ point of view tells the reader only what one character
   is thinking and feeling.

4. Third-person __d__ point of view tells the reader what all the characters
   are thinking and feeling.

5. In __b__ person point of view, the narrator is a character in the story.

6. A newspaper reporter would use the third-person __a__ point of view.

Answer the following questions about each version of "Ben and the Puffins"
by writing **Yes** or **No** on the line in the appropriate column.

	Story Version			
	1	2	3	4
7. Is the narrator a character in the story?	No	Yes	No	No
8. Is the narrator an outsider?	Yes	No	Yes	Yes
9. Do you know what Ben is doing?	Yes	Yes	Yes	Yes
10. Do you know what Ben is thinking?	Yes	Yes	No	Yes
11. Do you know what Ben's father is doing?	Yes	Yes	Yes	Yes
12. Do you know what Ben's father is thinking?	No	No	No	Yes

Decide if the point of view in each of the sections is:

- First-person point of view
- Third-person omniscient point of view
- Third-person limited-omniscient point of view
- Third-person dramatic point of view

Write your decision for each section on the line provided, then explain your answer.

13. Section 1: Third-person limited-omniscient point of view. The story is told through Ben's eyes, but the narrator is outside the story.

14. Section 2: First-person point of view. Ben is the narrator. He uses "I" and can't enter the minds of other characters.

15. Section 3: Third-person dramatic point of view. The narrator describes only what can be seen and heard, and doesn't know the characters' thoughts.

16. Section 4: Third-person omniscient point of view. The narrator is an all-knowing outsider who knows the thoughts of all the characters.

17. Rewrite the following sentences so that they are told entirely from Ben's third-person limited-omniscient point of view.

I enjoyed everything about living on the light station. I liked the way the waves broke on the rocks and the foghorn's mournful sound. I sometimes thought, "How could I ever live anywhere else?"

Ben enjoyed everything about living on the light station. He liked the way the waves broke on the rocks and the foghorn's mournful sound. He sometimes thought, "How could I ever live anywhere else?"

18. Rewrite the first paragraph of Section 1 of "Ben and the Puffins," telling the story from a first-person point of view.

I lived with my parents on a light station off Maine's coast. My father, the lighthouse keeper, faithfully climbed the winding lighthouse stairs to illuminate the lantern that warned ships away from the rocky shore. By 1901, when I was twelve, some lighthouses had begun the conversion to electric power.

19. Which version of the first paragraph of Section I do you prefer: third-person point of view or first-person point of view? Explain your answer.

Answers will vary. Possible answer: I prefer the first-person point of view,

because I see the story exactly as Ben sees it.

20. Reread Section 4 of "Ben and the Puffins." How would this section be different if it was retold from a third-person limited-omniscient point of view? What choice would the author have to make about the narrator? Use complete sentences to write your answer.

If Section 4 was retold from a third-person limited-omniscient point of view, the narrator

would only be able to see into the mind and thoughts of one of the characters.

The author would have to choose either Ben or his father to be the narrator.

Practicing Vocabulary

Write a word from the box to complete each sentence.

appalling	conversion	disappointment	illuminate	occasionally	overjoyed	solitary

21. Only _____occasionally_____ could Ben's father join him in bird-watching.

22. The _____conversion_____ from one power source to another was time-consuming.

23. The idea was so dreadful, Ben found it _____appalling_____ .

24. Ben was always _____overjoyed_____ to watch the unusual birds return to the island.

25. One year, Ben felt terrible _____disappointment_____ when only four birds arrived.

26. The lantern was used as a warning, not to _____illuminate_____ the shore.

27. The company of his parents made Ben's _____solitary_____ life less lonely.

Writing a Narrative

Use another piece of paper to continue this story of Ben and the puffins. What will happen next? What will Ben do to protect the puffins? Will he be successful? Before you begin, select the point of view from which you will write. You can pretend to be Ben and write from the first-person point of view, or you can write from one of the third-person points of view.

Identifying Text Structure

Text structure refers to the way a piece of writing is organized. Authors choose a particular text structure to fit their purposes and the type of information they are writing about.

There are two main kinds of writing–fiction and nonfiction. **Fiction** stories, which tell of imaginary people and events, are often organized in the time order in which they occur, or chronological order. **Nonfiction** tells of real people and events, or tells information about the real world. Nonfiction writers can use several different ways to organize their work. Following are some of the ways that a piece of writing can be organized:

Chronological Order	This form of text structure organizes a piece of writing by the order in which events occur. Fiction stories and novels are often organized this way. Nonfiction works that use chronological order can include biographies and autobiographies, and articles or books that describe historical events or time periods. Clue words such as **at first, later,** and **eventually,** as well as dates of important events, signal chronological order.
Cause and Effect	Nonfiction pieces can be organized by showing cause-and-effect relationships. Sometimes the causes and effects are directly stated. For instance, a newspaper article reporting that a government official has resigned will go on to state why the official resigned if the causes are known. Other times, either the cause or effect is not stated. Instead, the causes or effects are implied. Look for clue words such as **because, as a result,** and **therefore** to signal causes and effects.
Compare and Contrast	A piece of nonfiction writing that is organized by compare and contrast shows how two subjects are alike, different, or both alike and different. Look for clue words such as **similarly, like, in addition,** or **in the same way** to signal likenesses. Clue words such as **but, however, different, unlike,** or **on the other hand** show differences. The author may directly state the relationship between the two subjects, or the ways in which the subjects are alike and different may be implied.
Main Idea	Nonfiction writers often organize a paragraph, passage, or article by main idea and supporting details. The main idea is the writer's most important idea about the topic. It may be stated in a topic sentence or it may be implied. Supporting details give more information about the main idea.
Problem and Solution	This nonfiction text structure presents both a problem and the solution to the problem. An editorial might be arranged this way, with a problem stated at the beginning and the writer's suggested solution at the end.

Read the following paragraphs. Think about how the text is organized and what effect this has on the information presented.

Paragraph 1

Sarah Chang was born in Philadelphia in 1980. She began to take violin lessons when she was just four years old. She played so well that she was performing with local orchestras by the time she was five. Word of Sarah's talent spread to the conductor of the New York Philharmonic Orchestra. When he heard her play, he invited her to appear as a soloist with his famous orchestra. Sarah was just eight years old. After her momentous performance, the Philharmonic audience was silent. Then, suddenly, the crowd burst into cheers. Since that exciting day, Sarah has recorded several CDs and now appears with orchestras all over the world.

How is this passage organized? Explain your answer.

The passage is organized by chronological order. It tells of some important events in Sarah's life in the order in which they happened.

What might have been the author's purpose in choosing this text structure?

Possible response: to focus mainly on Sarah Chang's childhood and how she became famous.

Paragraph 2

I'm so excited! I'm going to play a violin solo at the Metropolitan Concert Hall next week, and I'll get to meet my idol, Sarah Chang! First, I want to ask her how she manages to devote so much time to scales. I've read that, unlike me, she really keeps up her scales. She has also managed to balance her music with her family and study time. I, however, have trouble doing that, and I would like her advice. Finally, I know she gets a lot of support from her parents and brother. My family supports me in the same way. I'd like her to know that we have something in common!

1. **How is this passage organized? Explain your answer.**

   The passage is organized by compare and contrast. The writer, who is a violinist, compares himself or herself to Sarah Chang in several ways.

2. **Did you use clue words to decide how the passage was organized? Explain your answer.**

   The clue words "unlike," "however," and "in the same way" help to signal that the piece is organized by compare and contrast.

Tip

As you read a story or article, think about how the text is organized and what that tells you about the author's purpose.

On Your Own

Read the following biography of another famous musician. As you read, think about how the text is structured and how this organization affects the tone of the writing.

Mozart:
The Wonderchild

Wolfgang Amadeus Mozart was one of Austria's most famous musicians. What is really interesting is that Mozart became famous at a very early age. When he was only six, he was performing all over Europe. In 1768, when he was twelve, he wrote his first opera. How did Mozart become so successful at such an early age?

The most important factor in Mozart's success was his talent. He was composing music by age five and wrote his first published works, four violin sonatas, at the age of eight. He could make up music at the keyboard, improvise songs to go with melodies composed by others, and play any piece of music in any style—even when blindfolded. His talent made him a great favorite with audiences, who called him the *wunderkind* (VUN-der-kint), a German word meaning *wonderchild*.

Furthermore, Mozart was successful because of the determination of his father. Leopold Mozart wanted young Wolfgang to be a composer, especially since the boy showed such early promise. The Mozarts were a musical family, and the house was always full of the sounds of instruments and singing.

Wolfgang learned to read and play music when he was a small child. His father decided to show him off to audiences when he was very young. He played in the courts and palaces of the major European cities. Although Wolfgang was already a favorite of the emperor of Austria, his father was always urging him to work harder and do better. Only a few musicians at that time became rich, but Leopold thought that his son deserved wealth and fame.

Finally, Wolfgang Mozart was successful because he genuinely loved music. As a child, he enjoyed surprising his father with little tunes he had written. Some were so technically challenging that even longtime professional musicians could not play them! By the time of his early death at age 35, Mozart had composed more than 600 works.

Today, Mozart's music is performed all over the world. There are Mozart festivals in many big cities every summer. Because of Mozart's great talent, the influence of his father, and his love for music, he is considered one of the most brilliant composers who ever lived.

Checking Comprehension

1. What do you think some of Wolfgang Mozart's character traits were when he was young?

   Possible answers: He was very obedient. He enjoyed performing. He was very

   creative and talented.

2. Imagine yourself in Mozart's place. Would you say your childhood was a happy one?
   Why or why not? [Drawing Conclusions/Critical]

   Answers will vary, but may include: Yes, because I would get to spend so much time with music.

   Yes, because I would be famous. No, because I would probably have to practice all the time

   instead of playing or making friends.

Practicing Comprehension Skills

3. What text structure is used in "Mozart: The Wonderchild"? Why do you think
   the writer chose this structure?

   The text structure is cause and effect. The writer wanted to explore how and why Mozart

   became famous at such a young age, rather than simply tell what he did.

Complete the chart to show the text structure used in "Mozart: The Wonderchild."
Fill in the blank on the left by giving another reason for Mozart's early fame. Fill in
the blanks on the right by writing the effects.

Causes	Effects
4. Mozart was talented.	Possible answers: He composed music by age five. He wrote his first published works at 8. He wrote an opera when he was 12.
5. Mozart's father encouraged him.	He learned to read and play music as a small child. He played for audiences when he was only six.
6. Mozart loved music.	Possible answers: He liked to surprise his father with new pieces he had written. He wrote more than 600 works.

7. What might a chronological approach to Mozart's life have told the reader that this article does not say?

Possible answers: It might have told us the date and place of his birth, the dates of some of his

famous musical compositions, the name of his wife and when they were married, what his life

was like as an adult, and what he died of.

Read the following letter to a newspaper. Think about how the text is organized and what effect this has on the information presented.

We Need an Orchestra Parents Association!

Dear Editor,

Our middle school orchestra is asked to play at events all around the state. Last week, however, we had to turn down an invitation to play because of lack of funds for a bus. It is expensive to transport an entire orchestra, plus instruments, to a distant town. Everyone felt bad about this decision. I have a solution: we need an Orchestra Parents Association. My friend in another town belongs to his school orchestra, and they have an OPA. This group of parents raises funds for the orchestra. They sell snacks at concerts and hold garage sales and raffles to raise money. We have many caring orchestra parents here in the middle school. Let's start our own Orchestra Parents Association!

8. Is this a fiction or nonfiction passage? Explain your answer.

It is nonfiction. It tells about real people and events.

9. Describe the text structure of "We Need an Orchestra Parents Association!" What effect does the text structure have on the information presented?

The text is organized by problem and solution. The writer identifies a problem, then suggests a

solution for the problem. The effect is to make the piece sound persuasive.

Read this newspaper article. Think about how the text is organized.

ORCHESTRA PARENTS ASSOCIATION FOUNDED AT READING MIDDLE SCHOOL

The first meeting of the Reading Middle School Orchestra Parents Association will be held on Tuesday, March 21, at 7:30 P.M. at the home of James and Georgia Lewis on 121 Smith Road. All interested parents of students in the middle school orchestra are invited to attend to discuss future fundraising ideas. Mr. and Mrs. Lewis are both cello players with the Metropolitan Orchestra. Their son, James Jr., plays the viola in the middle school orchestra.

10. Is this a fiction or nonfiction passage? Explain your answer.

   It is nonfiction. It tells about real people and events.

11. How is the article organized? Explain your answer.

   The article is organized by main idea and supporting details. The first sentence gives the main

   idea about the meeting. The other sentences give additional information about the meeting

   and the Lewis family.

Practicing Vocabulary

Choose the word from the box that best fits each
blank in the paragraph. Write the correct words on the blanks.

| challenging | composers | emperor | improvise | influence | melodies | urging |

One of my piano teacher's favorite ____composers____ is Mozart. Some of Mozart's ____melodies____ are extremely ____challenging____ for a young artist to play. I've learned a few Mozart pieces because my teacher was ____urging____ me to. My teacher says the composer's work was a strong ____influence____ on her career. However, I really prefer to ____improvise____ my own pieces. I'm glad I don't have a royal ____emperor____ to please, as Mozart did!

Writing a Paragraph
What are you good at doing? Do you write or draw, or play an instrument or a sport? On a separate sheet of paper, write a paragraph about your talent, using one of the text structures you learned in this lesson.

Understanding Author's Viewpoint

An **author's viewpoint** is the way an author looks at the subject he or she is writing about. Authors can choose to take a viewpoint that is either balanced or biased.

In **balanced writing**, the reader is presented with facts and opinions from more than one viewpoint. Readers are usually left to make up their own minds. This news report shows balanced writing: "The leader of the parents' organization reported on the study of Norwood's school lunches. He said the study showed the lunches were lacking in nutritional value. The president of the Make-a-Lunch Company responded, 'Our school lunches meet every nutritional standard.' "

In **biased writing**, the reader can detect a strong feeling for or against someone or something. The writer will present only one viewpoint or one side of an argument. The use of "loaded" words meant to bring out the reader's emotions is often a clue that biased writing is present. In this news report, the words *totally* and *blustered* indicate biased writing.: "The leader of the parents' organization said the study proved that the nutritional value of the Norwood School lunches was totally inadequate. In response, the Make-a-Lunch Company blustered about standards."

As you read this letter to a school newspaper, consider the author's viewpoint. Is it balanced or biased?

Dear Editor:
    Yesterday I read that our Congress is allotting billions more dollars for the space program this year. Aren't there more important things we could do with that money? For example, what about all the schools that lack funding for computers? What about the schools that can't offer special programs, such as art and music? Couldn't some NASA money be spent on funding for these things? It's outrageous to waste money sending people into space when there are far more meaningful ways to spend our money.
    Signed,
    Mary Lee, Montrose, AZ

Tip

Biased writing contains loaded words that try to slant a reader's view. Some examples of loaded words are *terrible, wonderful, horrible,* and *sensible.*

Does the writer of this letter have a balanced or biased viewpoint?

Biased _____

What evidence in the letter supports your judgment?

The author presents only one side of the argument. She uses loaded words such as

waste and *outrageous* to make readers feel strongly about her viewpoint.

On Your Own

Read this speech a sixth-grader gave to a school assembly. Watch for words the speaker uses to express a viewpoint. Judge for yourself if that viewpoint is balanced or biased.

Support Young Astronauts!

My fellow students, I am very interested in the space shuttle and our country's attempts to explore space. Recently, I read a newspaper article about toys that were taken into space, but they weren't taken for diversions. The astronauts used them for science experiments!

Astronaut John Casper had a ball that was attached to a cup with a string. He tried to get the ball into the cup. This task was much harder than it sounds because in space there is no gravity to pull the ball down.

Astronaut Mario Runco performed some experiments with a toy car and a track. On Earth, he had pushed a toy car around a circular track that stood on its side. The car went around the track until friction slowed the wheels to a stop. Then gravity caused it to fall off the track. In orbit, the car just stopped when the friction of the wheels made it stop. Because there is no gravity in space, the car stayed on the track and didn't fall off.

What is my point? If NASA is going to waste billions of critical dollars on the space shuttle program so people can play with toys in space, then they should send children like us on these missions!

If they want to test toys, they should go to the experts—kids!

There are obvious benefits to letting kids perform these experiments. Kids who are chosen would get fantastic training that they could use in their future. Back on Earth, they could share their enthusiasm. This, in turn, would make other kids support NASA. Remember, kids grow up to become voters! Most important, using kids to perform these experiments would allow the astronauts to spend their time on more crucial matters. NASA could also send two ninety-pound kids for every 180-pound adult.

Do you need more reasons? Think about this. Most kids play on sports teams, so we know about teamwork and playing by the rules. Finally, space travel may well become an everyday event in the near future. Children need to be prepared.

Please, fellow students, talk to your parents and your teachers. E-mail your senators and representatives. We desperately need to stand together on this important issue. Children belong in space!

Checking Comprehension

1. **What are some experiments on toys that were performed in space? How were they different in space?** [Drawing Conclusions/Critical]

   One experiment involved getting a ball into a cup. It was hard to do because there is no gravity in space. Another experiment involved pushing a toy car around a track. It stayed on the track because there is no gravity.

2. **What would be some benefits of using children as astronauts?** [Main Idea/Critical]

   They would get great training. They could make other kids enthusiastic about NASA. They would free up the astronauts' time. Kids are smaller than adults. They know about teamwork.

Practicing Comprehension Skills

3. **What is the author's viewpoint about sending children on space missions?**

   The author strongly believes that children should fly on these missions.

4. **Is the speech balanced or biased? Why do you think so?**

   Possible answer: It is biased. The author has a definite viewpoint, that children should fly on the space shuttle. The author uses loaded words and presents only one side of the issue.

5. **Give examples of loaded words in the speech.**

   Possible answers: waste, critical, obvious, fantastic, crucial, desperately, important

6. **Fill in the circle next to the sentence that does not express bias. Explain your answer on the lines provided.**

   ○ NASA is wasting billions of dollars so people can play with toys in space.

   ● Recently I read a newspaper article about toys that were taken into space.

   ○ Kids who are chosen would get fantastic training.

   ○ Children belong in space!

   Possible answer: This statement does not express bias. It states a fact. It contains no strong opinions or feelings and uses no loaded words.

7. Rewrite these sentences so that they present a more balanced viewpoint. Remember to show both sides of the issue, such as whether there could also be benefits in NASA's approach to the toy experiments.

   If NASA is going to waste billions of critical dollars on the space shuttle program so people can play with toys in space, then they should send children like us on these missions! If they want to test toys, they should go to the experts: kids! There are obvious benefits to letting kids perform these experiments.

   Possible answer: NASA spends billions of dollars on the space shuttle program. If testing toys

   is an important part of the program, perhaps NASA should include children, since children are

   experts on toys. However, it's also possible that there are benefits to having trained astronauts

   perform these experiments.

Practicing Vocabulary

Write the word from the box that belongs with each group of words.

| circular | critical | diversions | enthusiasm | experiments | friction | obvious |

8. rubbing, resistance, _____ friction _____

9. clear, plain, _____ obvious _____

10. round, like a circle, _____ circular _____

11. tests, trials, _____ experiments _____

12. eagerness, interest, _____ enthusiasm _____

13. amusements, pleasures, _____ diversions _____

14. important, crucial, _____ critical _____

Making the Reading and Writing Connection

Writing a Letter to the Editor
On another sheet of paper, write a letter to your local newspaper about an issue you care about. Before writing, decide whether your writing will show a balanced or a biased viewpoint. Be able to explain the language you used to indicate this.

Making Generalizations

A **generalization** is a conclusion that you can make after thinking about a number of examples or facts and what they have in common. Generalizations help you recognize an author's purpose and evaluate possible bias. Clue words that can signal a generalization include *all, none, most, many, always, everyone, never, sometimes, some, usually, seldom, few, generally, in general,* and *overall.*

Generalizations can be valid or faulty. A **valid** generalization is one that is supported by facts or logic. A **faulty** generalization is not completely supported by facts. As you read, look for generalizations the writer makes. Decide whether they are supported by facts.

Read the following paragraphs. As you read, think about generalizations the author makes. Also think about generalizations that you can make.

Crack! Lightning strikes a tree in the middle of the forest. Soon the dry underbrush is aflame. Before the fire can get out of hand, special firefighters are preparing to parachute from a plane. These firefighters, called smokejumpers, are usually in the air within ten minutes of the call.

Once the fire has been located and evaluated, smokejumpers jump to a safe spot nearby. Generally, smokejumpers begin by cutting down nearby sources of fuel for the fire and digging a trail that surrounds the fire. Both of these steps will usually contain the fire. Then the smokejumpers attack the fire itself, cooling it down with dirt and spading the burned area.

Decide whether the following sentence is a generalization. Explain your answer.

These firefighters, called smokejumpers, are usually in the air within ten minutes of the call.

The sentence is a generalization because it uses the word "usually" to show how long it takes the smokejumpers to get into the air.

Find a generalization in the second paragraph. Explain how you know it is a generalization.

Possible answers: "Generally, smokejumpers . . . ," "Both of these steps will usually contain. . . ." Clue words that signal a generalization are included.

Tip

Clue words can help you spot generalizations, but some generalizations do not include clue words. If you can mentally add a clue word to a sentence without changing the meaning, then the statement is probably a generalization.

What is it like to be a smokejumper—a firefighter who parachutes to the location of wildfires? Veteran smokejumper Arlen Cravens is manager of the Region 5 Smokejumper Base in Redding, California. As you read the following interview with Mr. Cravens, look for generalizations that he makes, as well as generalizations you can make from what he says.

An Interview with Smokejumper ARLEN CRAVENS

Q: Have you always been a smokejumper?
A: I started out as a hot shot. Hot shot crews are twenty-person firefighting teams. They work as a single unit and are called in to fight the largest, most difficult wilderness fires. The smokejumper mission is the initial attack. Our motto is: "Hit 'em hard and keep 'em small."

Q: What made you want to become a smokejumper?
A: When I was in eighth grade, I was failing English. My teacher said that the only way I would pass was if I wrote a three-page paper on what I wanted to be when I grew up. So I went to the school library for ideas. They had a row of about eight or ten file cabinets. I started at A in the first cabinet. When I got to S, I saw something that looked like a deep-sea diver. I thought, "That looks interesting." It turns out that it was a smokejumper from Redding. I was interested!

Q: Were you a parachutist before you became a smokejumper?
A: No, we look for experienced wildland firefighters. We train them to become parachutists.

Q: What's the best part about being a smokejumper?
A: The camaraderie. There is great camaraderie among our crew and among the other 360 American smokejumpers. Smokejumping also provides a sense of accomplishment. Another exciting part is not knowing where you'll end up at the end of a day. We are based in Redding, but by nightfall we may be fighting a fire anywhere from the southern California Sierras to central Oregon.

Q: Are there any women smokejumpers?
A: Nationally, there are more than 30 female smokejumpers.

Q: How do you feel when you get a call?
A: Excited. When you're not working on a fire, you're maintaining the gear or exercising. You never know when the alarm will sound. When it does, you are ready and eager to answer the call.

Q: How long are you typically at a fire?
A: Normally, we're there two days and two nights. A three-day supply of food and water is dropped by parachute when we jump. Smokejumpers fight fires without water, and that takes time. When we leave, we leave with the fire out. We dig up the dirt, then we get down on our hands and knees and feel every inch to make sure it is cool.

Q: What special equipment do you use?
A: We wear fire-resistant jumpsuits with padding. We use chain saws and crosscut saws. We are probably the last experts in the use of the crosscut saw. That's the one with handles at each end for two people to use.

Q: What qualities do smokejumpers need?
A: Smokejumpers need desire, tenacity, and the ability to set a goal and stick to it.

Checking Comprehension

1. How is a smokejumper's work different from that of a regular firefighter?

   Possible answer: Smokejumpers jump out of planes to reach a fire, instead of riding in a truck.

   They fight fires without water and don't leave the fire for days at a time.

   [Making Judgments/Critical]

2. What physical skills would someone probably need to be a smokejumper?

   Possible answer: A successful smokejumper would probably need to have both strength and

   endurance to fight a fire over several days.

Practicing Comprehension Skills

Fill in the circle next to each answer. Then explain your choice by writing your answer on the lines.

3. Which of the following is a generalization, not a simple fact?

   ● a. Normally, smokejumpers are at a fire for two days and two nights.   ○ b. The smokejumper mission is the initial attack.

   ○ c. Hot shot crews are teams of 20 firefighters.   ○ d. The smokejumpers in Region 5 cover the territory from the southern Sierras to central Oregon.

4. **Explanation:** Item a is a conclusion that can be made about a number of examples, so it is a generalization. The other choices are simple facts.

5. Which of the following generalizations is valid, based on facts in the interview?

   ○ a. Any parachutist can become a smokejumper.   ○ b. Smokejumpers usually use water to put out fires.

   ● c. Smokejumpers always need to be able to work well with others.   ○ d. All smokejumpers were on hot shot crews before they became smokejumpers.

6. **Explanation:** Smokejumpers do need to work well with others. They work together for days at a time, and they need to work in pairs to cut trees with a crosscut saw.

7. Which of the following generalizations is <u>faulty</u>, judging from the interview?

   ○ **a.** Smokejumping is often unpredictable work.

   ● **b.** In general, smokejumping is much like deep-sea diving.

   ○ **c.** Some smokejumpers are women.

   ○ **d.** Smokejumpers are usually busy, even when they are not fighting fires.

8. **Explanation:** <u>The interview suggests only that smokejumpers may look a bit like deep sea</u> <u>divers when they are dressed for a fire, not that the work is similar.</u>

9. Complete the following statement with a generalization you can make based on facts from the text or your previous knowledge and experience.

   All smokejumpers need to be <u>Possible answers: able to set a goal and stick to it, in great</u>

   <u>physical condition, able to jump from planes, able to use chain saws and crosscut saws.</u>

Practicing Vocabulary

Choose the word from the box that best fits each blank in the paragraph. Write the correct words on the blanks.

10.   When the request came into the dispatcher's office, the smokejumpers

were _____maintaining_____ their equipment. Quickly they suited up for

their _____mission_____ and boarded the plane. There was a friendly

spirit of _____camaraderie_____ as they prepared to spend three days

together in the rugged _____wilderness_____ . A _____smokejumper_____

is both a firefighter and a trained _____parachutist_____ , and soon the

crew was parachuting from the plane in small groups. They were ready to fight

the fire with great _____tenacity_____ .

camaraderie
maintaining
mission
parachutist
smokejumper
tenacity
wilderness

Writing an Advertisement
Create a recruiting poster for smokejumpers. Include generalizations about the work and about the kind of person who would find this job exciting and fulfilling. Use a separate sheet of paper for your poster.

Outlining

A good way to understand what you read is to make an **outline**. An outline is a list of information that shows how an author organized the different ideas in a piece of writing. Brief **headings** capture the most important information in an outline. Before you begin making an outline, you need to choose whether you will write all your headings as sentences, as phrases, or as key words.

A good outline shows how the author's main topics, subtopics, and important details are organized. A **main topic** is written next to **Roman numerals I, II, III,** and so on. Main topics are divided into two or more **subtopics**, which give more information about the main topic. Subtopics are written next to **capital letters A, B, C,** and so on. Important **details** give information to support the subtopics. They are written next to **numerals 1, 2, 3,** and so on.

Read the following passage and look at the outline beside it. Fill in the blank spaces with any missing main topics, subtopics, and details.

San Francisco's Cable Cars

On September 1, 1873, several people boarded a cable car in San Francisco. This trip was the first cable car ride in the United States.

Cable cars get their name from the long wire cord or cable that runs beneath the streets of the cars' route. The cable looks like a giant moving clothesline with a pulley at each end. A huge power source turns the pulleys and makes the cable pull the cars up and down the city's steep hills. Each car has a large, powerful claw under its floor. This claw grips the cable when the car is ready to move and lets go when the car needs to stop.

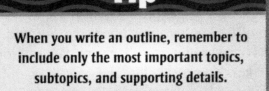

Tip

When you write an outline, remember to include only the most important topics, subtopics, and supporting details.

(Title)		San Francisco's Cable Cars
(Main Topic)	I.	The first U. S. cable car
(Subtopics)	A.	Year 1873
	B.	Place San Francisco
(Main Topic)	II.	How cable cars work
(Subtopic)	A.	Cable below streets
(Details)	1.	Power turns pulleys
	2.	Pulleys move cable
(Subtopic)	B.	How cable cars stop and go
(Details)	1.	Claw beneath car grips cable to go
	2.	Claw beneath car releases cable to stop

Read the following article about the New York City subway system. As you read, think about the most important information you would include in an outline of this article.

ALL ABOARD! A Trip Through New York's Subways

At the turn of the twentieth century, New York City was a busy place. The city was growing so quickly that new houses and apartment buildings were going up every day. Downtown, the sidewalks were jammed with shoppers, workers, travelers, and newly arrived immigrants from Europe. Horses and carriages filled every bit of empty space in the streets. Fierce winter snowstorms and the merciless summer heat exhausted those New Yorkers who had to travel on foot. What could be done?

An underground railroad, or subway, seemed to be the solution to these problems. Railroads moved on their own tracks, so they never sat in traffic jams. Powered by strong engines, railroads could do the work of many horses. Horses had to be fed and cared for, and they could get sick or go lame. However, if an engine failed, it could be repaired or replaced. Building the railroad under the ground made perfect sense. It would ease congestion on the crowded streets of Manhattan. Most of the city's major business districts were located in this borough, which is on a small and narrow island.

A subway was not a new idea to New Yorkers. The first subway in the world had opened in London back in 1863. However, the question of who would build and own a subway in New York City had never been decided. In 1888, New York's mayor, Abram Hewitt, proposed a law that said the city government should build and own the subway. This idea was finally accepted. Building a subway would be backbreaking work for 12,000 people, but many New Yorkers were eager for steady work, even if it was hard.

In 1904, the mayor of New York City put on his good coat and a top hat and guided the first train north from City Hall in downtown Manhattan to Grand Central Station on 42nd Street. It then ran west to Times Square, the midpoint of the modern city. From Times Square the train went north again up Broadway to 145th Street. The total distance was a little over nine miles, and it took just 26 minutes. That same day, 100,000 excited New Yorkers rode the brand-new train. The fare was just 5¢.

By 1913, the subway was so popular that officials made plans to extend the system. The cost, over $300 million, was sky-high. Up to that time, the only building project that had cost more was the Panama Canal. However, the expansion was worth the money. When it was finished, there were 656 miles of track—still the longest in the world.

Today, the New York City subway remains the most efficient way to get around the city 24 hours a day. The population has continued to grow, and traffic jams have grown as well. Every day, millions of New Yorkers descend below the city streets to travel quickly and safely to their destinations. However, the fare is now much more than a nickel!

Checking Comprehension

1. Why was a subway system needed in New York City? [Main Idea/Critical]

   Possible answer: The long distances between places in the city made

   a transit system necessary.

2. What is one of the benefits of the New York City subway system? [Cause and Effect/Critical]

   Possible answer: Because the subways are so convenient, fewer people drive.

Practicing Comprehension Skills

3. Complete an outline of the article by filling in the missing topics, subtopics, and details.

<u>All Aboard: A Trip Through New York's Subways</u>

I. Need for a new transportation system

  A. Busy sidewalks and streets

  B. Walking in extreme weather unpleasant

II. Benefits of a subway

  A. No traffic jams

  B. Trains stronger and easier to maintain than horses

  C. Would ease congestion

III. Building the subway

  A. Question of ownership

    1. Mayor Abram Hewitt's idea

    2. Proposed in 1888

  B. Provided work for 12,000 people

IV. The first New York subway

  A. Year was 1904

  B. Ran from City Hall to Broadway and 145th Street

    1. Route about nine miles

    2. Took 26 minutes

  C. 100,000 riders

  D. 5-cent fare

V. The subway today

  A. 656 miles of track

  B. Runs 24 hours a day

  C. Used by millions

On the line below, list a detail from the article that is not closely related enough to the topic to belong in an outline.

4. <u>Possible answers: the fact that the first subway opened in London in 1863; what the mayor</u> wore on opening day

5. If the article had an additional paragraph at the end containing a new main topic, how would that topic be indicated on the outline?

<u>It would be written as a brief phrase next to the roman numeral VI.</u>

6. Fill in the blanks in the paragraph.

Main topics are written next to <u>Roman numerals I, II, III, etc.</u> . Main topics are divided into

two or more <u>subtopics</u> , which are written next to <u>capital letters A, B, C, etc.</u> .

Important <u>details</u> give information to support the <u>subtopics</u>

and are written next to <u>numerals 1, 2, 3, etc.</u> .

Practicing Vocabulary

Choose the word from the box that best matches each clue. Write the word on the line.

7. <u>repaired</u>   antonym for *broke*

8. <u>immigrants</u>   antonym for *emigrants*

9. <u>subway</u>   synonym for *underground train*

10. <u>merciless</u>   antonym for *kind*

11. <u>congestion</u>   synonym for *fullness*

12. <u>midpoint</u>   synonym for *center*

13. <u>exhausted</u>   antonym for *refreshed*

congestion

exhausted

immigrants

merciless

midpoint

repaired

subway

Writing an Outline

Write a short nonfiction article about a topic that interests you. Use the Internet or an encyclopedia if you need ideas or facts. Be sure to organize your article so that it contains main topics, subtopics, and details. Then trade papers with a partner. On another sheet of paper, make an outline of your partner's article as your partner outlines what you wrote.

Persuasive Devices and Propaganda

If you've ever listened to an advertisement on radio or television, you have probably come across **propaganda**. Propaganda is the spreading of ideas in order to convince people to believe, do, or buy something. You can find propaganda in political speeches and in most advertising. Five **persuasive devices** often used in propaganda are shown in the chart below.

When a writer's purpose is to persuade you, he or she presents evidence to convince you. Some evidence is more valid than others. To become a wise reader, you should look at the evidence the writer offers and decide whether or not you can trust that evidence.

Device	Definition	Example
Testimonial	A testimonial is something a person says to recommend someone or something.	Basketball pro Hoop Hooper says, "I wear Pro-Rite shoes in every game. So should you!"
Bandwagon	This device suggests that many people are buying or doing something, so it must be the right thing to do.	Last year, 40,000 Americans bought Fast-Tek Mountain Bikes. What are you waiting for?
Loaded Words	Loaded words try to slant a reader's view of a product or person. Loaded words have strong connotations that are not necessarily true.	Refreshing, delicious, nutritious — Bright Star Lemonade is one unique drink! Mmmm!
Vague Generalities	Vague generalities are statements that are purposely broad or vague. They give few specific details and offer little evidence to back up their claims.	Moe Mullins is the best candidate for mayor, because Moe gets results!
Sweeping Generalizations	Sweeping generalizations give some sort of "truth" but offer little evidence. They speak for a large group or overstate a situation. They often include such words as *always*, *never*, *all*, *no one*, *none*, and *everyone*.	At Val's Diner, you'll never be disappointed. Val's always serves the best meals at the lowest prices!

Circle the name of the propaganda device that each statement uses.

Candidate Mary Brown is independent, hardworking, and courageous.

    testimonial   bandwagon   (loaded words)

Champion dog trainer Rory Rolfe says, "My dogs roll over and beg for Doggie Yum-Yums!"

    (testimonial)   vague generalities   sweeping generalizations

Read the following radio ad for Petster's Pet Shop. Look for persuasive devices as you read.

Studies show that people with pets are happy people. That's why more and more Americans are becoming pet owners. Perhaps the time is right for you to share your life with a pet. At Petster's Pet Shop, we are ready to help you take that important step.

Stop by our clean, pleasant shop anytime. Get to know our happy family of pets. Talk to our caring pet professionals.

Now, don't just take our word for it. Listen to what Dr. Dan Noto, radio's famous pet vet, had to say: "For pet perfection, go to Petster's!" That's right, Dr. Dan! No one knows more about pets than we do. Our pets always make the best pets. So make Petster's *your* pet center today. You'll never be lonely again!

What persuasive device does this sentence from the ad illustrate? Explain your answer.

"Studies show that people with pets are happy people."

vague generalities; the sentence makes a broad statement with little evidence

What persuasive device is used in this sentence? How do you know?

"That's why more and more Americans are becoming pet owners."

bandwagon; the sentence suggests that many people are buying pets, so it is the right

thing to do.

What persuasive device is mainly used in this paragraph from the ad?

"Stop by our clean, pleasant shop anytime. Get to know our happy family of pets. Talk to our caring pet professionals."

loaded words

What two persuasive devices are used in paragraph 3 of the ad? How do you know?

testimonial and sweeping generalization. The advertiser has a

famous radio "pet vet" recommend its store. The words *no one,*

always, and *never* are used.

Tip

If an author's purpose is to convince you to believe, do, or buy something, the writing is propaganda. Once you identify propaganda, think about facts and ideas that the author fails to mention.

"World Traveler"

Nutribeef Dog Food Ad

EXTERIOR: HIGH ON A SNOWY MOUNTAINTOP—DAY

A dog sits on the side of a mountain. He sniffs the air, sniffs it again, then runs down the snowy slope.

EXTERIOR: DESERT IN AFRICA

The dog runs across desert sands.

EXTERIOR: EIFFEL TOWER

The dog makes a circuit around the Eiffel Tower in Paris and sniffs again.

EXTERIOR: SHIP IN NEW YORK HARBOR NEAR THE STATUE OF LIBERTY

The dog passes the Statue of Liberty, still sniffing.

EXTERIOR: STREETS OF NEW YORK CITY

The dog runs up and down streets of New York City in pursuit of the delicious aroma. He stops and sniffs. Then he spies a luxurious apartment building and trots toward it. A woman holding a bag of groceries enters the building. The dog follows her inside.

INTERIOR: APARTMENT—DAY

The woman opens her grocery bag and pulls out a can of Nutribeef dog food.

WOMAN (to the dog): "I bet you're hungry, boy."

DOG: "Woof, woof!"

WOMAN: "Here's a bowl of scrumptious and nutritious Nutribeef dog food!"

The woman puts dog food in a bowl. The dog eats hungrily.

VOICE-OVER (Narrator): "Dogs will travel any distance for a delicious bowl of Nutribeef Dog Food. It's right on the label: Nutribeef contains meaty chunks of real beef. What dog doesn't love beef? Dogs know that Nutribeef is the tastiest dog food made. They flock from all over the world to get a bite of Nutribeef, because it's worth it! Nutribeef also has all the nutrition your dog ever needs. More and more dog owners are choosing Nutribeef. Shouldn't you choose it, too?"

Checking Comprehension

1. What point is this commercial trying to make? [Main Idea/Inferential]

   Dogs will travel a long distance for Nutribeef. The dog in the commercial travels over

   mountains, over a desert, through France, and across the ocean to get the food.

   [Making Judgments/Critical]
2. Would you be influenced by this advertisement? Explain why or why not.

   Answers will vary. Some students may say the humor in the ad could make them remember the

   dog food and want to buy it. Others will say they wouldn't be convinced to purchase the dog

   food because the persuasive devices are obvious and lack supporting evidence.

Practicing Comprehension Skills

Fill in the circle before the persuasive device used in each sentence. Then on each line, write the words that gave you clues about the device used.

3. Dogs know that Nutribeef is the tastiest dog food made.

   ○ testimonial   ● vague generality   ○ bandwagon   ○ sweeping generalization

   Dogs know; tastiest

4. More and more dog owners are choosing Nutribeef.

   ○ testimonial   ○ loaded words   ● bandwagon   ○ sweeping generalization

   More and more dog owners

5. Here's a bowl of scrumptious and nutritious Nutribeef Dog Food!

   ○ vague generality   ○ testimonial   ● loaded words   ○ bandwagon

   scrumptious and nutritious

6. Nutribeef has all the nutrition your dog ever needs.

   ○ testimonial   ○ loaded words   ○ bandwagon   ● sweeping generalization

   all the nutrition; ever needs

7. Give an example of a testimonial the television script writer might
    have included in this advertisement.

    Possible answer: Animal expert John Smith of the World-Famous Animal Clinic says, "Nutribeef

    dog food is the only food we ever give our dogs."

8. Think about the name *Nutribeef*. Would you agree that this made-up
    word is an example of a loaded word? Why or why not?

    Possible answer: Yes, the name is a loaded word. Most people would associate the first part—

    "Nutri"—with *nutrition* and *nutritious*, words that generate positive feeling. As an ingredient of

    dog food, "beef" also has positive connotations.

Suppose you wanted to persuade people to switch dog food brands to Nutribeef.
Think of a sweeping generalization and a bandwagon device you might
use to persuade them. Write your answers on the lines below.

9. **Sweeping Generalization**

    Possible answers: Everyone who cares about their dog buys Nutribeef; Nutribeef is always

    rated number 1; There's no reason not to buy it—none whatsoever!

10. **Bandwagon**

    Possible answers: Every day, thousands of dog owners are switching to Nutribeef;

    Your neighbors feed their dogs Nutribeef—you should, too!

Rewrite these statements, providing facts that could be used to support them.

11. **Nutribeef has all the nutrition your dog ever needs.**

    Possible answer: A recent study showed that Nutribeef has all the ingredients your dog needs

    for good nutrition.

12. **More and more dog owners are choosing Nutribeef.**

    Possible answer: Surveys show that nine out of ten dog owners choose to buy Nutribeef

    instead of other brands.

13. Look back at the commercial for Nutribeef. Are any of the claims it makes valid, supported by facts or evidence? Explain your answer.

   Possible answer: One of the claims is valid. Nutribeef probably does contain some real beef,

   since it's listed on the label.

14. Circle the dog food names below that use loaded words.

   (Yummywoof Crunchies)

   Blank Brand Dog Food

   (Doggy Delight)

   (Healthy Pup Dog Food)

   Jake's Dog Food

Practicing Vocabulary

Choose the word from the box that best completes each analogy. Write the word on the line.

15. outdoor : indoor :: exterior : _____ interior _____

16. velvety : touch :: _____ scrumptious _____ : taste

17. straight line : one way :: _____ circuit _____ : around

18. meager : poverty :: _____ luxurious _____ : wealth

19. quest : search :: _____ pursuit _____ : chase

20. rest : sleeping :: _____ nutrition _____ : eating

21. seeing : scenery :: hearing : _____ voice-over _____

circuit
interior
luxurious
nutrition
pursuit
scrumptious
voice-over

Reading AND Writing CONNECTION

Writing an Advertisement
On another sheet of paper, write a radio or television advertisement for a product that pet owners might buy for their pets. When you have finished, share your work with a partner. Identify the persuasive devices in each other's work.

Literary Elements: Character

Understanding the characters in a story can help you comprehend the story as a whole. As you read, you can find clues to the characters' traits or personality characteristics. Some characters are confident; some are shy. Some characters are generous; others are mean-spirited.

There are several ways an author can show the traits of the characters in a story. What a character is like can be revealed by:

- **what the character *says***
- **what the character *does***
- **what the *narrator or other characters* say about the character**
- **how others *act* toward the character.**

Read the following story. As you read, look for clues that tell you about the characters.

"Hey, Alex," Marta said. "Do you want to work on our science project after school today?"

"I can't," answered Alex. "My grandfather is coming over to help me build a doghouse for Buster. We're going to construct it out of sod, the way the Nebraska pioneers built their homes."

"Why don't you tell him we have to work on the science project?" Marta asked.

"No, I promised I'd be home when he arrives, and I always keep my promises," Alex said. "Why don't you come over and help us? We can finish the science project on Saturday."

Marta grinned and nodded. "You have great ideas, Alex. It's a deal."

Fill in the circle next to all the answers that are correct.

Which of the following traits best describes Alex?

- ○ dishonest   ● considerate
- ○ snobbish   ○ musical

How does the reader learn about Alex's character?

- ● by what other characters say about him
- ● by what he says and does
- ● by how other characters act toward him
- ○ by what the narrator says about him

To understand characters in the stories you read, think about whether they have anything in common with you, the people you know, or other characters you've read about.

Read the following diary entries. As you read, think about how the author reveals information about the characters James and William.

From the diary of James Jacobsen

August 3, 1894

Dear Diary,

Today we had exceptional weather. We have made fine progress on our journey, but the trail is monotonous, and my feet are blistered from walking beside the wagon. Pa hopes we will be more prosperous in our new home in Nebraska than we were in the East. That hope is what keeps us going.

The Kelleys joined our wagon train last week. I have found a new friend in William Kelley, who shares my interest in fishing. Mama says she disapproves of William, though. He made quite a stir when he put a baby rattlesnake in Mrs. Kelley's laundry. The Kelleys plan to settle near Bellevue, Nebraska, which is our destination as well.

September 10, 1894

Dear Diary,

Tomorrow we begin work on the "soddy." Mama can't wait for it to be finished so that we can move out of the wagon. Poor Mama. I'd help her more, but Pa needs my assistance. Tomorrow my muscles will be tested as we cut and load blocks of sod for the house.

Pa has discovered that although our oxen did a fine job pulling the wagon all the way from Pennsylvania, they are too slow to cut sod properly. He has struck a deal with Mr. Kelley. We will help each other build our soddies. William Kelley will help us this week. I am glad, for he is the only boy near my age for miles around.

September 11, 1894

Dear Diary,

This morning Pa and I explored our claim for a good place to start cutting the sod.

I felt very proud when he listened respectfully to my views. William and I rode on the sod cutter as ballast while the Kelleys' horse pulled it along. Our weight makes the sod cutter cut through the thick prairie grass to make even bricks of sod. The roots are just deep enough to hold the dirt together. William and I were matched in strength as we piled the sod on a wheelbarrow and wheeled it back to the site of the soddy. When I went to the pump for a drink, William tipped the wheelbarrow, and some pieces of sod fell to the ground. Pa was furious with him, for we had to cut more sod to replace the broken pieces. He has been grumbling about going to help the Kelleys with their soddy next week.

September 30, 1894

Dear Diary,

Earlier this week we could see smoke in the distance. We were fearful that the wind might blow the fire in our direction across the dry prairie grass, but a rainstorm started and we were saved. We found out later that William Kelley had been playing with an oil lamp, and the dry branches and twigs on the roof of their new soddy caught fire. No one was injured, but Mama says William is a careless, tiresome boy.

Checking Comprehension

1. Do you think the Jacobsens could have built their home without the help of others? Explain. [Drawing Conclusions/Critical]

   Possible answers: Yes, but it would have taken more time; no, they needed the Kelleys' horse to cut the sod.

2. How do you think the relationship between James and William might develop? What makes you think so? [Making Predictions/Critical]

   Possible answer: They will probably be friends because there are few boys their age nearby.

   However, their personalities are quite different, so they may not be that close.

Practicing Comprehension Skills

Put a checkmark in the box for each of the ways that the characters of James and William are revealed. Then write an example from the diary for each way you chose.

		James	William
3.	By the character's own words	✔ James tells in his own words that he feels sorry for his mother.	☐
4.	By the character's actions	✔ James helps his family.	✔ William places a snake in the laundry, tips over the cart, and plays dangerously with a lamp.
5.	By what others say about the character	☐	✔ James says he is glad William lives nearby; Mama disapproves of him and calls him careless and tiresome.
6.	By how others act toward the character	✔ Pa listens with respect to James's views.	✔ Pa acts angry with William.

Complete the Venn diagram to compare James Jacobsen and William Kelley. In the left section, write two character traits that apply only to James. In the right section, write two character traits that apply only to William. In the middle section, write character traits that both boys share. Answers will vary. Possible answers:

James

7. responsible _____

_____

8. hard-working _____

_____

Both

9. like to fish _____

_____

10. strong _____

_____

William

11. mischievous _____

_____

12. careless _____

_____

Practicing Vocabulary

Choose a word from the box. Write it on the line next to the matching definition.

13. _____ disapproves _____ doesn't admire

14. _____ monotonous _____ boring, all the same

15. _____ ballast _____ extra weight

16. _____ exceptional _____ excellent

17. _____ tiresome _____ annoying

18. _____ destination _____ goal

19. _____ prosperous _____ successful

| ballast |
| destination |
| disapproves |
| exceptional |
| monotonous |
| prosperous |
| tiresome |

Writing a Character Sketch

Try to recall an interesting character you read about in a book or story. What made that character memorable? On another sheet of paper, write a character sketch to show what the character is like. Be sure to reveal some of the character's traits through things he or she says and does, things the narrator or other characters say about the character, and your own descriptions.

Literary Elements: Plot

When you talk about the **plot** of a story, you're talking about the series of events that move the story forward. The chart below shows the parts of the plot.

Part of the Plot	Description
Background	information you need to know about the setting and characters
Conflict or problem	a struggle between two forces, whether between two or more characters or within an individual
Rising action	the events that build to the climax
Climax	where the characters face the conflict directly
Outcome or resolution	where the action winds down and the conflict is resolved

Think about the important elements of plot as you read the following story.

Captain Liang Tan had just finished inspecting the orbiting satellites. Her spaceship was finally headed home. Suddenly a control light warned that the ship's heat shield was loose. If Captain Tan went back into the Earth's atmosphere, her craft could explode.

She contacted Mission Control. "All functions are normal, Captain," the team reported. "Your control light must be in error. Proceed with reentry."

Captain Tan had flown with this control team since 2038, and she trusted them. Still, her pulse rate began climbing as she started the reentry engines.

The reentry went smoothly. At last the ship settled on the pad. Captain Tan was fine, but this had been the most difficult mission of her career.

Tip

As you read, think about how events move a story toward a solution to the problem. During the rising action, the conflict or problem builds up, leading toward the story's climax and resolution.

What is the problem in this story?

A control light indicates that the spaceship's heat shield is loose,

which means that the ship could explode during reentry.

List two events that are part of the story's rising action.

Possible answers: Captain Tan contacts Mission Control, who

reports that functions are normal. She starts the reentry engines.

As you read the following play, think about the different parts of the plot: background (setting and characters), problem, rising action, climax, and outcome or resolution.

Kids in Space
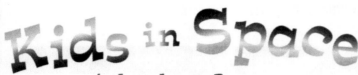

by Joyce Annette Barnes

Characters

Captain	Commander's Mom
Commander	Narrator

Narrator: It is the year 2150. Two officers stand at the helm of a small but powerful spacecraft as it hurtles through the vast darkness of a faraway galaxy.

Commander *(speaking into a recording device)*: Commander's Log: It has been one hundred days since our launch from the International Space Station. We are the first kids in space, and our mission is to continue the search for new planets in the universe where humans can live. Captain, what is the status of our Reusable Launch Vehicle?

Captain: We're traveling at warp speed, and in two days we'll reach our destination planet. All systems are at peak level. Everything appears normal, Commander. In fact, the whole journey has been like a very long field trip. But—wait! What is that on the radar screen?

Commander *(peering at the control panel)*: An unidentified presence is on the screen. We've picked up a signal from 3,000 miles away. *(Looks out the window)* Who knows what's waiting for us out there? It could be anything! I wish I'd studied harder for that test on alien encounters!

Captain: What should we do, Commander?

Commander: Proceed with caution, Captain. We can't get distracted from our mission. Still, we must check this out and make sure it poses no threat to us.

Narrator: The engine slows as the spacecraft approaches the foreign object.

Captain: Commander, I can see something through the window now. It's a small light that looks vaguely familiar.

Commander: Yes, Captain. I have it in view. Look at that! It appears to be flashing like a neon light. Could it be—?

Captain *(excitedly)*: I don't know, Commander. There's no earthly reason for it.

Commander: It's a sign! I can't quite make out the letters. Captain, check it out with the Environmental Analyzer.

Captain: Yes, Commander! *(Pushes a button.)*

Narrator: The Captain sets off activity on an instrument panel. Within seconds, results flash on a computer screen.

(Both the Commander and the Captain react with delight, sniffing the air.)

Captain and Commander: It's a pizza restaurant! *(They give each other a high five.)*

Captain: All right! There *is* intelligent life in the universe!

Commander: Well, I don't think any harm will come if we stop for a couple of slices. Just one minute. *(Presses a button)* Mom?

Commander's Mom *(offstage voice)*: Yes, dear?

Commander: Can we get some pizza?

Commander's Mom: As long as you don't spoil your appetite for dinner.

Commander: Take her down, Captain.

Captain: Yes, Commander!

Checking Comprehension

1. In what ways are the Captain and Commander in this play like kids today?

   Answers will vary, but students are likely to note that the characters mention field trips,

   studying for tests, loving pizza, and asking permission before doing things.

[Drawing Conclusions/Inferential]

2. Why do the Captain and Commander think there is intelligent life in the universe?

   They think that there is intelligent life in the universe because there is a pizza restaurant

   in space.

Practicing Comprehension Skills

3. Complete the diagram of *Kids in Space* by filling in the blank lines.
Answers shown are sample responses. Student responses may vary.

Background

Setting: Aboard a spacecraft in outer space in the year 2150

Main Characters: Commander, Captain, Narrator, and Commander's Mom.

Climax: The presence

turns out to be a pizza

restaurant.

Rising Action: The Commander

and Captain approach the

object and analyze it.

Problem: The Commander

and Captain face a mysterious,

unidentified presence.

Resolution: They decide to

visit the pizza restaurant.

List three events that lead the story to its climax.

4. <u>The Commander sees an unidentified object on the radar screen.</u>

5. <u>The spacecraft approaches the object and the kids examine it.</u>

6. <u>The Captain checks out the object with the Environmental Analyzer.</u>

7. Circle the letter next to the sentence that states the story's climax.

   a. An unidentified presence is on the screen.   **b.** Is it possible, so far away from Earth?

   (c.) It's a pizza restaurant!   **d.** Yes, Commander!

8. Explain your answer to question 12 on the lines provided.

   <u>Answer c is the climax. The characters face the conflict directly.</u>

Practicing Vocabulary

Write the word from the box that belongs in each group.

9. steering mechanism, controlling position, <u>helm</u>

10. seems, looks, <u>appears</u>

11. speeds, rushes, <u>hurtles</u>

12. faintly, somewhat, <u>vaguely</u>

13. recyclable, can be used again, <u>reusable</u>

14. possible, of this world, <u>earthly</u>

15. not recognized, unknown, <u>unidentified</u>

appears
earthly
helm
hurtles
reusable
unidentified
vaguely

Writing a Science Fiction Story
Plan a science fiction story that takes place later in this century. It might be a space adventure or another type of futuristic tale. Prepare to write the story by identifying its setting, characters, problem, rising action, climax, and resolution. Outline your plot elements on another sheet of paper.

Literary Elements: Setting

The **setting** is the time and place in which a story occurs. Writers sometimes tell you exactly where and when the action takes place. At other times, a writer gives you clues about the setting through details. For example, if a story is set long ago, the author may tell about the characters traveling the countryside in a stagecoach pulled by horses. These details give you clues about where and when the events occur.

Setting can be an important part of the plot of a story. The setting often has an effect on what the characters do and what happens to them. The setting can also set up the **mood**, or feeling, of the story. A mood may be sad, dreamlike, eerie, or lighthearted, for instance. When you read a story, ask yourself, "Is the plot affected by the setting? Does the choice of setting help to create a mood? Could these same events occur in a different time or in a different place?"

Read the following story. Pay special attention to details that describe setting. Ask yourself how the setting affects the events and the characters.

The Civil War was over at last. Many former slaves took their dreams of freedom and opportunity to the Wild West. In 1865, Eddie Perkins was only fourteen years old. Newly freed, Eddie left the Georgia plantation where he'd spent his childhood and found work as a cowboy in Kansas.

Eddie's work as a cowboy was very demanding. He spent days and nights in the saddle as he tended huge herds of cattle on the open range. The work was also dangerous as he faced wild animals and outlaws.

Eddie enjoyed his work and became well-known for his skills. By 1875 he had won a riding, roping, and shooting contest in a town in the Dakota Territory called Ready, earning him the nickname of "Ready Eddie."

Where and when does this story take place?

It takes place in the Wild West after the Civil War, from about

1865 to 1875.

Think about how setting affected Eddie's story. How would a cowboy's life be different in 1975 instead of 1875?

Possible answer: By 1975, the West was no longer "wild" and

wouldn't have offered Eddie the same freedom. He also would have

developed different skills working as a cowboy in 1975.

Tip

Remember that setting means both when and where a story takes place. The time and place in which a story is set can sometimes have an effect on the characters, the plot, and the mood.

Read the following adventure story. Identify the setting and think about how it affects the events of the story.

Day Hike

"Turn here!" said my sister Rosa as our car neared Mount Benton. "This place looks great!" she shrieked as we parked in front of the lodge.

In winter, the lodge was snowbound, but now, in May, the rocky ground was only spotted with ice. The sun sparkled on a lake nestled behind the lodge. The smooth surface of the water reflected the mountain as well as some puffy clouds in the sky. Paul directed Rosa and me into the lodge, where we signed the hikers' log. Paul listed exactly the trail we would take to Lookout Point, noting that we planned to return by about 2:00 P.M.

Rosa had chattered constantly during our entire trip. She was thrilled about this wilderness trek with our favorite uncle. At 24, Paul was nine years older than my sister and 12 years older than I was.

The hike was Paul's idea. He thought that a wilderness experience would help bring us closer.

I was not as excited about this hike as the others. The "great outdoors" makes me kind of nervous. I was willing to go along with Paul and Rosa and hope for the best, though I'd been reading up on survival skills just in case.

As we were about to leave, the park ranger warned, "Storm clouds are forecast. If they move in, you'd better head down. It gets cold very fast."

Paul assured him that we would be careful, and we started up the trail. We quickly shed our jackets. Paul cracked jokes, and Rosa asked me questions about the various plants and animal tracks we saw along the trail. As we climbed, the air thinned. We donned our jackets once again. I got a little dizzy

from altitude sickness, so I rested, drank some water, and felt better.

"Look at nature's spectacle!" Paul exclaimed as he swept his arm across the view.

What I noticed was quickly changing weather. Clouds began obscuring the sights.

"Check out those clouds, Paul," I said.

"We're in the mountains, Ramon!" he answered matter-of-factly. "We're just closer to the clouds."

We kept going. At Lookout Point there wasn't much looking out to do. By then it was a white world of clouds, fog, and now, a blizzard. Suddenly Paul seemed eager to descend. We followed wordlessly until he stopped.

"I can't see," Paul called, sounding more worried and uncertain than I liked. "I've lost the trail."

I felt more confident now, because I recalled advice from my survival book. "We should stay put," I said firmly. "There's no sense roaming around in circles. When we don't return on time, the patrols will search for us."

Paul and Rosa didn't argue. We huddled together, shared trail mix, and talked.

By 4:00, a patrol found us and soon zoomed us down the trail on their snowmobiles.

I guess Uncle Paul got his wish. That hike really did bring the three of us closer together!

Checking Comprehension

1. **What happened that put the three hikers in danger?** [Cause and Effect/Critical]

   The weather changed, becoming cold and snowy. The hikers could no longer see the trail.

   _____

2. **Why was the patrol able to rescue the hikers?** [Drawing Conclusions/Critical]

   Paul had written in the hikers' log what trail they were taking and when they would return.

   The hikers waited on that trail so the patrol would know where to find them.

Practicing Comprehension Skills

3. **Where and when does this story take place?**

   It takes place in the present on a May afternoon on a hiking trail on Mount Benton.

4. **What details from the story tell the setting?**

   Mount Benton, lodge, May, trail, Lookout Point, 2:00 P.M., outdoors

5. **How do you think the story would change if it were set 100 years ago?**

   There might not have been a patrol. There would have been no snowmobiles to rescue the

   characters. They might have been in much more serious danger.

Fill in the circle before the correct answer.

6. **How did the setting affect the mood of the story?**

   ○ The appearance of the lodge made the story feel sad.

   ● The snow falling on the mountain trail made the mood tense.

   ○ Rosa's chatter in the car made the mood joyous.

   ○ The setting did not affect the mood of the story at all.

7. **Which of the following details does not tell more about the mountain setting?**

   ○ the view from Lookout Point   ○ the plants and animals

   ● the car   ○ the trail

Use the chart below to explain how the weather on the trail affected Paul's and Ramon's behavior in different ways. Write your answers on the lines provided.

Effect of weather on Paul's behavior	Effect of weather on Ramon's behavior
8. When the weather became stormy at Lookout Point, Paul's behavior changed from confident to uncertain.	9. Once the weather became so stormy that the characters had to stop, Ramon became more confident, because he had studied survival skills.

Practicing Vocabulary

10. Choose the word from the box that best completes each blank in the paragraph. Write the word on the line.

altitude	donned	hikers'	huddled	log	nature's	obscuring

"From the top of this mountain, you'll see _____nature's_____ finest entertainment!" our guide said as he signed the _____log_____ . "We have great weather, and there's no danger of fog _____obscuring_____ the trail." We all _____donned_____ our hats as protection from the sun. As we started to climb the mountain, another group of hikers began to descend it. We met that group at the halfway point and _____huddled_____ around the _____hikers'_____ leader. She warned us that the high _____altitude_____ might make us feel faint as we continued our climb.

Writing a Narrative Paragraph
Think about an outdoor adventure you have had, or make up one that sounds exciting. On a separate sheet of paper, write a narrative paragraph about the adventure. Make the setting clear by stating when and where the story takes place and by including details that reveal the time and place.

Literary Elements: Theme

Most fiction writers have a "big idea" in mind when they write a story. This "big idea" that the writer wants you to know is called the story's theme. Some themes are directions for living life, such as "Don't sweat the small stuff." Other themes are observations about the world, such as "Appearances can be deceiving." A story's theme is not always stated directly. Sometimes you must figure it out for yourself. Often you can use skills such as drawing conclusions to help you.

Some stories will have one major theme, as well as one or more minor themes. A story about a character who finds a lost puppy, wishes she could keep it, and decides to find the rightful owner might have a major theme of "Honesty is the best policy." A minor theme in the story might be "Don't bite off more than you can chew" when the character has trouble finding the owner because she neglects to ask anyone for help.

Read the following story. As you read, think about the theme the author is trying to communicate.

Molly woke up early. She'd been looking forward to the field trip to the animal shelter ever since Mr. Bernstein had announced it.

"Sometimes," Mr. Bernstein had said, "people do not respect animals as living things. They purchase a little bunny or kitten because they think it's cute. When the animal gets bigger and isn't quite as cuddly or eats too much food, the owner doesn't want it anymore. Then some people just let the animal go, expecting it to be able to fend for itself." Mr. Bernstein hoped that his students would learn to treat animals responsibly.

Put a checkmark next to the sentence that best states the theme of this passage.

_____ Everyone should have a pet.

_____ Teachers who care are the best teachers.

_____ Many animals are abandoned or mistreated.

__✔__ Animals are living beings and should be treated with respect.

What might be a minor theme in this passage?

Possible answer: Think ahead before you get a new pet.

Tip

As you look for the theme of a story, ask yourself, "What is the author's 'big idea'? What is the message that could be applied to other stories or to my own life?"

Secrets of the Swamp

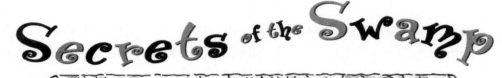

Leotie Johnson knew something most twelve-year-olds did not know: she knew about orchids. Her family grew them and shipped them all over the world.

Leotie's father had taken her on several orchid-finding trips in the swamplands near their Florida home. This time they were looking for a species so rare, some people thought it was extinct. Commonly called the ghost orchid, it bloomed only once a year. The ghost orchid had no leaves at all; its roots wrapped themselves around a tree. The flower was a beautiful papery white, and the side petals tapered into long, fluttery tails.

When they set off, Leotie had been excited at the prospect of finding the ghost orchid, but she was growing irritable from the insects and the intense humidity. As she walked—or rather, sloshed—through the swamp in her snake-proof boots, her legs ached and her head hurt. She felt miserable.

She kept her eyes open for alligators and snakes. These swamps had both. Though her father had taught her how to protect herself if she were ever threatened by an alligator or a poisonous snake, she certainly didn't want to encounter one.

Suddenly her dad signaled her to stop. A few feet ahead, basking on a tree limb, was a four-foot-long snake. Leotie froze. The snake had the brown coloration and thick body of the poisonous cottonmouth.

"Think, Leotie," her father said calmly. "Look at its face."

Leotie forced herself to take a good look at the snake. No dark brown band ran across the side of its head. "It's a water snake," she said, breathing again as the harmless snake slithered down the tree and disappeared under the water.

"Plenty of water snakes die every year because people think they're cottonmouths. They don't take a moment to look. They just react with fear and kill a snake that has a right to be left alone in its native habitat."

As they continued their slow trek through the swamp, Leotie's dad stopped abruptly and said excitedly, "There! The ghost orchid! Isn't it beautiful?"

Leotie stared in awe at the pure white orchid, set against the dark bark. Instinctively, she reached out to touch the white petals, then picked up her camera instead. "Dad, will growers ever be able to cultivate them?" she asked.

"Well, Leotie, I don't know. These plants are endangered, so it's against the law to collect them from the wild. All we can do is take some pictures."

"Even if we can never grow them," Leotie said, "we'll always have the memory of seeing at least one!"

Checking Comprehension

1. **What do you know about Leotie and her family from reading this story?** [Character/Inferential]

   Answers will vary, but may include: They appear to be a close family since Leotie and her father

   enjoy doing things together. They are very concerned about plants and animals. They are

   unwilling to take the endangered plant, so they must respect nature.

2. **Why did Leotie leave the snake alone?** [Drawing Conclusions/Critical]

   Answers may include: Her father helped her realize it was a harmless water snake.

   She did not believe it was right to hurt a snake that was no danger to her.

Practicing Comprehension Skills

3. **What do you think the main theme is in "Secrets of the Swamp"?**

   Possible answer: People should have respect for plants and animals in their native habitats.

4. **Give some details from the story that support the theme you identified.**

   Answers will vary, but may include: Leotie's father doesn't immediately try to kill the snake.

   He encourages Leotie to think before she reacts. Leotie knows better than to touch the orchid,

   which could harm or destroy it. Leotie and her father do not want to take the endangered

   orchid out of its habitat.

5. **Put a checkmark next to the sentence that expresses a minor theme of the story.**

   _____ Cottonmouths and water snakes are often confused.

   _____ Swamps are very humid and uncomfortable.

   __✓__ Sharing common interests can bring parents and children closer together.

   _____ Some orchids are very rare.

6. If Leotie had expressed another minor theme of the story in dialogue, which of the following might she have said?

○ "I'm so hot and tired, Dad. Let's go home."

○ "Snakes make me very nervous."

○ "I wish the day would come when growers can cultivate orchids."

● "Finding the orchid was worth all the trouble. I'm glad we didn't give up."

7. Think about the theme of this story. Could you apply it to other situations or other stories you have read? Explain.

Answers will vary, but students should realize that the theme could be applied to many other

situations. They may give examples such as practicing low-impact camping. They may refer to

novels or nonfiction works about protecting wild animals.

Practicing Vocabulary

Write a word from the box to complete each sentence.

abruptly	basking	cultivate	encounter	humidity	irritable	miserable

8. When the _____humidity_____ is high, there is a lot of moisture in the air.

9. Sweltering summer days can seem _____miserable_____ if you are not used to the heat.

10. Because snakes are cold-blooded, you will often find them _____basking_____ in the sun for warmth.

11. To _____cultivate_____, or raise, orchids requires dedication and knowledge.

12. After three hours of walking, some hikers began to get _____irritable_____ .

13. The group heard a strange noise and _____abruptly_____ stopped to look around.

14. No one wants to _____encounter_____ a dangerous animal when hiking.

MAKING THE Reading AND Writing CONNECTION

Writing a Realistic Story
Think about a theme you would like to express to others. On another sheet of paper, write a realistic story that expresses your theme. Decide whether you want to state the theme in your story or let your readers figure it out for themselves.

Synonyms

Think about these two sentences:

The stubborn dog refused to move an inch.

The determined dog refused to move an inch.

The words *stubborn* and *determined* are synonyms, but each has a slightly different meaning. Careful writers choose just the right word for each situation. **Synonyms** are useful because they are words with similar, though not usually identical, meanings. The right synonym is the one that will best convey the writer's meaning, mood, and tone.

Notice synonyms as you read and think about why the author has chosen them. The synonyms can change the intensity, strength, seriousness, or other characteristics of the people, place, things, and actions being described. They can also help a writer to avoid repeating the same words.

Read the following paragraphs. As you read, notice synonyms that are used and think about how they create specific meanings.

Guide dogs lead blind or visually impaired people on streets, in stores and offices, and other places. These dogs must be strong and healthy, with friendly, calm, and confident personalities. They must also be intelligent, recognizing situations in which they should disobey their handlers.

Imagine that a dog and handler are walking down a sidewalk when suddenly the dog sits down. The person commands the guide dog to go forward, but the dog refuses. When the person insists, the dog still does not obey. Instead it pushes the person away. Why didn't the dog follow the command? A car is backing out of a driveway in front of the pair. Dog and handler are a team—a partnership built on trust and love.

Find a synonym in the second paragraph for the word "obey." Why do you think the author chose not to use "obey" twice?

follow; using a synonym helped the author to avoid repetition

In the last two sentences, how are the meanings of *pair, team,* and *partnership* alike or different?

Possible answer: A *pair* just describes two people or things with

something in common. *Partnership* and *team* suggest working

together.

Tip

Synonyms are words with similar, though not usually identical, meanings. Synonyms can change the strength, seriousness, or other characteristics of the people, places, things, or actions being described.

On Your Own

As you read the following article, look for synonyms and think about how they show the author's exact meaning.

Puppy People

Imagine taking an adorable puppy into your family. You love and train it throughout its first year, knowing that at the end of the year, you'll have to give it up. That's just what puppy raisers do. Puppy raisers raise guide dogs for blind and visually impaired people.

When a potential guide dog puppy is about eight weeks old, it goes to live with a family, sleeping inside the house as a member of the family. It's fine if the family has lots of children or other pets, since a guide dog needs to learn how to behave no matter who or what else is around.

The puppy raiser's responsibility is not to turn the puppy into a guide dog, but to make the dog a well-behaved family member. That means someone must spend quality time with the puppy, including playing with it and patting, grooming, and training it. Training the puppy involves housebreaking it, not permitting it to chew shoes or furniture, and encouraging it to be quiet and calm.

Guide dogs take blind people into a complex world. There are many distractions that could keep the dog from working. The puppy raiser helps the puppy become socialized, or well-behaved in groups, by exposing it to lots of new environments and praising it when it stays calm. Visits to the park, mall, and bus stop are all valuable field trips for the puppy. Since guide dogs may have to travel in cars, buses, planes, ferries, and other vehicles, puppy raisers try to give their puppies useful experiences of this nature too. Many puppy raisers even take their puppies to work with them. Learning to be calm and disciplined in a work situation is important for a guide dog.

Although the puppy raiser is not responsible for training the puppy to be a guide dog, the puppy can be taught simple commands. Daily training sessions teach the dog such easy commands as "Sit," "Down," and "Stay." The one command the puppy is not taught is "Heel," because a guide dog stands in front of the handler, not at the handler's side.

Dogs love to eat, but it is crucial for future guide dogs to learn to dine only from their own bowls. They cannot be distracted by the sight and smells of food while they are working, so there can be no begging at the table and no handouts from strangers.

When the dog is between a year and eighteen months old, the puppy raiser's job is over. The dog is now ready to do its real work. The family members have committed their time, energy, and care. When their work is done, they always feel sad to give up the dog they have loved so much. They can do it only because they know someone else needs the dog more than they do.

Checking Comprehension

[Drawing Conclusions/Critical]

1. Why is it so important for a guide dog to learn to be calm and well-behaved?

    Possible answer: If the dog is noisy or easily distracted, it might not concentrate on its job.

2. Would you like to be a puppy raiser? Why or why not? [Making Judgments/Critical]

    Possible answers: Yes, because I like dogs and this is an important job. No, because I would be

    too sad when the dog had to leave.

Practicing Comprehension Skills

Match the words from the article "Puppy People" on the left with their synonyms on the right by writing the correct letter in the blank space.

____c____ 3. disciplined   a. useful

____d____ 4. eat   b. easy

____a____ 5. valuable   c. well-behaved

____e____ 6. over   d. dine

____b____ 7. simple   e. done

Choose the synonym that best completes the sentence. Write it in the blank.

8. I work with my puppy every day to _____teach_____ her simple commands.

    educate   teach   instruct

9. It's important for a dog to avoid distractions while he is _____working_____ .

    working   employed   active

10. Taking the puppy on a plane provided a valuable _____experience_____ for her.

    occurrence   experience   adventure

11. How is a potential guide dog like and unlike a future guide dog?

    Possible answer: Both a potential guide dog and a future guide dog are not yet guide dogs.

    However, a potential guide dog might be one someday, and a future guide dog will likely be one.

STRATEGY: Understanding Synonyms   113

The author of "Puppy People" uses the word *calm* and its synonym *quiet*. What other words have meanings similar to *calm*? Brainstorm synonyms or find them in a thesaurus. Organize them in the synonym web below so that the most similar words are grouped together in the same spoke.

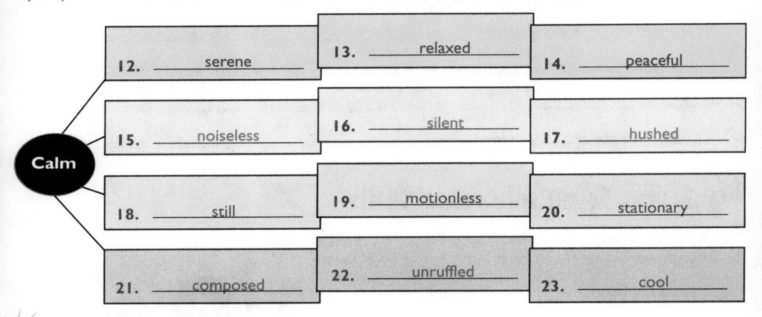

Calm

12. ___serene___   13. ___relaxed___   14. ___peaceful___

15. ___noiseless___   16. ___silent___   17. ___hushed___

18. ___still___   19. ___motionless___   20. ___stationary___

21. ___composed___   22. ___unruffled___   23. ___cool___

Practicing Vocabulary

Choose the word from the box that is a synonym for each word listed below. Write the synonym on the line.

24. ___permitting___ allowing

25. ___crucial___ important

26. ___distractions___ interruptions

27. ___complex___ complicated

28. ___adorable___ charming

29. ___exposing___ showing

30. ___committed___ devoted

adorable

committed

complex

crucial

distractions

exposing

permitting

MAKING THE Reading AND Writing CONNECTION

Writing a Description
Think about a pet you know—your own or someone else's. On another piece of paper, write a paragraph that describes the pet's physical traits and personality. Use a thesaurus to choose the most precise words you can find.

Antonyms

Antonyms are words with opposite meanings, such as *hot* and *cold*, *top* and *bottom*, *wise* and *foolish*. When an author points out contrasts between ideas, characters, settings, or other things, you can expect to find antonyms.

The prefixes *un-*, *in-*, *dis-*, and *im-* can change words into their antonyms. For example, *able* and *unable*, *decisive* and *indecisive*, *trust* and *distrust*, and *possible* and *impossible* are all antonyms.

Pay attention to antonyms in the stories and articles you read. They can help you understand how characters, ideas, or other things are different.

Read the diary entry below. Notice how antonyms give opposite meanings.

Sunday, April 12

Dear Diary,

I just returned from my visit with Jenny. When she moved away, we promised to be best friends forever, but she's changed so much! Jenny and I were once so similar, but this weekend, we seemed very different.

We spent the whole weekend playing quiet games instead of our usual noisy fun. She doesn't even like basketball anymore! When it was time to go home, I left eagerly rather than reluctantly. I felt unhappy at first, but then Mom said it was normal for friendships to change. I'm sure glad Beverly moved into our building last week!

Reread the diary entry to find the antonym for each word listed below. Write the antonym on the line.

different   similar

quiet   noisy

eagerly   reluctantly

unhappy   glad

Choose two antonym pairs from the list above. Change one word so that the pair still shows antonyms. For example, if the antonym pair were *hot/cold*, other antonym pairs could be *hot/cool* or *warm/cold*.

Possible answers: different/alike, silent/noisy, enthusiastically/

reluctantly, sad/glad

Tip

Some negative prefixes, such as *dis-*, *un-*, *in-*, and *im-*, turn base words into their antonyms. When you see a word with a negative prefix, think about its antonym to figure out the meaning.

Read the following story. Notice the contrasts that are pointed out with antonyms.

The Other Mr. Franklin

Denise passed by and waved to her neighbor Mr. Franklin as he packed his car with two big suitcases. "He must be going on a long trip," Denise decided as he waved back. She thought no more about it until two days later, when she noticed that Mr. Franklin's back door was open. "Thieves!" thought Denise, but then she saw Mr. Franklin emerge from the doorway. "It's peculiar," Denise thought, "that he packed so much for such a short trip."

Denise waved to Mr. Franklin, but he didn't wave back, which certainly seemed out of the ordinary. Mr. Franklin had always been cordial. Not waving seemed almost unfriendly.

After school the next day, Denise saw Mr. Franklin working on the new shelves in his garage. His cat was in the front yard. It was very unusual for the cat to be outdoors.

"Hello, Mr. Franklin," Denise said.

"Hello to you, young lady," he replied.

"Is everything okay with you?" asked Denise.

"I'd say that everything's just right!" said Mr. Franklin.

That night Denise told her mother, "Something is wrong with Mr. Franklin."

"Is he ill?" asked her mother.

"He seems healthy, but he's just not himself."

"I've got the answer," offered Denise's brother, Ray. "We read a story about something like this in school. A normal guy went through another dimension, and he started acting really abnormal. Even his dog didn't recognize him."

"I don't think that's the problem," Denise said, "but I do feel as if I'd met another Mr. Franklin."

The next day, Denise saw Mr. Franklin get into his car. "Didn't Mr. Franklin's old car used to be a dull red?" she asked. "That one is so bright."

"Maybe he bought a new car," said Denise's mother. "Sometimes there's a simple explanation for things that seem complicated."

Denise couldn't stop thinking about Mr. Franklin's strange behavior. In her imagination, the neighbor she had known was the genuine Mr. Franklin, and this new neighbor was the false Mr. Franklin. False Mr. Franklin had a hurried gait; genuine Mr. Franklin strolled in a leisurely way. Genuine Mr. Franklin always wore a hat; false Mr. Franklin never wore one. Genuine Mr. Franklin watered his garden in the morning; false Mr. Franklin watered in the evening. Something seemed wrong.

Two weeks later, Mr. Franklin rang the doorbell. He held out a wrapped parcel and said, "This is a gift from my wonderful trip to Africa." Denise knew this was the genuine Mr. Franklin.

"Did you meet my brother?" Mr. Franklin asked. "He house-sat for me while I was gone."

"Ah…are you and your brother identical twins, by any chance?" asked Denise.

"Ever since the day we were born," said Mr. Franklin.

"Then I *did* meet the other Mr. Franklin," Denise said with a smile.

Checking Comprehension

1. Why is Denise concerned about her neighbor? [Cause and Effect/Critical]

   Possible answer: Mr. Franklin doesn't seem to be his usual self. He is doing things he's never

   done before, and he doesn't even seem to know Denise.

2. How do you think Denise feels at the end of the story? [Drawing Conclusions/Critical]

   Possible answer: She feels relieved to know that the real Mr. Franklin was just on a trip and

   embarrassed that she didn't figure out his brother was visiting.

Practicing Comprehension Skills

Read the word in the center circle. Fill in each surrounding circle with
an antonym from the story.

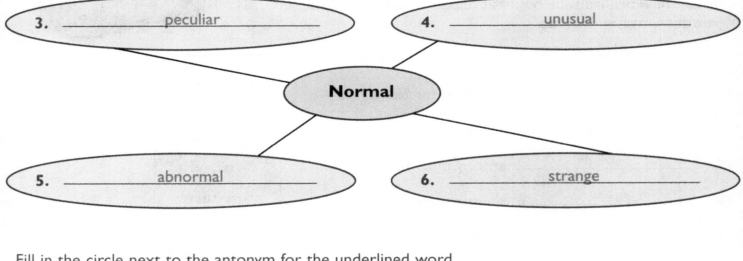

3. _____peculiar_____

4. _____unusual_____

Normal

5. _____abnormal_____

6. _____strange_____

Fill in the circle next to the antonym for the underlined word.

7. The solution to the mystery was <u>simple</u> rather than _____ .

   ○ brief   ○ wide   ● complicated   ○ hopeful

8. Denise thought that Mr. Franklin was <u>healthy</u>, not _____ .

   ○ healthful   ○ genuine   ● ill   ○ ordinary

9. Mr. Franklin's car was <u>bright</u> red instead of _____ red.

   ○ new   ○ shiny   ○ red   ● dull

Complete each analogy with an antonym from the story:

10. *lengthy* is to *brief* as *long* is to _____<u>short</u>_____ .

    edge   endless   short

11. *Often* is to *rarely* as *always* is to _____<u>never</u>_____ .

    generally   never   usually

12. *Error* is to *correction* as *wrong* is to _____<u>right</u>_____ .

    right   incorrect   dull

13. *Worn* is to *fresh* as *old* is to _____<u>new</u>_____ .

    false   real   new

Practicing Vocabulary

Choose the word from the box that best matches each clue.
Write the word on the line.

14. _____<u>leisurely</u>_____ antonym for *rushed*

15. _____<u>shelves</u>_____ synonym for *racks*

16. _____<u>explanation</u>_____ synonym for *reason*

17. _____<u>cordial</u>_____ antonym for *rude*

18. _____<u>thieves</u>_____ synonym for *robbers*

19. _____<u>peculiar</u>_____ antonym for *common*

20. _____<u>parcel</u>_____ synonym for *package*

cordial
explanation
leisurely
parcel
peculiar
shelves
thieves

MAKING THE Reading AND Writing CONNECTION

Writing a Contrast Essay
Use another piece of paper to write about two people, animals, places, or things that are opposites in some ways. Use antonyms to point out differences.

Using Figurative Language

We call expressions that can't be understood from the usual, everyday definitions of their words **figurative language**. Writers often use such expressions to give a clearer picture of what they mean. There are several types of figurative language.

Type of Language	Definition	Example
simile	a comparison of unlike things using words such as *like* or *as*	Young Hercules wrestled *like a lion cub.*
metaphor	a comparison of unlike things without any words of comparison	With his *muscles of iron* Hercules defeated each enemy.
idiom	a phrase that cannot be understood using ordinary definitions	He refused to *back down* from his enemies.
personification	giving human characteristics to animals or things	The golden apples *winked* in the sunlight.
hyperbole	an exaggeration that is used for emphasis	Hercules was *so hungry he could eat a horse.*

Read the following Greek myth. Notice how descriptive expressions help create a picture.

Hera, the queen of the gods, was jealous of the mighty Hercules. She forced Hercules to serve a wicked king. To win his freedom, Hercules had to perform 12 difficult tasks called *labors*.

Task eleven was for Hercules to collect some golden apples as bright as the sun. Near the apple orchard, Hercules found Atlas, a giant who supported the heavy sky on his shoulders. "I'll get the apples for you," Atlas said, "but you must hold up the sky."

Hercules suspected that Atlas had a trick up his sleeve. When Atlas had fetched the apples, Hercules said, "Take the sky back for a moment while I make a cushion for my shoulder." As Atlas took back the sky, Hercules picked up the apples and ran away at lightning speed.

In the passage above, find examples of the following types of figurative language and write them on the lines provided.

Simile: _apples as bright as the sun_

Idiom: _had a trick up his sleeve_

Hyperbole: _ran away at lightning speed_

Tip

As you read, pay attention to figurative language. Think about why the author chose to use a certain expression. Try to form a mental picture of the person or thing being described.

Read the following story. Look for figurative language the author uses. Use the description to form a picture in your mind.

The Labors of Stacy

by Norma Johnston

"Playing Hercules in *The Labors of Hercules* will be Stewart Potter," Mrs. Minter announced, "and the narrator, Athene, will be Roxie Grant."

Stacy ducked her head as waves of disappointment crashed over her. She didn't even get a part! "It's no big deal," she told herself—but the play, the culmination of the annual sixth-grade Greek and Roman festival, *was* a big deal. When the bell sounded, everyone else in her language arts class stampeded for the door.

Mrs. Minter sat down next to Stacy. "I know you're disappointed," she said gently, "but I really need you for something more important: props manager. You can ask other students to assist you— Greg's already volunteered."

Stacy swallowed hard. "I'll do the best I can, I promise."

To Stacy's surprise, "running props" was fun. With gold paint, Stacy and Greg transformed garbage pail lids into shields. They covered football and bicycle helmets with gold and silver foil. Best of all, Stacy and Greg made enormous mythological monsters out of craft paper and mounted them on poles. The monsters grimaced and smirked as they swooped around the stage.

When she wasn't making props, Stacy attended rehearsals. Stewart didn't know his lines, and Stacy prompted him so often she knew them by heart.

By the day of the play, everyone had the jitters. At the dress rehearsal, watching Stewart clowning around as usual, Mrs. Minter looked as grave as a judge.

"Stewart, watch that pole!" she said sharply— seconds before Stewart tripped. The cast stared in horror as Stewart lay groaning on the stage.

"I need to help Stewart," Mrs. Minter announced succinctly. She suspended the rehearsal by saying, "I'll see the rest of you at six."

By six o'clock, neither Stewart nor Mrs. Minter was in the classroom. Everyone fell silent when Mrs. Minter walked in alone. "Stewart won't be able to perform tonight," she said.

"What about our play?" someone blurted. "No one else knows Hercules' lines."

"Stacy does," Greg said placidly.

"A girl playing Hercules?" Roxie drawled.

"Why not?" Greg inquired. "Stacy knows the play inside out."

"Will you do it, Stacy?" Mrs. Minter asked.

Stacy nodded weakly.

After donning her costume, Stacy hardly recognized herself inside Hercules' beard and helmet. Once she was out on the stage, the play claimed her completely. When she pulled off her artificial beard during curtain call, everybody gasped. Applause and cheers rained on her.

Stacy changed and was walking outside to meet her parents when a voice said, "Hey, you were good!" She jumped. It was Stewart, on crutches.

"Thanks," said Stacy dryly. "What are you doing here?"

"Wild horses couldn't drag me away— not even the ones Hercules tamed." He gave her a smile and a wink; then he was gone. Stacy rolled her eyes and ran toward her waiting parents.

Checking Comprehension

1. Which character takes the school play more seriously, Stacy or Stewart? Explain your answer. [Comparing and Contrasting/Critical]

   Stacy takes the play more seriously. She works hard, whether making props or helping Stewart

   memorize his lines. Stewart doesn't learn his part and clowns around at rehearsals.

2. How does Stewart's injury affect Stacy's contribution to the play? [Cause and Effect/Critical]

   Stacy is called on to take over the part of Hercules. She not only gets to be in the play as she

   had hoped, but she also performs the starring role.

Practicing Comprehension Skills

Fill in the circle that names the type of figurative language shown by the words in italics.

3. Stacy knows the play *by heart*.

   ● idiom   ○ hyperbole   ○ metaphor   ○ simile

4. Stacy *hardly recognized herself* inside Hercules' beard and helmet.

   ○ personification   ○ idiom   ○ metaphor   ● hyperbole

5. Fill in the circle next to the example of personification.

   ○ Stacy ducked her head.

   ○ Stacy and Greg transformed garbage pail lids into shields.

   ○ Everyone else in her language arts class stampeded for the door.

   ● The monsters grimaced and smirked as they swooped around the stage.

Identify the types of figurative language in the following sentences and tell what each expression means.

6. "Stacy knows the play inside out." "Knows the play inside out" is an idiom. It means that

   Stacy knows everything there is to know about the play.

7. "Wild horses couldn't drag me away."

   "Wild horses couldn't drag me away" is hyperbole. It means that nothing could have

   prevented him from being there.

Look at the following sentences. On the blank line, write an **M** if the sentence is an example of a metaphor and an **S** if the sentence is an example of a simile. Circle the things the simile or metaphor is comparing. The first example has been completed for you.

8. __M__ (Waves) of (disappointment) crashed over her.

9. __S__ Mrs. Minter looked as (grave) as a (judge).

10. __M__ (Applause and cheers) (rained) on her.

11. __M__ (Everyone in class) (stampeded) for the door.

Practicing Vocabulary

Choose a word from the box that best replaces the underlined word or words. Write the word on the left.

culmination	grave	grimaced	placidly	stampeded	succinctly	suspended

12. _____stampeded_____ When the tickets went on sale, the fans <u>rushed to</u> the box office.

13. _____culmination_____ The <u>highest point</u> of weeks of rehearsing came when the audience stood and cheered.

14. _____grimaced_____ Stacy <u>frowned</u> at the thought of Stewart's injury.

15. _____placidly_____ Although everyone else seemed worried, the director spoke <u>calmly</u>.

16. _____succinctly_____ The critic's short review <u>briefly</u> summarized the performance.

17. _____grave_____ The teacher looked <u>serious and concerned</u> as she announced the problem.

18. _____suspended_____ After the blizzard, school was <u>temporarily closed</u> for two days.

Making the Reading and Writing Connection

Writing a Descriptive Paragraph
On another sheet of paper, write a paragraph that describes a time when you performed in public. Perhaps you performed in a play or a recital, competed in a sports event, or made a presentation. To help your readers picture the event and understand your feelings, use at least three examples of figurative language.

Analogies

Do you know what an **analogy** is? It is a comparison. An analogy shows that a relationship between one pair of words is similar to the relationship between another pair. For example, the relationship between *big* and *large* is similar to the relationship between *small* and *tiny* because both pairs are **synonyms**. The comparison can be expressed with words or with dots. The dots stand for the words *is to* and *as*.

big is to large as small is to tiny   **big : large :: small : tiny**

Analogies can show many different relationships in addition to showing synonyms. Some more of those relationships can be found in the chart below.

Opposites	**Cause and Effect**
summer : winter :: hot : cold	ice : slip :: sun : burn
Categories	**Part-to-Whole**
canary : bird :: poodle : dog	branch : tree :: nose : face

Read this paragraph about tarantulas. Look for an analogy.

If you are a mouse, you want to stay out of the way of a tarantula. That's because a tarantula is to a mouse as a fox is to a chicken. A tarantula comes out at night to hunt. Because it has poor vision, a tarantula searches for its victims by touch. When a tarantula finds a tasty meal, it bites its victim and releases a paralyzing venom with its large fangs. A tarantula's bite is not deadly to humans, but it does hurt.

Write a cause-and-effect analogy you found in the paragraph.

A tarantula is to a mouse as a fox is to a chicken.

On the line, write the word that completes the analogy. Then, in each box, identify the kind of analogy you have completed.

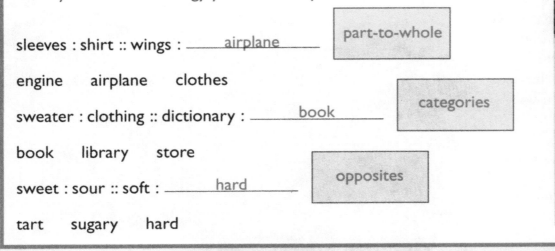

sleeves : shirt :: wings : ___airplane___   [part-to-whole]

engine   airplane   clothes

sweater : clothing :: dictionary : ___book___   [categories]

book   library   store

sweet : sour :: soft : ___hard___   [opposites]

tart   sugary   hard

Tip

To figure out what an analogy means, you must figure out the relationship between the first pair of words. Then compare the second pair using the same relationship.

Read a story about a boy who finds a tarantula. Look for analogies as you read.

Rain Forest Discoveries

Jason peered outside his wooden hut into the darkness of the rain forest's dense growth. The night was as dark as the day had been bright. However, the darkness couldn't dim his happiness at being on vacation in South America with his father.

Jason ran his fingers over the inside of the mosquito netting that surrounded his bed. Then he saw a small, furry, brown spider slowly climbing the wall beside his bed.

His father was snoring in the bed next to him. Jason tiptoed over to the bureau, not wanting to disturb the spider or wake his father. He picked up his father's empty eyeglass case, very slowly moved it above the creature's body, and scooped it up. Now he would have his very own South American pet, a native tarantula.

The next day, Jason and his father were on the river at dawn to see the macaws at the clay bank. Hundreds of these large parrots with blue, green, yellow, and red feathers clung to the clay bank, and Jason watched them with fascination. They flew about and shrieked loudly when provoked. The sight was spectacular, and it was lunchtime before they returned to the hut. Jason immediately checked inside the eyeglass box, but it was empty!

He looked everywhere in the room, in the shower next door, and on the porch outside.

"What are you looking for?" Jason's father asked.

"Um, well," Jason hedged. He was not sure his father would approve of his new acquisition. His father treasured nature the way Jason treasured his coin collection.

"A tarantula, perhaps?" Jason's dad pointed to the spider crawling on the rafter above.

Jason reached up to touch it, but his dad stopped him. "I wouldn't grab that if I were you!" he said. "If that spider gets frightened, it might give you a nasty bite."

"My friend Alex has a tarantula that doesn't bite."

"Alex's tarantula is probably tame. This spider lives in the jungle."

"You mean I can't take it home with me?"

"Think about it. Is it better off here in the rain forest, or locked up in your bedroom?"

Jason thought about his room back home and gazed out at the forest. His father's earnestness convinced him. He said, "I guess I was being thoughtless. To a tarantula, our house would be the same as a prison is to a person."

"Good thinking, Jason," his dad said.

Jason gently placed a piece of cardboard under the spider and ushered it to the safety of a large leaf on the edge of the forest. The spider slowly walked to freedom.

Checking Comprehension

1. Why does Jason agree to let the tarantula go? [Drawing Conclusions/Critical]

   He realizes it would be thoughtless to take the spider out of its environment.

2. Why do you think Jason wanted to keep the tarantula as a pet? [Making Inferences/Critical]

   Possible answer: They are fun to watch, and they are unusual.

Practicing Comprehension Skills

Read the incomplete analogies below. On the line, write the word that completes the analogy. Then, in each box, identify the kind of analogy you have completed: synonyms, categories, opposites, cause and effect, or part-to-whole.

3. empty : full :: big : _____small_____

   | opposites |

   container   enormous   small

4. pine forest : North America :: _____rain forest_____ : South America

   | part-to-whole |

   wood   macaws   rain forest

5. macaw : parrot :: collie : _____dog_____

   | categories |

   dog   insect   doghouse

6. tarantula : bite :: bee: _____sting_____

   | cause and effect |

   eat   sting   venom

7. remember: _____recall_____ :: bother : disturb

   | synonyms |

   recall   sameness   forget

8. dawn : sun :: _____evening_____ : moon

   | cause and effect |

   morning   evening   clock

9. Finish this analogy from "Rain Forest Discoveries." Then explain what it means.

house : _____tarantula_____ :: prison : person

A tarantula isn't free in a house and a person isn't free in a prison.

Express the following sentences from "Rain Forest Discoveries" as analogies.

10. The night was as dark as the day had been bright.

night : dark :: day : bright

11. His father treasured nature the way Jason treasured his coin collection.

his father : nature :: Jason : coin collection

Practicing Vocabulary

Use the words in the box to fill in the blank in each sentence.

acquisition	earnestness	fascination	happiness	hedged	provoked	ushered

12. Jason _____ushered_____ the spider to its freedom.

13. He wondered if his father would like his new _____acquisition_____ , the tarantula.

14. Because he didn't know how to answer his dad, Jason _____hedged_____ his reply.

15. They watched in _____fascination_____ as the macaws flapped their bright wings.

16. Jason took coin collecting seriously, and his father treated the subject of nature with the same _____earnestness_____ .

17. Jason felt intense _____happiness_____ when he learned he was going on the trip.

18. When the macaws shrieked, you knew something must have _____provoked_____ them.

Writing a Description
On another sheet of paper, write a paragraph that describes something in nature. In your description, make several comparisons. When you finish, write one of the comparisons as an analogy.

Connotation and Denotation

Imagine that you are about to take a test that is described as *difficult*. You might think to yourself that the test is very hard. Now imagine that the same test is described as *challenging*. Perhaps to you a *challenging* test is an interesting one that brings out your best abilities. Although *difficult* and *challenging* mean nearly the same thing, they suggest different ideas.

We call a dictionary meaning of a word its **denotation**. We call the ideas or feelings you may associate with that word its **connotation**. While the denotation of a word will be the same for everyone, its connotation can change.

Connotations can be **positive** (thinking or feeling that something is good) or **negative** (thinking or feeling that something is bad). Context clues can tell you whether an author meant for a word to have positive or negative connotations. Connotations can also change according to a reader's experiences. In the example above, *difficult* has a negative connotation, while *challenging* has a positive one.

As you read the following passage, think about how word connotations affect the message.

Tina and Ana needed to perform volunteer work as part of a project. Because both girls had good grades in math, they decided to tutor young children in the neighborhood. Tina wrote this notice.

Tutoring by Tina and Ana
Do your children need more practice with math skills? We can help most school kids do well. At the end of each meeting, we will test your child's progress.

"I have a few changes to suggest," Ana said. After she changed some words, the notice read:

> Do your children need practice with math skills? We can help most students excel. At the end of each meeting, we will evaluate your child's work.

Tip

While the denotation of a word can be found in a dictionary, a word's connotation cannot. A connotation is more personal and can be influenced by your own experience.

Read each of the following sentences. Underline the words in parentheses that have the more positive connotation.

We can help most (school kids, <u>students</u>) (do well, <u>excel</u>).

At the end of each meeting, we will (<u>evaluate</u>, test) your child's (<u>progress</u>, work).

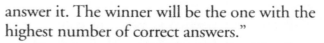

On Your Own Read the following story. As you read, think about the connotation and denotation of some of the words.

The Quiz Show

It was a dismal, rainy Saturday. Tami, Amy, Van, and Diego had already flipped through all the TV channels. They couldn't find anything worth watching.

"Let's play dominos," Van suggested.

"I have another idea," Diego said. "Let's play a game. We all like quiz shows. Why don't we make one up?"

"Good idea, Diego," Tami said. "Should we just make up some trivia questions?"

"I know!" Amy said. "We've been studying connotation and denotation in language arts class. Let's call our game 'What's the Difference?' The questions can be based on words that mean practically the same thing but bring different pictures to people's minds."

"Like what?" asked Diego. "Do you mean words like *heroes* and *heroines*?"

"No, heroes and heroines are really the same thing—you just use one word for males and the other for females. I mean words like *solos* and *performances*. They both mean some type of public presentation, but would you rather make solos or performances?"

"Performances," Diego replied promptly.

"That's because when I say *solos*, you think of performing by yourself with lots of people watching. *Performances* don't sound as pressured," Amy continued.

"I get it," said Tami. "I'll be the moderator, and you three can be the contestants. I'll ask a question, and the first one to knock on the table gets to answer it. The winner will be the one with the highest number of correct answers."

Everyone agreed to Tami's rules. Her first question was, "What's the difference between the words *gale* and *breeze*?"

Van knocked first. He said that both words describe how air can move, but that *breeze* has connotations of a gentle, pleasant wind, and *gale* has connotations of a strong, more unpleasant wind.

By 1:00, the score was exactly even. Amy, Van, and Diego all knew the connotations and denotations of words like *unusual* and *extraordinary*, *frigid* and *chilly*, and *nosy* and *inquisitive*. They also knew the differences between *aroma* and *odor*, *walk* and *strut*, *home* and *hut*, *oration* and *speech*, and *restaurant* and *diner*.

"Speaking of diners, I'm getting hungry," Amy said. "Look! It stopped raining. Let's go out and get something to eat."

"What is the difference between a hamburger and chopped steak?" asked Diego as they strolled toward the street—or was it a boulevard?

Checking Comprehension

1. Why did the four friends make up a quiz show? [Cause and Effect/Critical]

   It was a dismal, rainy Saturday. They couldn't go outside, and there was nothing to watch on TV.

2. Where do you think the story takes place? Explain your answer. [Setting/Critical]

   It's probably set in the home of one of the four characters, because it's a Saturday and there are

   references to a television and a table.

Practicing Comprehension Skills

Read each pair of words. Describe how their denotations are similar. Explain what their connotations suggest to you.

3. chilly/frigid

   Possible answer: Both refer to the cold. *Chilly* suggests a slightly cool feeling. *Frigid* gives the

   image of a miserable, unbearable kind of cold.

4. restaurant/diner

   Possible answer: Both are places to eat. A restaurant sounds large and formal. A diner sounds

   smaller and less expensive.

5. oration/speech

   Possible answer: Both are oral presentations. A speech can be of any length and on any

   subject. An oration suggests a longer, more formal presentation.

Read each of the following sentences. Then underline the word in parentheses that has the more positive connotation.

6. When the teacher finished his speech, the (nosy, inquisitive) student had many questions.

7. From the open restaurant door, the four friends could smell the wonderful (odor, aroma) of pizza.

8. Welcome to my cozy (home, hut).

Read the italicized words below each sentence. Then, on the line, rewrite each group in order from the least strong to the strongest degree of meaning. The first example has been done for you.

9. It was too ___cool, chilly, frigid___ outside to ride bikes.
    chilly   frigid   cool

10. They could not take a walk because it was ___sprinkling, raining, pouring___ .
    raining   sprinkling   pouring

11. The weather was ___strange, extraordinary, unbelievable___ for that time of year.
    strange   unbelievable   extraordinary

12. It was ___possible, likely, probable___ that the rain would stop soon.
    probable   likely   possible

Practicing Vocabulary

Write the word from the box that belongs with each group.

aroma	contestants	dismal	heroes	moderator	oration	solos

13. champions, winners, ___heroes___

14. participants, players, ___contestants___

15. single parts, perfomances, ___solos___

16. fragrance, scent, ___aroma___

17. judge, referee, ___moderator___

18. gloomy, dreary, ___dismal___

19. speech, lecture, ___oration___

Writing a Descriptive Paragraph
On another sheet of paper, write a paragraph describing an indoor game or sport you enjoy playing. When you have finished, go back and circle each word that has a positive connotation for you. Underline each word that has a negative connotation.

Using a Map

Different features on a map are there to make the map easier for you to use. One standard feature found on most maps is a map **key**. The key lists special symbols, or pictures, and tells what each one stands for. Capitals and major routes are some of the features a key might show. The arrows on a **compass rose** show north, south, east, and west. The **scale** helps you estimate distances by showing a length on the map that is equal to a set number of miles or kilometers.

Not all maps give you the same information. **Road maps** display roads and highways. **Political maps** show boundaries such as state lines or the borders of countries. **Physical maps** show physical features of a land area such as rivers, valleys, and mountains. Other maps have special purposes, such as showing populations or industries.

Read the following paragraph. As you read, look at the map to help you understand what you read.

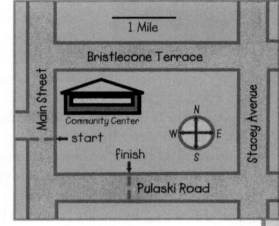

Carlos was thrilled. Today was the day of the race, and after training hard for weeks, he was ready. Excitedly, he traced the route in his mind. From the starting line on Main Street, he would jog north the first mile to Bristlecone Terrace. Then he would turn east at the community center and run two and a half miles. When he reached the corner at Stacey Avenue, he would make another right. Keeping up that pace for another mile and a half, he'd eventually see Pulaski Road. One more turn westward, and he could finally put on the speed. At that point, he'd have only a mile and a half to go until the finish line!

To turn east onto Bristlecone Terrace, which way did Carlos have to turn?

_____ right _____

In what direction is Carlos going when he runs along Stacey Avenue?

_____ south _____

Carlos runs the last mile and a half on what street?

_____ Pulaski Road _____

Tip

Use the scale of miles to estimate distances. For example, if the scale on a map shows that one inch equals 250 miles, measure the number of inches from one point to another. Then multiply the number of inches by 250 to estimate the actual distance in miles.

As you read the following article about Lance Armstrong's win in the 1999 Tour de France, refer to the map to help you visualize the route.

LANCE ARMSTRONG
AGAINST THE ODDS

Cancer can be one of the scariest words in the world. To Texas-born Lance Armstrong, a professional bicycle racer, it could have been a death sentence. At the very least, it could have been the end of his career—but it wasn't.

In 1996, at the age of 24, Lance learned he had a rare form of cancer that had spread to his brain and lungs. Doctors gave him only a 50-50 chance of recovery. After surgery and chemotherapy, Lance began his comeback. He pushed himself in training until he was winning races again. By 1999, he was ready to tackle the Tour de France, a grueling team bicycle race that goes up and down mountains and through hairpin turns in all kinds of weather. Think about bicycling 2,500 miles (about 4,000 kilometers) in 21 days!

The Tour is run in stages, or time periods. Lance won the qualifying race, and then the real race began. The first stage, from Montaigu to Challans, is relatively flat. Lance and his teammates were ahead. By the end of Stage 2, they had lost their lead. They weren't able to regain it again until Stage 8, in Metz.

Stage 9 was the first "mountain stage." It began in Le Grand Bornand, in the Alps. That day's ride was a course of about 132 miles (213.5 kilometers). Lance and his teammates pushed themselves as they had never done

before and enjoyed a six-minute lead as they reached the town of Sestrières.

Stage 9 was the turning point in the race. With a commanding lead, Lance and his team stayed ahead for the next eleven days. After pedaling through the Alps, they cycled through several stages that weren't too precipitous. Then came Stage 15, which began in Saint-Gaudens—the first of two days of climbing up the Pyrénées Mountains. The final stages took the team across western France and along the cobblestones of Paris's main avenue up to the finish line. Lance was the winner: the rider with the lowest time for all the stages overall. In 2000 this remarkable athlete again competed in the Tour de France—and once again, he won!

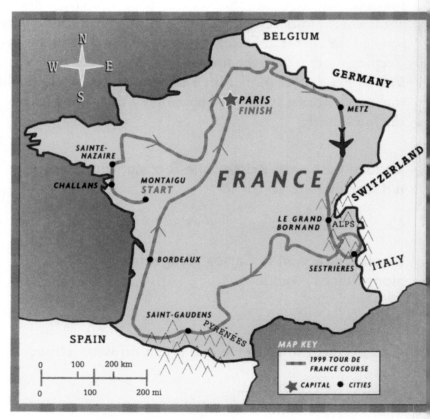

Checking Comprehension

1. Why is this selection entitled "Lance Armstrong: Against the Odds"?

    Lance Armstrong, a professional cyclist, had cancer. Doctors thought he might die. Lance battled

    the cancer, regained his strength, and came back to win the Tour de France.

2. What do you think Lance Armstrong is like as a person? [Making Judgments/Critical]

    Possible answers: Lance Armstrong has to be a physically fit and strong athlete. He showed great

    courage, determination, and will to live.

Practicing Study Skills

Use the map on page 132 to answer each question. Fill in the circle
next to the correct answer.

3. In which general direction did the cyclists ride from Le Grand Bornand
    to Sestrières?

    ○ northeast   ○ northwest   ● southeast   ○ southwest

4. Through which of these cities did the cyclists go between
    Saint-Gaudens and the finish line in Paris?

    ○ Sestrières   ○ Metz   ● Bordeaux   ○ Le Grand Bornand

5. If you could travel in a straight line from Paris to Metz, how far
    would you go?

    ○ about   ● about   ○ about   ○ about
      600 miles   200 miles   5 miles   3,000 miles

6. In what part of France are the Pyrénées Mountains?

    ● south   ○ northwest   ○ northeast   ○ east

7. Number the cities below from 1 to 4 in the order in which
    the 1999 Tour de France riders passed through them.

    __1__ Metz   __3__ Bordeaux   __4__ Paris   __2__ Saint-Gaudens

Using the map on page 132, write your answers to the following.

8. What is the capital of France? How do you know?

   Paris; the capital is indicated with a star

9. Where is the country of Switzerland located in relation to France?

   It borders France to the east.

10. The Pyrénées Mountains lie partly in France and partly in what other country of Europe?

    Spain

Practicing Vocabulary

Write the word from the box that belongs in each group.

commanding	grueling	precipitous	qualifying	relatively	scariest	surgery

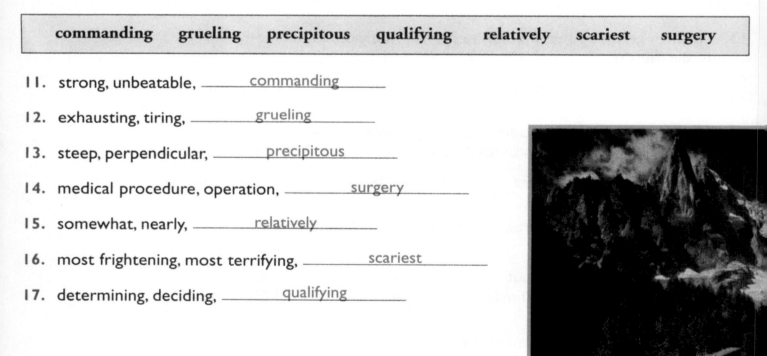

11. strong, unbeatable, _____commanding_____

12. exhausting, tiring, _____grueling_____

13. steep, perpendicular, _____precipitous_____

14. medical procedure, operation, _____surgery_____

15. somewhat, nearly, _____relatively_____

16. most frightening, most terrifying, _____scariest_____

17. determining, deciding, _____qualifying_____

Write a Journal Entry
Imagine that you just won an important race. On a separate sheet of paper, write a journal entry about it. Describe the race, the difficulties you encountered, and the way it felt to win. Include a small map to show the route of your race.

Understanding Charts and Tables

Have you ever traveled on a bus, train, airplane, or ship? All these forms of transportation run according to **schedules**. Most schedules show **departure times**, or the times the vehicle leaves, and **arrival times**, or the times it arrives.

Different schedules are organized in different ways and contain different information. The following schedule is arranged as a **timetable**—a special kind of table that presents information about arrivals and departures. To read a timetable, look at the headings, then read down the columns and across the rows to find the information you need.

Read the advertisement and the accompanying timetable. Notice how the timetable is set up. Use the advertisement and timetable to answer the following questions.

CRANBERRY POINT EXCURSION TRAIN
Daily Schedule**

Read down	Departures		
Cranberry Center	9:00 A.M.	1:00 P.M.	5:00 P.M.
Old Stone Bridge	9:30 A.M.	1:30 P.M.	5:30 P.M.
Cranberry Bay	10:30 A.M.	2:30 P.M.	6:30 P.M.
Cranberry Village*	11:45 A.M.	3:45 P.M.	7:45 P.M.

* The return to Cranberry Center takes 30 minutes

**Daily April–September; Saturdays, Sundays, & Holidays only, March & October; closed November–February

CRANBERRY POINT RAILROAD
Take a Scenic Journey Back in Time

Your family will enjoy a leisurely ride along the ocean peninsula to Cranberry Point. You'll have plenty of time to explore at stops in historic Cranberry Village, beautiful Cranberry Bay, and the unique Old Stone Bridge. Come ride with us!

Three departures daily from Edgar Station at Cranberry Center.

When are the "three departures daily" that are mentioned in the advertisement?

9 A.M., 1 P.M., and 5 P.M.

How much time is there between the departure at Cranberry Bay and the departure at Cranberry Village?

1 hour and 15 minutes

If you leave Cranberry Village at 7:45 P.M., what time will you arrive back at Cranberry Center?

The train will arrive at Cranberry Center in 30 minutes, or at

8:15 P.M.

Tip

All timetables are different, so look carefully to figure out departure and arrival times. Look for any notes and for symbols and the key that explains them.

On Your Own

As you read the passage, look at the timetable to find the information that is mentioned.

A Day at WESTORIA

"I vote for Dinosaur Park!" said Rob, reading the poster at the bus terminal. "I could stay there all day long." He was visiting his aunt, uncle, and cousin for the weekend, and the family had decided to sightsee at Westoria.

"It's essential that I see the crafts market," said Aunt Wilma.

"Attraction Number 5, Mystery Mine—that's where I want to go. I love mysteries!" Ellen said.

"I heard that the Museum of Rocks and Minerals is a real gem," said Uncle Otto jokingly. "But seriously, we need to look carefully at the bus schedule. We have to be realistic about how many attractions we can visit in one day if we plan to spend much time at each one."

"I'm sure that if we approach this creatively, we can figure something out to please each of us," said Aunt Wilma. Hastily, she added, "I see that Crafts Marketplace is the first stop. It's only half past eight now. We can take the nine o'clock bus."

"If I stay on that bus I'll be at Dinosaur Park in two hours," Rob said, studying the timetable.

"Each of us seems to have a different attraction in mind," said Uncle Otto. "What should we do?"

"How about if we split up?" suggested Ellen. "Dad and I can go to the museum and the mine. Mom and Rob can see the crafts and dinosaurs."

"That's a good compromise," said Uncle Otto as the others nodded agreeably. "At 4:45," he added, "we'll meet at Attraction Number 3 to soak our weary feet."

Welcome To WESTORIA
Sightseeing Bus Route

1 Crafts Marketplace
2 Museum of Rocks & Minerals
3 Whirlpools
4 Dinosaur Park
5 Mystery Mine

$4.95 per ticket.
One ticket buys as many trips as you want!

Read Down To Attractions	Westoria Sightseeing Bus Timetable			
Terminal	9:00 A.M.	10:30 A.M.	12:00 P.M.	1:00 P.M.+
1 Crafts Marketplace	9:30 A.M.	11:00	12:30	1:30+
2 Museum of Rocks & Minerals	10:00	11:30	1:00	2:00+
3 Whirlpools	10:15	11:45	1:15	2:15+
4 Dinosaur Park	11:00	12:30 P.M.	2:00	3:00+
5 Mystery Mine	11:30	1:00	2:30	3:30+
To Terminal				
5 Mystery Mine	11:45 A.M.	1:30 P.M.	3:30 P.M.	4:30 P.M.+
4 Dinosaur Park	12:15 P.M.	2:00	4:00	5:00+
3 Whirlpools	1:00	2:45	4:45	5:45+
2 Museum of Rocks & Minerals	1:15	3:00	5:00	6:00+
1 Crafts Marketplace	1:45	3:30	5:30	6:30+
Terminal	2:15	4:00	6:00	7:00+
+ Saturdays and Sundays Only				

Checking Comprehension

1. What problem is the family trying to solve? [Plot/Inferential]

   They can't spend a lot of time at all the attractions on the bus route, and each wants to see a

   diffferent attraction.

2. Do you agree that the family's solution is the best one? [Making Judgments/Critical]

   Answers will vary. The family's compromise is to have each pair see two sites before they meet

   at a third. Students who disagree may offer an alternative solution so that the family can stay

   together; by timing the bus departures, for example, they can visit four out of the five attractions.

Practicing Study Skills

Refer to the passage and the table to fill in the circle before the right answer.

3. The bus that leaves the Terminal at noon arrives in Dinosaur Park at 2:00 P.M.
   When does the next bus stop at that attraction?

   ● one hour later   ○ two hours later   ○ six hours later   ○ half an hour later

4. At what time should Ellen and Uncle Otto leave the Museum of Rocks
   and Minerals to reach Attraction 5 at one in the afternoon?

   ○ 9:25 A.M.   ○ 9:30 A.M.   ● 11:30 A.M.   ○ 12:30 P.M.

5. What is the latest bus that Ellen and Uncle Otto can take from the Mystery
   Mine to reach the Whirlpools by the agreed-upon time of 4:45?

   ● 3:30 P.M.   ○ 2:30 P.M.   ○ 3:00 P.M.   ○ 4:00 P.M.

Refer to the passage and the tables to write the answers to these questions.

6. Rob and Aunt Wilma finish their tour of the Crafts Marketplace in two hours.
   Do they have time for lunch before boarding the bus to Dinosaur Park?
   Explain your answer.

   Yes, they arrived at Crafts Marketplace around 9:30, so it's now 11:30. The next bus to

   Dinosaur Park doesn't leave till 12:30, so they have an hour for lunch.

7. How would the family have to change their plans if they visited Westoria on a weekday?

   On weekdays, the last bus leaves the Whirlpools at 4:45 P.M. They would have to meet there

   earlier than 4:45 in order to spend any time there.

8. The family reached the whirlpools at 4:45. How much time did they have to spend there? Explain your answer.

They have one hour until the train leaves for the terminal at 5:45.

9. Complete the chart to show how the family could have visited four attractions in one day. In the last column, write the amount of time spent at each attraction.

Attraction	Arrive	Depart	Time Spent
1. Crafts Marketplace	9:30 A.M.	11:00	1 1/2 hours
2. Museum of R & M	11:30	1:00 P.M.	1 1/2 hours
3. Whirlpools	1:15	2:15	1 hour
4. Dinosaur Park	3:00	5:00	2 hours

Practicing Vocabulary

Choose the word from the box that best completes each analogy. Write the word on the line.

10. unwanted : necessary :: useless : _____essential_____

11. crawl : slowly :: run : _____hastily_____

12. frown : unhappily :: smile : _____agreeably_____

13. nap : sleep :: tired : _____weary_____

14. train : station :: bus : _____terminal_____

15. paint : artistically :: think : _____creatively_____

16. selfish : argue :: generous : _____compromise_____

agreeably

compromise

creatively

essential

hastily

terminal

weary

Writing a Story
On another piece of paper, write a story in which transportation plays an important part. Create a table that will help readers keep track of the routes and times mentioned in your story.

Using Graphs

A **graph** gives you information as a picture. Writers often use graphs to make information in articles clearer. You are likely to find graphs as you read newspapers, magazines, and advertisements. Your science, math, and social studies books often use graphs, too.

Sometimes a graph's information appears in the form of a line or lines. A **line graph** can help you understand how something has changed over a period of time. Pay attention to the labels on the **horizontal** axis, or line at the bottom, and the **vertical** axis, or line at the left. They tell you what information is being presented.

Read this article on the weather pattern known as La Niña. Notice how the line graph helps you see how La Niña affects weather far away.

La Niña is part of the cycle of changing ocean temperatures known as El Niño. In a "La Niña" year, the average sea temperature in the central Pacific Ocean drops at least half a degree Celsius for six months or more. At the same time, winds from the west are quite strong. La Niña occurs every four to ten years.

La Niña affects weather in America. Winter weather in a "La Niña" year is usually cooler than usual in the northeast. In much of the southern U.S., however, the weather is warmer and drier.

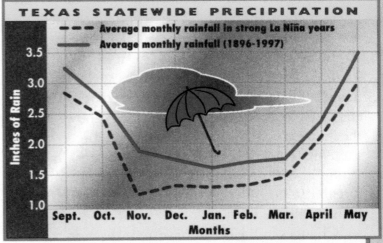

The graph above compares average rainfall in Texas overall with rainfall during strong "La Niña" years. Averages for each month from September through May are given for the period from 1896-1997.

Look at the graph. Answer the questions on the lines.

During the time period from 1896-1997, was there more or less rain in Texas during strong "La Niña" years? Explain your answer.

Less rain. The line for average monthly rainfall in La Niña years

is below the one showing average rainfall overall.

Look at the amount of rain in an average month of May in Texas compared to the amount of rain in a strong "La Niña" year. About how much less rainfall than the average can Texans expect in May of a strong "La Niña" year?

about half an inch

Tip

When you read a line graph, the vertical axis and the horizontal axis will be labeled with information. Pay attention to these labels to know what information the graph presents.

Read the article about El Niño. Notice that the graph provides information that supports certain ideas in the article.

What Is El Niño?

For centuries the sailors of Peru noticed something that happened each December. The normally cool water along the coast was replaced by a warmer ocean current. Fish were harder to find in this part of the Pacific Ocean. The sailors called this phenomenon "El Niño." The period when these ocean waters were colder is called "La Niña."

In most years, the warming from El Niño is small. It lasts for only a few months and is confined to a narrow strip of ocean along the coast of Peru and Ecuador. Every four to seven years, however, the increase is pronounced. Near the equator, the sea temperature may rise by several degrees. In a strong El Niño year, much of the eastern Pacific Ocean can heat up. A strong El Niño can last for many months.

Changes in the ocean have an impact on the atmosphere. Because of this, a powerful El Niño has dramatic effects on the world's weather. Fierce rainstorms soak the coastal regions of Peru and Ecuador, causing floods. In southeast Asia and Australia, however, the same El Niño causes extremely dry weather. In Australia, droughts related to El Niño often cause wildfires.

El Niño also disrupts weather in the United States, especially in winter. People in the Northeast can thank El Niño if it feels like spring in January. To the Southeast and Gulf Coast, the phenomenon will probably bring more rain than normal. A moderate El Niño usually causes dry conditions in the western United States. A strong El Niño, by contrast, brings very wet weather there.

Predictions about El Niño can't be made easily. The same is true of La Niña, which is part of the same weather cycle as El Niño although it has an opposite effect on the world's weather. However, scientists do agree on how to measure El Niño and La Niña. They take the ocean's temperatures along part of the equator. If the temperature averages more than half a degree Celsius (.9 degrees Fahrenheit) above normal for at least six months, it's an El Niño year. If the temperature averages less than half a degree Celsius below normal, it's a La Niña year.

The graph shows changes in the average annual temperatures in Boston, Massachusetts, before and after the start of an El Niño cycle.

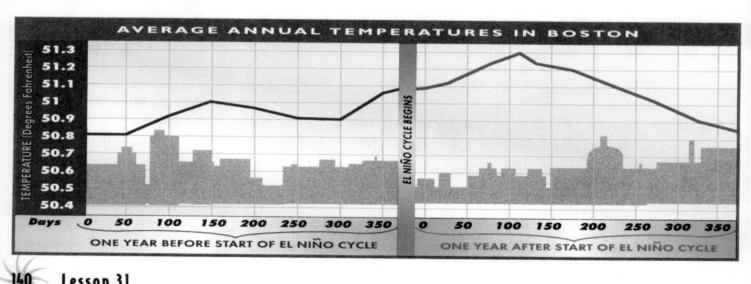

AVERAGE ANNUAL TEMPERATURES IN BOSTON

TEMPERATURE (Degrees Fahrenheit)

51.3 51.2 51.1 51 50.9 50.8 50.7 50.6 50.5 50.4

EL NIÑO CYCLE BEGINS

Days 0 50 100 150 200 250 300 350 | 0 50 100 150 200 250 300 350

ONE YEAR BEFORE START OF EL NIÑO CYCLE | ONE YEAR AFTER START OF EL NIÑO CYCLE

Checking Comprehension

1. **What is the difference between La Niña and El Niño?** [Comparing and Contrasting/Critical]

   El Niño is a period of warmer ocean currents in part of the Pacific Ocean. La Niña is a period

   of cooler ocean currents there. They are part of the same weather cycle, but they have

   opposite effects on the world's weather.

2. **Why might people in the northeastern United States enjoy the effects of a strong El Niño more than people on the West Coast?** [Cause and Effect/Inferential]

   Possible answers: A strong El Niño causes spring-like weather instead of the usually cold winters

   of the Northeast; on the West Coast, however, a strong El Niño causes very wet weather.

Practicing Study Skills

The graph on page 140 shows changes in average annual temperatures in Boston. It includes periods before and after the start of an El Niño cycle. The blue line shows average temperatures for a year before the start of an El Niño cycle. The red line shows average temperatures for a year after the start of an El Niño cycle.

Study the graph. Then fill in the circle next to the correct answer.

3. The graph shows that *following* the start of an El Niño cycle, temperatures in Boston:

   ○ usually stay exactly the same.　　● rise by several tenths of a degree.

   ○ fall by about ten degrees.　　○ rise by about ten degrees.

4. *Before* the start of an El Niño cycle, annual temperatures in Boston:

   ○ average between about 0 and 32 degrees Fahrenheit.　　● average between about 50.8 and 51.1 degrees Fahrenheit.

   ○ average between about 50.4 and 51.3 degrees Fahrenheit.　　○ average between about 0 and 365 degrees Fahrenheit.

5. Averaged over a year, the warmest temperatures in Boston occur:

   ● about 120 days after the start of an El Niño cycle.　　○ about a year after the start of an El Niño cycle.

   ○ about a year before the start of an El Niño cycle.　　○ long after the El Niño cycle has ended.

6. The La Niña cycle has a *cooling* effect on Boston temperatures. We could expect a graph showing average annual temperatures in Boston before and after the start of a La Niña cycle:

● to dip down, instead of up, after the start of the cycle.

○ to be flat, showing no change.

○ to look exactly like the graph for an El Niño cycle.

○ to show temperatures on the horizontal axis and days on the vertical axis.

Look at the graph on page 140. Then write the answer on the line.

7. What information does the horizontal axis provide?

<u>days (or years) before and after the start of an El Niño cycle</u>

8. What information does the vertical axis provide?

<u>temperatures in degrees Fahrenheit</u>

Building Vocabulary

Choose the word from the box that best matches each definition. Write the word on the line.

9. <u>phenomenon</u> an unusual event

10. <u>pronounced</u> clearly marked

11. <u>disrupts</u> disturbs

12. <u>easily</u> simply

13. <u>confined</u> limited

14. <u>probably</u> almost certainly

15. <u>droughts</u> periods of very dry weather

> **confined**
>
> **disrupts**
>
> **droughts**
>
> **easily**
>
> **phenomenon**
>
> **probably**
>
> **pronounced**

MAKING THE Reading AND Writing CONNECTION

Writing a News Story
Write a news story about an unusual weather event or disaster. The event can be real or imaginary. You might describe a heat wave in winter, a flooding rainfall, or a record-breaking drought. Be sure to tell who, what, when, where, and why in your story. Then make a graph to give additional information about the story. Use another sheet of paper for your story and your graph.

Using a Dictionary

When you read, you may come across a word you don't know. You can find the meaning of the word in a **dictionary**. The words a dictionary lists are called *entry words*, and they appear in alphabetical order. *Guide words* at the top of each dictionary page tell you the first and last words that appear on that page.

Following each entry word, you will find the *pronunciation*, or way to say the word, and usually its *part of speech*, such as noun or verb. You will also find one or more *definitions* and sometimes *example sentences* that use the word in context. Many dictionary entries will include an *etymology*, or word history, as well.

Read this dictionary entry for the word *browse*.

guide words	**brown ➤ brutish**
entry word	**browse** (brouz) *verb* 1. to nibble at leaves, twigs, shoots, etc. [Cows like to *browse* in a grassy field.] 2. to look through something in a casual way [I'm going to *browse* in the shops on Main Street.] (probably from the Middle French word *brouts*, plural of *brout*, sprout)

pronunciation

definitions

etymology

example sentence

Which dictionary definition of *browse* is used in this sentence?

I needed to find out more about robots for a science report, so I decided to browse different websites about robots.

definition #2 _____

Fill in the circle before the correct answer or answers.

Look back at the guide words for the definition of *browse*. Which of these words would you be most likely to find on the same dictionary page as browse?

- ● brownie   ○ broom
- ● brush   ○ bucket

According to the dictionary definition, from what language does the word *browse* probably come?

- ○ Old Latin   ● Middle French
- ○ Greek   ○ Old Norse

Tip

To find a word quickly, use the guide words at the top of each dictionary page. Think about alphabetical order to find the guide words your word will fall between. When you find the right page, again use alphabetical order to find your entry word.

Read the following article about robots. Look for words from robot technology that are now familiar terms.

ROBOTS

The word *robot* describes an amazing variety of machines. *Robots* have various skills, sizes, and shapes. They have different levels of intelligence. When people hear the word *robot*, they often think of a human-like creation out of a science fiction movie. In reality, most robots do not look like humans but are machines designed to do specific jobs. Many are just "smart arms." Their only human-like parts are an arm and hand that can perform jobs.

Robots are hardier than humans in many ways. They can go where humans can't go and can do work that is dangerous or repetitive. They don't require air, food, water, or comfortable temperatures. For this reason, they are perfect for work in outer space, under the sea, or in hazardous places on Earth. Robots work tirelessly. They never need a lunch break!

A robot's brain is a computer that can be programmed to perform tasks. Actually, a robot is simply a computer that moves. Sensors collect information from the robot's surroundings and send it to the computer brain. The sensors work like a human's eyes, ears, nose, and skin. One of the commonest types of sensor is a small camera that acts as the robot's eyes.

The "body" of a robot is a mix of machinery, motors, and power sources. Humans can control the "body" in various ways. They might push buttons, tilt joysticks, move a computer mouse, or give verbal orders. The operator's signals sometimes travel through a cable. More often they are sent by remote control using radio waves.

Robots no longer live only in the world of science fiction. Modern robotics has produced all sorts of mechanical workers. They guard museums at night, run errands in hospitals, milk cows, and explore the universe. Many manufacturers have robotized their factories. A lawn equipment company has already invented a turtle-shaped "mobot" that mows grass. Maybe someday your personal "sewbot" will mend your clothes and a "cookbot" will make your meals!

Checking Comprehension

1. Why are robots better suited for certain jobs than humans are? [Main Idea/Inferential]

   Robots can go to dangerous places where humans can't go. Robots work tirelessly and don't

   need air, food, water, or comfortable temperatures.

2. How are a robot's sensors like a human's sensory organs? [Comparing and Contrasting/Critical]

   Like a human's eyes, ears, nose, and skin, a robot's sensors perceive the surrounding

   environment and send signals to its brain/computer.

Practicing Study Skills

Use the dictionary entries to complete the following items.

---

robot ➤ rod

robot (rō´ bät) *noun* **1.** a machine, often imaginary, made to look and work like a human being **2.** any machine that can be programmed to perform and repeat tasks automatically **3.** a person who acts or works automatically, like a machine (from *robota,* meaning *forced labor,* first used in a play by Czech writer Karel Capek)

robotics (rō bä´ tiks) *noun* the science or technology of producing or using robots

robotize (rō´ bə tīz) *verb* **1.** to make something automatic, especially a factory process [The factory owner decided to *robotize* the assembly line.] **2.** to make somebody act in an automated, unemotional way; to turn (a person) into a robot

---

3. What is the difference between *robot, robotics,* and *robotize?* Include their parts of speech in your answer.

   Robot is a noun that means a machine or person that performs tasks automatically.

   Robotics is a noun that means the science of producing or using robots.

   Robotize is a verb. To robotize something means to make it automatic.

Look back at the guide words. Fill in the circles before all the words that answer the question.

4. Which of the following words might appear on the same dictionary page as *robot*?

   ● rock　　　○ roam　　　● robust　　　○ rodent

Fill in the blanks on the lines provided.

5. The word *robot* comes from the term *robota*, which was first used in a Czech

   _____play_____ . It originally meant _____forced labor_____ .The part of the

   dictionary entry that gives this word history is called the _____etymology_____ .

On the lines provided, write an example sentence for each of the three definitions of the word *robot*.

6. Definition #1: <u>Possible answer: My story is about a robot that becomes a famous athlete.</u>

7. Definition #2: <u>Possible answer: A robot performed the repair on the space shuttle.</u>

8. Definition #3: <u>Possible answer: The character in the movie was such a robot—he carried out</u>

   <u>orders without ever questioning them!</u>

Practicing Vocabulary

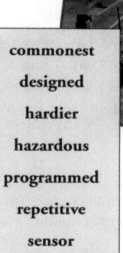

Choose the word from the box that completes each analogy.

9. eye : human :: _____sensor_____ : robot

10. built : assembled :: instructed : _____programmed_____

11. weaker : feebler :: stronger : _____hardier_____

12. safe : secure :: risky : _____hazardous_____

13. unusual : interesting :: _____repetitive_____ : boring

14. houses : built :: machines: _____designed_____

15. biggest : smallest :: rarest: _____commonest_____

> **commonest**
> **designed**
> **hardier**
> **hazardous**
> **programmed**
> **repetitive**
> **sensor**

MAKING THE
Reading
AND
Writing
CONNECTION

Writing a Narrative Paragraph

Choose one of the following words and look it up in a dictionary.

　　power　　program　　sense　　remote　　signal

You will find that the word has more than one meaning. Write a narrative paragraph in which you use two meanings of the word to tell a story.

Using an Encyclopedia

To do research for a report, you might first look in an **encyclopedia**. If you were looking for an article on the Olympic Games in a print encyclopedia, you would look in the volume whose guide letters include the letter O. The **guide words** at the top of each page will name the first and last **entries**, or articles, on the two pages. To use a CD-ROM or on-line encyclopedia, you would type "Olympic Games" into a search box.

If the entry you need is a long one, check its section **headings**. They describe what that section is about. After you read an article, check to see if any **cross-references** are given. Cross-references direct you to other encyclopedia articles about the subject. In a print encyclopedia, cross-references are at the end of an entry and are introduced with the words *See also*. If you come upon a cross-reference with parentheses, the words in parentheses are the title of a section heading—for example, *See also* **Winter Sports (Ice Hockey)**. CD-ROM or on-line encyclopedias have electronic links to cross-references.

Read this excerpt from an encyclopedia article on the Winter Olympics. Pay attention to the section heading and the cross-references.

Winter Olympics — guide words

entry words

Winter Olympics have been held since 1924. While many events make up the Winter Olympic Games, the events fall into only seven categories. These categories are bobsledding, luge, skating, ice hockey, curling, skiing, and biathlon.

section heading

Bobsledding

The first Olympic bobsledding race took place at the first Winter Olympics. The games were held in France in 1924. The first crews were made up of four people. In the 1932 Olympics in the U.S., races for two-person crews were added. Bobsled runs are at least 1,500 meters long (about 1,640 yards). They have 15–20 turns. The first run in the U.S. was built near Lake Placid, New York, for the 1932 Winter Olympics.

See also **Bobsledding (History); Lake Placid, New York.** — cross-references

What section heading is shown in this portion of the encyclopedia entry?

<u>Bobsledding</u>

Which cross-reference is to an article about the site of the first U.S. bobsled run?

<u>Lake Placid, New York</u>

Tip

When you research a topic in an encyclopedia, use the section headings to find the exact information you want. Use cross-references to find more information.

As you read the following encyclopedia article titled "U.S. Olympic Women's Ice Hockey Team," pay attention to the section headings and the cross-references.

United States Olympic Women's Ice Hockey Team is the U.S. entry in a medal sport first played at the 1998 Winter Olympics.

History

For years, women ice hockey players and coaches from teams around the world petitioned the International Olympic Committee to be included in the Winter Olympics. Membership on women's teams climbed steadily upward. The first women's world championship was held in March 1990. Then, in 1992, the International Olympic Committee announced that it would include women's ice hockey as a medal sport. Women ice hockey players first competed in the Olympics in 1998, in Nagano, Japan.

World Championships Established Rivalry

The 1997 Women's World Championships in ice hockey served to qualify teams for the 1998 Olympic Games. The top five countries from that tournament were Canada, the U.S., Finland, China, and Sweden. Japan, as host country, would also compete at Nagano. The Canadian team had beaten the U.S. team in all four world championships since 1990. The U.S. team was runner-up each

time. Team USA knew they would face formidable competition in the 1998 Winter Olympics. They were determined to avoid another defeat by Canada.

Two Pioneers

The first U.S. Olympic Women's Ice Hockey Team included two pioneers in the sport. They were Karyn Bye and team captain Cammi Granato. When she was fourteen, Bye had played ice hockey on a boys' team in Wisconsin. She wore a jersey that read "K. L. Bye." In the 1998 Winter Games, the 26-year-old Bye would play forward and serve as alternate captain. Team captain Granato was already a seasoned pro. She had been voted the U.S.A. Women's Hockey Player of the Year in 1996.

Historic Game 6

A series of wins at Nagano moved Team U.S.A. toward

an expected showdown with the Canadian team. Game 6 was the first gold medal game in the history of women's ice hockey. As expected, the Canadian and American women battled fiercely during the first period of the game. The score stayed at 0–0. In the second period, American forward Gretchen Ulion broke the tie with a goal. Toward the end of the third period, with the score 2–0, the Canadians scored their only goal. With just seconds remaining in the game, Sandra Whyte scored the American team's third and final goal. The final score was U.S. 3, Canada 1.

See also **Winter Olympics; Ice Hockey; Canada (Winter Sports).**

1998 Winter Olympics U.S. Women's Ice Hockey Results			
U.S.	5	China	0
U.S.	7	Sweden	1
U.S.	4	Finland	2
U.S.	10	Japan	0
U.S.	7	Canada	4
U.S.	3	Canada	1

Checking Comprehension

1. Why was winning the 1998 gold medal in ice hockey so important for the U.S. women's ice hockey team? [Drawing Conclusions/Critical]

It was the first time women's ice hockey was part of the Winter Olympics games. The U.S. won

against Canada, the world champions.

2. What factors might have caused the International Olympic Committee to agree to make women's ice hockey an Olympic sport? [Making Judgments/Critical]

Possible answer: They were under pressure from women players and coaches, and there were

already women's world championship games.

Practicing Study Skills

Write your answers to these questions in the blanks.

3. How many section headings does this article contain? __4__

List the section headings on the lines below.

4. History

5. World Championships Established Rivalry

6. Two Pioneers

7. Historic Game 6

8. How many cross-references appear at the end of this article? __3__

Fill in the circle or circles next to the correct answer for each item.

9. Which cross-reference would you look up to find out more about the various events at the Winter Olympics Games?

   ● Winter Olympics   ○ Ice Hockey

   ○ Canada (Winter Sports)   ○ Two Pioneers

10. Look at the table that goes with the article. Which country scored the highest number of goals in a game against the U.S.?

   ○ Japan   ○ Finland   ● Canada   ○ Sweden

11. Which section or sections would you read if you wanted to find out if the U.S. team beat Canada?

- ● the table showing game scores
- ● Historic Game 6
- ○ Two Pioneers
- ○ Canada (Winter Sports)

12. Use the section headings in the article to write a brief summary of the entry "United States Olympic Women's Ice Hockey."

Possible answer: Women ice hockey players first competed in the 1998 Olympics in Nagano,

Japan. The U.S. team was one of six to play in the 1998 Olympics. They faced stiff competition

from Canada, who had won four world championships. The team included two important

players, Karyn Bye and Cammi Granato. Team USA won steadily and beat Canada in Game 6

to win the gold medal.

Practicing Vocabulary

Write a word from the box that belongs with each group.

13. experienced, capable, _____seasoned_____

14. in the direction of, nearer to, _____toward_____

15. requested, asked, _____petitioned_____

16. loss, failure, _____defeat_____

17. council, advisory board, _____committee_____

18. higher, above, _____upward_____

19. difficult, fierce, _____formidable_____

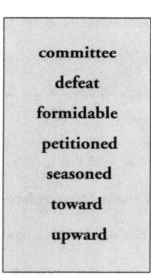

committee

defeat

formidable

petitioned

seasoned

toward

upward

Writing a Summary
Choose a sport to research in an encyclopedia. Use section headings in the article to write a summary of the information in the article. Then describe additional information you could find by using any cross-references. Write your summary on another sheet of paper.

Using a Library Card Catalog/ the Internet

All libraries use systems to organize their books and magazines so that you can find them easily. You've probably used one system, the **card catalog**, many times. Some libraries have a print card catalog. This set of cards lists all the books in the library. It contains three sets of alphabetized cards: title, subject, and author cards. **Title** cards give you the book's title first. **Subject** cards list each nonfiction book by its subject. They give you the subject of the book first. **Author** cards give you the author's name first.

TITLE CARD

006/Pim	Virtual Reality
	Pimentel, Ken.
	Virtual Reality: through the
	new looking glass
	New York, McGraw-Hill, 1995
	438 p. illus.

SUBJECT CARD

006/Pim	VIRTUAL REALITY
	Pimentel, Kim.
	Virtual Reality: through the
	new looking glass
	New York, McGraw-Hill, 1995
	438 p. illus.

AUTHOR CARD

006/Pim	Pimentel, Kim.
	Virtual Reality: through the
	new looking glass
	New York, McGraw-Hill, 1995
	438 p. illus.

If your library uses a computerized catalog system, the search process is similar to using a card catalog. You must first decide whether to search the database by author, title, or subject. Then you type in your selection and look at the choices.

AUTHOR: Jefferis, David
TITLE: Cyber Space: virtual reality and the
    World Wide Web
PUBLISHED: New York, NY: Crabtree Pub., c 1999
    Paging: 32 pp.: ill. Notes: Includes index
CALL NUMBER: J004 JEF—J. Nonfiction—In

How does a catalog card or database lead you to a book on the shelf? If the book is fiction, the card or database will show an **F** or **Fic.** Books of fiction are arranged on the shelves alphabetically by author's last name. If a book is nonfiction, the card catalog or database will show its call number. This **call number,** made up of numbers and letters, appears on the spine of the book. The books are placed on the shelf in order of their call numbers.

Library call numbers are part of the *Dewey Decimal System*. This system classifies nonfiction books into ten main groups shown on the chart below.

Dewey Decimal System			
000-099	General Reference Works	500-599	Pure Science
100-199	Philosophy	600-699	Technology
200-299	Religion and Mythology	700-799	The Arts
300-399	Social Sciences	800-899	Literature
400-499	Language	900-999	General Geography and History

Write *author, title*, or *subject* to tell how you would search for each book in the library.

A novel by Virginia Hamilton _____ author _____

Books about opera _____ subject _____

The book *Computer Games and How to Win Them* _____ title _____

A book about the Grand Canyon _____ subject _____

Use the information you've just learned to help you complete the chart below.

What You Need	Where to look: Subject, Title, or Author	Call Number Section
A book of Greek myths	subject	200-299
A book called *An Introduction to Sculpture*	title	700-799

Today, many students search the **Internet** for information. Online, you can use encyclopedias, atlases, almanacs, and magazines. In addition, thousands of organizations post information on their home pages. To find what you need, your computer has software called a *search engine*. Search engines that are programmed for students and young people are especially useful.

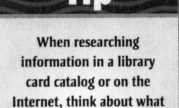

To start an Internet search, type in a keyword to describe what you're looking for. The search engine then finds articles that contain that word. Be careful, though. If your keyword is too broad, you'll get far too many listings that aren't useful. Looking though them all would be a waste of time.

You can refine, or narrow, your search by using a specific keyword or keywords. If you must research Monarch butterflies, for example, don't enter *insects* or *butterflies*. Instead, enter *Monarch butterflies*. Then all the listings will tell about the one species you need to know more about. You can also refine your search by entering more than one keyword. If you need to know where Monarch butterflies migrate, enter *monarch butterflies* and *migration*. Then only information with all those words will be listed. You can also use a phrase within quotation marks, such as "*migrating Monarch butterflies,*" to refine a search.

Read the following paragraph. Think about keywords you could enter in a search engine to find more information on the subjects mentioned.

Video games were created years before you were born, but they have come a long way in a short time. The first video game, *Pong*®, appeared in 1972. It was a very simple game similar to Ping-Pong. The screen was black and white, and the sounds were quite basic. Yet Pong was so successful that it started the video game industry. Nearly any video game you play today can be traced back to the success of Pong. In less than thirty years, we have gone from the simple game of Pong to 3-D virtual reality games that put players in the middle of the action.

Jake wants to learn more about the history of video games. When he used the keywords "video games," he got thousands of responses. How should he refine his search?

Possible answers: "history of video games," "first video games"

What keywords might you use to search the Internet for information about amusement parks that feature virtual reality rides?

Possible answer: "virtual reality" and "amusement parks"

Tip

When researching information in a library card catalog or on the Internet, think about what you already know and what you need to know. Then make your selection and look at your choices.

As you read this article about virtual reality, think about the subject areas you could look up to find out more about some of the ideas that are discussed.

VIRTUAL REALITY: THE LOOK OF THE FUTURE

Although the idea of virtual reality (VR) has been around for a long time, it has only become a common term in recent years. VR is easier to describe than to define. It is an artificial environment for your senses. You can view a VR environment on a computer screen by looking at a 3-D world. You can also have a complete "immersion" in an environment, using such devices as a data glove and a head-mounted display. If you saw the movie *Tron*, you saw "live" actors immersed in a VR environment: they were inside a video game.

Games, however, are only one side to virtual reality. VR has many useful applications. For example, the U.S. government uses VR for many aspects of training. Instead of sending armed forces recruits out on submarines or planes, which is risky and expensive, recruits can be trained in a room. There, trainees participate in a VR program, such as steering a ship or landing a plane on an aircraft carrier. NASA also uses VR to simulate space travel for astronauts in training. Local governments train employees with VR too. Police and firefighters use VR to teach trainees to handle different situations from traffic accidents to fires in high-rise buildings.

Virtual reality also has numerous uses outside the government. It is becoming common for doctors to learn new surgical techniques using VR. The procedure can be introduced with no risk to a real patient. Airline companies can use VR to design new planes and train pilots to fly them. People who study weather use VR to simulate hurricanes, tornadoes, and other weather events so they can better understand them.

In the years ahead, science will depend on VR even more. Engineers will build virtual bridges. Astronomers will tour virtual galaxies. Scientists will look inside a virtual atom. If you want to study art or literature, VR will be there too. VR programs will take you through the great art museums and libraries of the world.

Checking Comprehension

1. Why is virtual reality used in job training? [Summarizing/Critical]

   <u>To put an inexperienced trainee in a "virtual" situation is probably less expensive and less</u>

   <u>dangerous than many real situations.</u>

2. How might virtual reality be important in the future? [Making Predictions/Critical]

   <u>Possible answer: The use of VR could lead to important scientific breakthroughs.</u>

Practicing Study Skills

Read each item. Think about words you might use in a database search by subject to find library books that would provide useful information. Write the words on the line.

3. how engineers use virtual reality in aircraft design <u>aircraft design</u>

4. how filmmakers create special effects with computers <u>special effects</u>

5. which search engines are most useful for kids surfing the Internet <u>children Internet</u>

Use the following card catalog card to answer questions 6-8. Write your answers on the line.

025.04GRA	Online Kids
	Gralla, Preston. Revised Edition
	Online Kids: a young surfer's guide to cyberspace
	NY, John Wiley & Sons, Inc., 1995, 1999
	276 p.

6. What type of card is this? <u>title card</u>

7. When were the two editions of the book published? <u>1995 and 1999</u>

8. Based on its call number, *Online Kids* would be shelved with what category of books in the library? <u>general reference works</u>

Suppose you are planning some Internet searches. Look at each group of keywords below. Circle the most specific keywords in each group.

9. (blue whale migrations)   blue whales   whales and dolphins

10. weather   (tornadoes)   storms

Fill in the circle before the correct answer.

11. Denise wants to write a report about how virtual reality computer software is used in medical schools to help train doctors to perform surgical and other medical procedures. She is using the Internet to find information. Fill in the circle next to the search phrase that would probably bring the best results.

○ Virtual reality computer software   ○ Surgical and medical procedures

● Virtual reality medical education   ○ Computerized training

Practicing Vocabulary

12. Complete the paragraph with words from the box. Write the word on the lines.

applications	becoming	environment	galaxies	immersion	introduced	trainees

Often we think of virtual reality as only a form of entertainment. Increasingly, however, VR is ____becoming____ a useful educational tool. Virtual reality will have many ____applications____ when it comes to training doctors, pilots, and other specialists. Pilot and astronaut ____trainees____ could learn to fly on the ground with VR. After having been ____introduced____ to the basics in this way, they could begin training in the air more safely. Just about any setting or ____environment____ can be created with VR, including a complete ____immersion____ in the artificial experience. So whether you become a submarine commander or an astronaut traveling to distant ____galaxies____, you might get your early training with virtual reality.

Writing a Summary
Using either a library card catalog or the Internet, do some research on the subject of virtual reality to help you brainstorm ideas about how VR could be put to use in a sixth-grade classroom. On a separate piece of paper, write a summary of your ideas.

Level F Glossary

abruptly (ə brupt´ lē) *adverb* suddenly, without warning

acquisition (ak´ wə zish´ ən) *noun* something gained

admiration (ad´ mər ā´ shən) *noun* a feeling of delight and approval for beauty, skill, or other pleasing qualities

adorable (ə dôr´ ə bəl) *adjective* very attractive and likable

agreeably (ə grē´ ə blē) *adverb* in a pleasing or pleasant way

aloof (ə lo͞of´) *adjective* keeping oneself apart or at a distance

alternate (ôl´ tər nit) *noun* a person or thing that takes the place of another if needed; substitute

altitude (al´ tə to͞od) *noun* the height of a thing above Earth's surface or above sea level

antisocial (an´ ti so´ shəl) *adjective* not liking to be with other people

aperture (ap´ ər chər) *noun* opening; gap; hole

appalling (ə pôl´ iŋ) *adjective* shocking or horrifying

appears (ə pirz´) *verb* has the look of being; seems

applications (ap´ li ka´ shənz) *noun* acts of putting something to use

aroma (ə rō´ mə) *noun* a pleasant smell; fragrance

attempts (ə tempts´) *noun* tries or attacks

authentic (ô then´ tik or ä then´ tik) *adjective* genuine; real

ballast (bal´ əst) *noun* heavy material that is carried in a ship, balloon, or vehicle to keep it steady

basking (bask´ iŋ) *verb* staying in a warm, pleasant place

becoming (bē kum´ iŋ) *verb* coming to be

bisected (bi sekt´ əd or bi´ sekt əd) *verb* cut into two parts

brainchild (brān´ chī ld´) *noun* someone's idea or invention

brooded (bro͞od´ əd) *verb* kept thinking in a troubled way

brutal (bro͞ot´ l) *adjective* cruel and without feeling; savage

camaraderie (kä´ mə rä´ dər ē) *noun* friendliness and loyalty among fellow workers

candidate (kan´ di dāt or kan´ di dət) *noun* a person who seeks a political office or an honor

captivated (kap´ tə vāt əd) *verb* attracted; interested

captures (kap´ chərz) *verb* represents or records in lasting form

catapulted (kat´ ə pult əd) *verb* threw with great force

challenging (chal´ ənj iŋ) *adjective* calling for skill or effort

chaotic (kā ät´ ik) *adjective* very confused or disordered

chided (chīd´ əd) *verb* found fault with; blamed

chivalry (shiv´ əl rē) *noun* the qualities that a knight was supposed to have, including courage and politeness

circuit (sʉr´ kət) *noun* a course around an area

circular (sʉr´ kyə lər) *adjective* having the shape of a circle

classic (klas´ ik) *adjective* of the highest quality or rank

comical (käm´ i kəl) *adjective* funny or amusing

commanding (kə mand´ iŋ) *adjective* powerful

committed (kə mit´ əd) *verb* pledged or promised

committee (kə mit´ ē) *noun* a group of people who are chosen to do something

commonest (käm´ ən ist) *adjective* most often seen or heard

complex (käm pleks´ or käm´ pleks) *adjective* made up of parts connected in a way that is hard to understand

composed (kəm pōzd´) *adjective* calm or peaceful

composers (kəm pō´ zərz) *noun* people who compose music

compromise (käm´ prə mīz) *noun* an ending of an argument brought about by each side giving up something

confined (kən fīnd´) *verb* kept within limits

confounds (kən foundz´) *verb* throws into confusion

congestion (kən jes´ chen) *noun* overcrowding; clogging

contestants (kən test´ əntz) *noun* people who take part in a contest

conversion (kən vʉr´ zhən) *noun* the act or process of converting, or changing; change

cordial (kôr´ jəl) *adjective* warm and friendly

counterproductive (kount´ ər prə duk´ tiv) *adjective* producing results opposite to the desired ones

cowering (kou´ ər iŋ) *verb* crouching in fear or shame

creatively (krē āt´ iv lē) *adverb* in an imaginative way

critical (krit´ i kəl) *adjective* important to the outcome of a situation

crucial (kro͞o´ shəl) *adjective* of the greatest importance; needed in order to decide something

culmination (kul´ mə nā´ shən) *noun* the most important phase or stage; peak

cultivate (kul´ ti vāt) *verb* to grow from seeds or other plant parts

defeat (dē fēt´) *noun* failure to win

defender (dē fend´ ər) *noun* someone who acts, speaks, or writes in support of another person

deflate (di flāt´) *verb* to let air or gas out of an object

delay (dē lā´) *noun* the act of putting off to a later time

descend (dē send´) *verb* to move down to a lower place

deserted (dē zʉrt´ əd) *adjective* abandoned; empty of people

designed (dē zind´) *verb* set apart for a certain use

destination (des´ ti nā´ shən) *noun* the place that a person or thing is going to

devoured (dē vourd´) *verb* ate up in a hungry way

disappointment (dis ə point´ ment) *noun* feeling that something wanted, expected, or promised failed to happen

disapproves (dis ə pro͞ovz´) *verb* has a feeling against

disguises (dis gīz´ əz) *noun* things used to hide a person's identity

dismal (diz´ məl) *adjective* dark and gloomy

disrupts (dis rupts´) *verb* interrupts the orderly progress of

distractions (dis trak´ shənz) *noun* things that draw away the mind or attention to something else

distributed (dis trib´ yo͞ot əd) *verb* gave out in portions

diversions (di vʉr´ zhənz or dī vʉr´ zhənz) *noun* things that a person turns to for fun in order to relax; pastimes

donned (dänd) *verb* put on clothing

droughts (drouts) *noun* long periods of dry weather

E **earnestness** (ʉr´ nəst nəs) *noun* seriousness or sincerity

earthly (ʉrth´ lē) *adjective* having to do with life on earth

easily (ē´ zi lē) *adverb* without trying too hard

electronics (ē lek´ trän´ iks or el´ ek trän´ iks) *noun* the science that deals with the action of electrons and their use in devices

embellished (em bel´ isht) *verb* made a story more interesting with fictional additions

emperor (em´ pər ər) *noun* a person who rules an empire

encounter (en koun´ tər) *verb* to meet unexpectedly

enthusiasm (en tho͞o´ zē az´ əm) *noun* a strong interest

environment (en vī´ rən mənt) *noun* all the things and conditions that surround a person, animal, or plant

essential (ē sen´ shəl) *adjective* most important or necessary

estimated (es´ ti māt´ əd) *verb* made a general but careful guess about the size, quality, value, or cost of

exceptional (ek sep´ shə nəl) *adjective* outstanding

exhausted (eg zôst´ əd or eg zäst´ əd) *verb* made very tired

experiments (ek sper´ i mənts) *noun* tests that are used to find out or prove something

explanation (eks´ plə nā´ shən) *noun* something that shows the meaning of; reason

exposing (eks pōz´ iŋ) *verb* causing to know about or experience

F **facial** (fā´ shəl) *adjective* having to do with the face

familiar (fə mil´ yər) *adjective* well-known

fascination (fas´ i nā´ shən) *noun* a very strong interest

focus (fō´ kəs) *verb* to adjust the eye or a lens in order to make a clear image

footsore (fo͝ot´ sôr´) *adjective* having feet that hurt from much walking

formally (fôr´ mə lē) *adverb* in a way that follows usual rules or customs exactly

formidable (fôr´ mə də bəl) *adjective* hard to overcome

friction (frik´ shən) *noun* the force that slows the motion of two surfaces that touch each other

G **gadgets** (gaj´ əts) *noun* small, mechanical devices

galaxies (gal´ ək sēz) *noun* very large groups of stars

grave (grāv) *adjective* dignified; solemn

grimaced (gri māst´ or grim´ əst) *verb* twisted the muscles of the face to express pain or unhappiness

grueling (gro͞o´ əl iŋ) *adjective* very tiring; exhausting

H **happiness** (hap´ ē nəs) *noun* the condition of being happy

hardier (har´ dē ər) *adjective* more capable of surviving under bad conditions; stronger

hastily (hās´ ti lē) *adverb* quickly; in a hurry

hazardous (haz´ ər dəs) *adjective* dangerous

hedged (hejd) *verb* avoided giving a direct answer

helm (helm) *noun* the wheel or tiller by which a ship is steered

heroes (hir´ ōz or hē´ rōz) *noun* people who are looked up to

hikers' (hīk´ ərz) *adjective* belonging to people who take long walks, especially in the country or in woods

huddled (hud´ əld) *verb* crowded or pushed close together

hull (hul) *noun* the sides and bottom of a boat or ship

humidity (hyo͞o mid´ i tē) *noun* the amount of moisture in the air

hurtles (hʉrt´ əlz) *verb* moves with great speed or force

I **illuminate** (i lo͞o´ mi nāt´) *verb* give light to; light up

immersion (i mʉr´ zhən) *noun* the state of getting deeply involved or absorbed in

immigrants (im´ i grənts) *noun* people who come into a country to make a new home

immigrants (im´i grənts) *noun* people who come into a country to make a new home

improvise (im´prə vīz) *verb* to make up and perform at the same time, without preparation

impulsively (im pul´siv lē) *adverb* without thinking

infancy (in´fən sē) *noun* the earliest stage of something

influence (in´flōō əns) *noun* the power to act on or affect persons or things in ways that are either good or bad

ingredients (in grē´dē ənts) *noun* the things that make up a mixture

instantaneously (in´stən tā´nē əs lē) *adverb* in an instant

instinct (in´stiŋkt) *noun* a way of behaving that is natural to an animal or person from birth

interior (in tir´ē ər) *noun* the inside or inner part

Internet (in´tər net) *noun* a network of computers from around the world that are connected for sharing information

introduced (in trə dōōst´) *verb* brought into use

irritable (ir´i tə bəl) *adjective* easy to anger or annoy

L
lax (laks) *adjective* not strict; careless

legendary (lej´ən der´ē) *adjective* having to do with a legend

leisurely (lē´zhər lē) *adverb* without hurry

leveled (lev´əld) *verb* knocked to the ground

liberty (lib´ər tē) *noun* being free from control

lifeboats (līf´bōts) *noun* sturdy boats used for saving lives at sea or along the shore

log (lôg) *noun* the record of a trip or voyage

luxurious (lug zhōōr´ē əs) *adjective* giving a feeling of comfort and pleasure

M
magnitude (mag´ni tōōd) *noun* great size

maintaining (mān tān´iŋ) *verb* keeping or keeping up

melodies (mel´ə dēz) *noun* series of musical tones that make up tunes

merciless (mur´si ləs) *adjective* without pity; cruel

midpoint (mid´point) *noun* the place in the exact middle

miserable (miz´ər ə bəl) *adjective* very unhappy; sad

mission (mish´ən) *noun* a special duty or piece of work that a person or a group is sent out to do

moderator (mäd´ə rā´tər) *noun* person in charge of a discussion or debate

monotonous (mə nät´n əs) *adjective* having little change; boring

N
nature's (nā´chərz) *adjective* belonging to the physical world

nutrition (nōō trish´ən) *noun* food; nourishment

O
obscuring (äb skyōōr´iŋ) *verb* hiding from view

obtain (äb tān´) *verb* to get through effort

obvious (äb´vē əs) *adjective* easy to see or understand; clear

occasionally (ō kā´zhə nə lē) *adverb* once in a while

optional (äp´shən əl) *adjective* allowing one to make a choice; not required

oration (ô rā´shən) *noun* a formal public speech delivered on a special occasion

overhead (ō´vər hed) *adjective* above one's head

overjoyed (ō vər joid´) *adjective* very happy; delighted

overwhelming (ō vər hwelm´iŋ) *adjective* overcoming completely

P
parachutist (per´ə shōō´tist) *noun* a person who jumps from an aircraft using a parachute

parcel (pär´səl) *noun* a wrapped package; a bundle

peal (pēl) *noun* a loud sound that echoes

peculiar (pi kyōōl´yər) *adjective* odd or strange

permitting (pər mit´iŋ) *verb* giving consent to; allowing

perspective (pər spek´tiv) *noun* a certain point of view in understanding or judging things

petitioned (pə tish´ənd) *verb* made a serious written request

phenomenon (fə näm´ə nän) *noun* an unusual person or thing

placidly (plas´id lē) *adverb* calmly and quietly; peacefully

platform (plat´fôrm) *noun* all the plans and goals of a political candidate or party

poorly (pōōr´lē) *adverb* badly; not well

precipitous (pri si´pə təs) *adjective* very steep, perpendicular

pried (prīd) *verb* released by force

probably (präb´ə blē) *adverb* almost certainly

programmed (prō´gramd) *verb* given a set of instructions

pronounced (prō nounst´) *adjective* clearly marked; definite

propels (prō pelz´) *verb* pushes or drives forward

prosperous (präs´pər əs) *adjective* successful or thriving

provoked (prō vōkt´) *verb* annoyed or made angry

pupil (pyōō´pəl) *noun* the opening in the center of the eye

pursuit (pər sōōt´ or pər syōōt´) *noun* the act of chasing after someone or something

Q **qualifying** (kwäl´ i fi´ iŋ) *verb* proving fit for some activity

R **recap** (rē kap´) *verb* to review by a brief summary

relatively (rel´ ə tiv lē) *adverb* compared to something else

remote (rē mōt´) *adjective* far off from a particular place

repaired (rē perd´) *verb* put into good condition again; fixed

repetitive (ri pet´ ə tiv) *adjective* repeating; saying or doing something again

resentfully (rē zent´ fə lē) *adverb* with a feeling of bitter hurt

retina (ret´ n ə) *noun* the inner layer of the lining of the eyeball

retrieved (rē trēvd´) *verb* found and brought back

reusable (rē yoo´ zə bəl) *adjective* capable of being used again

reviewed (rē vyood´) *verb* went over or studied again

roaming (rōm´ iŋ) *verb* traveling about with no special purpose

S **scariest** (sker´ ē əst) *adjective* causing the most fear

scrumptious (skrump´ shəs) *adjective* delicious

seasoned (sē´ zənd) *adjective* better because of age or experience

sensor (sen´ sər) *noun* device that reacts to heat, light, pressure, etc.

serene (sə rēn´) *adjective* calm or peaceful

shelves (shelvz) *noun* thin, flat pieces of a material that are fastened against a wall or built into a frame so as to hold things

shifted (shif´ təd) *verb* changed from one position to another

shrewd (shrood) *adjective* clever or sharp in practical matters

signatures (sig´ nə chərz) *noun* people's names written by those people

sites (sīts) *noun* places on the Internet that have information on specific topics

smokejumper (smōk´ jum´ pər) *noun* a firefighter who parachutes to forest fires

solitary (säl´ i ter´ ē) *adjective* living or being alone

solos (sō´ lōz) *noun* performances by one person alone

somber (säm´ bər) *adjective* dark and gloomy or dull

spectacularly (spek tak´ yə lər lē) *adverb* in a showy way

stampeded (stam pēd´ əd) *verb* moved in a sudden rush of animals or people in one direction

steamship (stēm´ ship) *noun* a ship that is powered by steam

subway (sub´ wā) *noun* an underground railway that is usually powered by electricity

succinctly (sək siŋkt´ lē) *adverb* in few words; briefly

superheated (soo´ pər hēt´ əd) *adjective* heated to an extreme degree or to a very high temperature

superstitious (soo´ pər stish´ əs) *adjective* influenced by fearful beliefs

surgery (sur´ jər ē) *noun* the treating of disease or injury by cutting into and removing or repairing parts of the body

survivors (sər viv´ ərz) *noun* people or things that survive

suspended (sə spend´ əd) *verb* stopped for a time

T **technology** (tek näl´ ə jē) *noun* science as used in everyday life

tenacity (ti nas ´ə tē) *noun* persistence in working toward a goal

terminal (tur´ mi nəl) *noun* a main station

thieves (thēvz) *noun* people who steal in a secret way

tiresome (tir´ səm) *adjective* tiring; boring; annoying

toward (tôrd or twôrd) *preposition* in the direction of

trainees (trā nēz´) *noun* people who are receiving training

tutor (toot´ ər) *verb* to act as a private teacher

U **unidentified** (un´ i den´ ti fid) *adjective* not known or recognized

upward (up´ wərd) *adverb* from a lower to a higher place

urging (urj´ iŋ) *verb* encouraging strongly

ushered (ush´ ərd) *verb* showed the way or brought in

V **vaguely** (vāg´ lē) *adverb* in a way that is unclear

versus (vur´ səs) *preposition* in a contest against

visual (vizh´ oo əl) *adjective* having to do with sight or used in seeing

vital (vīt´ l) *adjective* very important

voice-over (vois´ ō´ vər) *noun* the voice of an offscreen narrator, announcer, or character

W **weary** (wir´ ē) *adjective* tired

wilderness (wil´ dər nəs) *noun* a wild area; land that has no settlers and is covered with wild plants and trees

wispy (wis´ pē) *adjective* thin; slight

wistfully (wist´ fə lē) *adverb* with a feeling of longing

worthy (wur´ thē) *adjective* deserving; having merit